Cardboa

MW01296779

until the day I die

Just one last box and all my Magic cards will finally be sorted.
Oops!-- Oh, no!...
At least we can be consoled that he died surrounded by the Magic cards he loved and with a smile on his face...

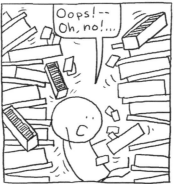

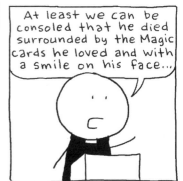

A collection of comics about the world's most addictive game.

Cardboard Crack until the day I die

Copyright © 2014

Check out these other Cardboard Crack books:
Cardboard Crack
I will never quit Cardboard Crack
Cardboard Crack anytime, anywhere

Cardboard Crack is in no way affiliated with or endorsed by Wizards of the Coast LLC. Wizards of the Coast, Magic: The Gathering, and their respective logos are trademarks of Wizards of the Coast LLC. All rights reserved.

This book collects comics that originally appeared online between June 9, 2014 and October 18, 2014, and can also be viewed at:
cardboard-crack.com
facebook.com/CardboardCrack

For information write:
cardboardcrack.mtg@gmail.com

Printed in the U.S.A.

For the people who make
magic by making Magic.

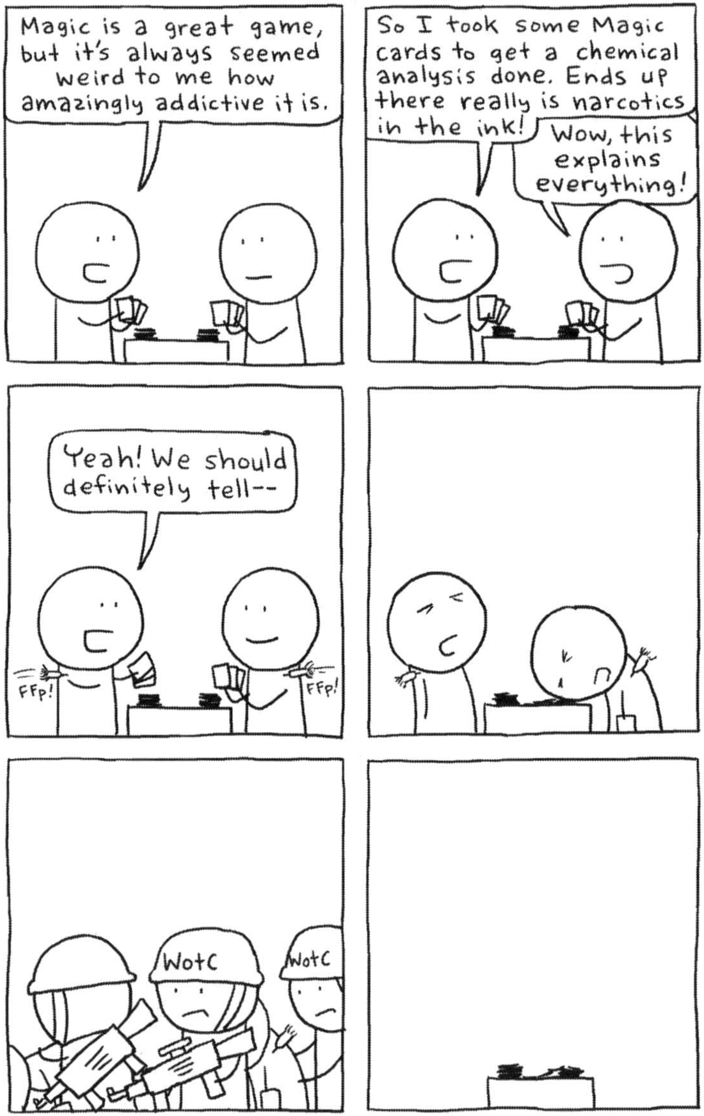
Magic is a great game, but it's always seemed weird to me how amazingly addictive it is.
So I took some Magic cards to get a chemical analysis done. Ends up there really is narcotics in the ink!
Wow, this explains everything!
Yeah! We should definitely tell--
FFp!
FFp!
WotC
WotC

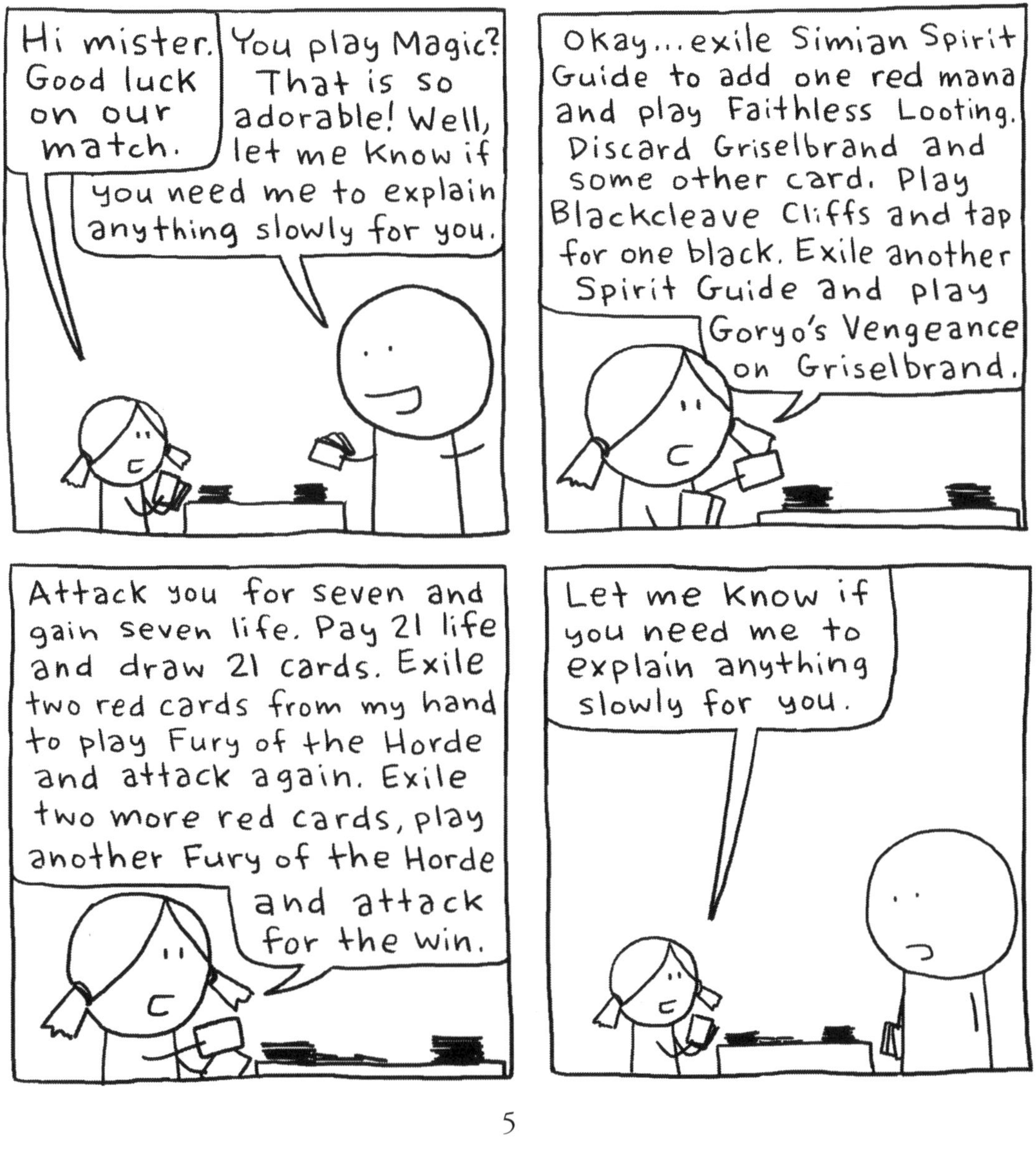
Hi mister. Good luck on our match.
You play Magic? That is so adorable! Well, let me know if you need me to explain anything slowly for you.
Okay... exile Simian Spirit Guide to add one red mana and play Faithless Looting. Discard Griselbrand and some other card. Play Blackcleave Cliffs and tap for one black. Exile another Spirit Guide and play Goryo's Vengeance on Griselbrand.
Attack you for seven and gain seven life. Pay 21 life and draw 21 cards. Exile two red cards from my hand to play Fury of the Horde and attack again. Exile two more red cards, play another Fury of the Horde and attack for the win.
Let me know if you need me to explain anything slowly for you.

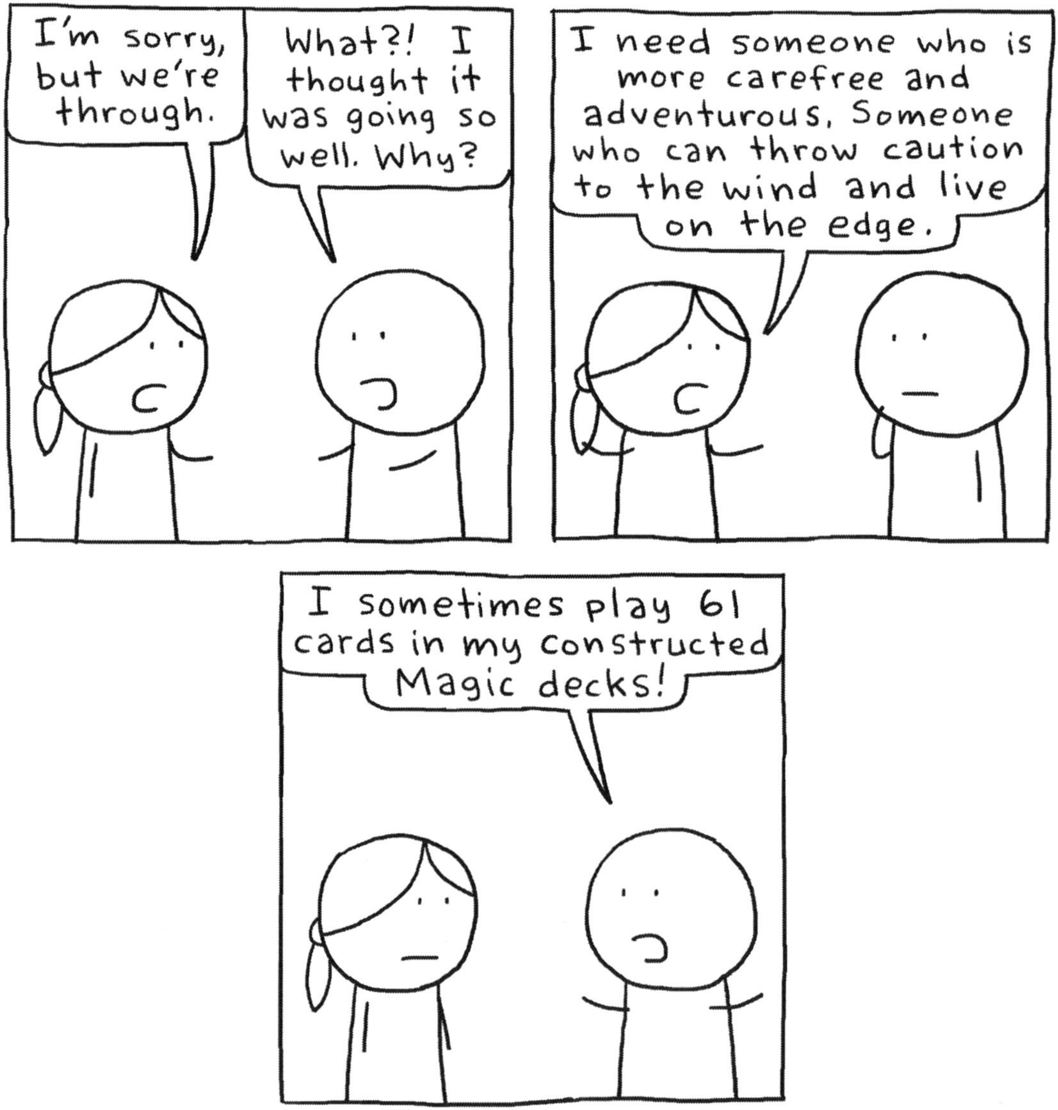
I'm sorry, but we're through.
What?! I thought it was going so well. Why?
I need someone who is more carefree and adventurous. Someone who can throw caution to the wind and live on the edge.
I sometimes play 61 cards in my constructed Magic decks!

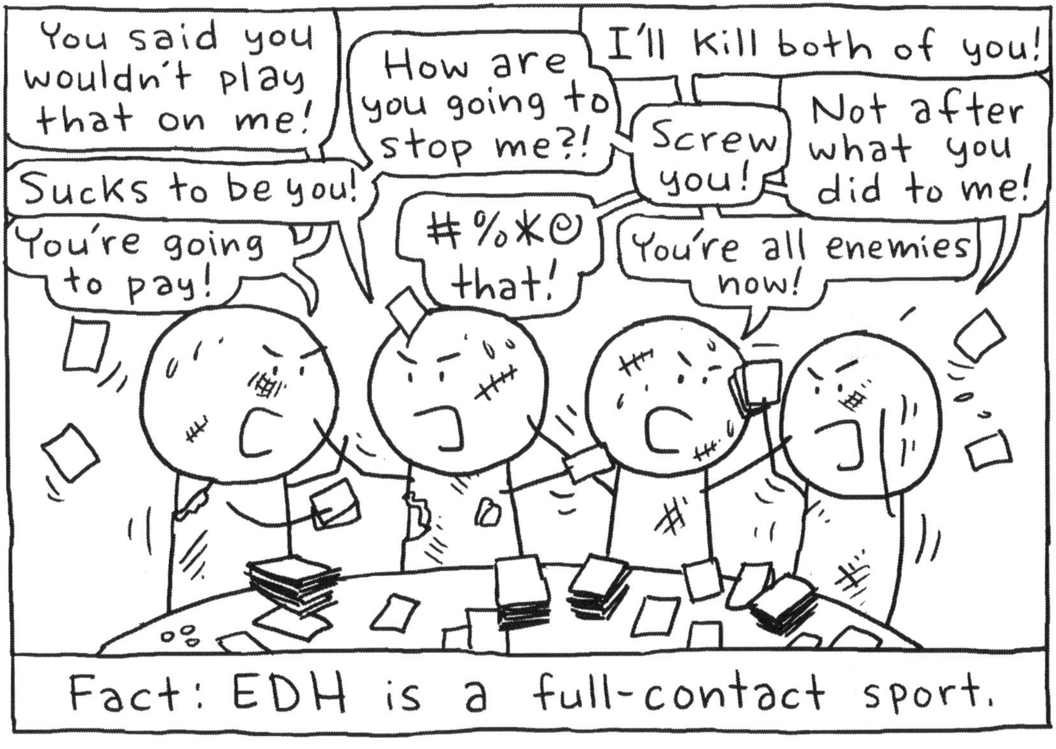
You said you wouldn't play that on me!
Sucks to be you!
You're going to pay!
How are you going to stop me?!
#%*@ that!
I'll kill both of you!
Screw you!
Not after what you did to me!
You're all enemies now!

Fact: EDH is a full-contact sport.

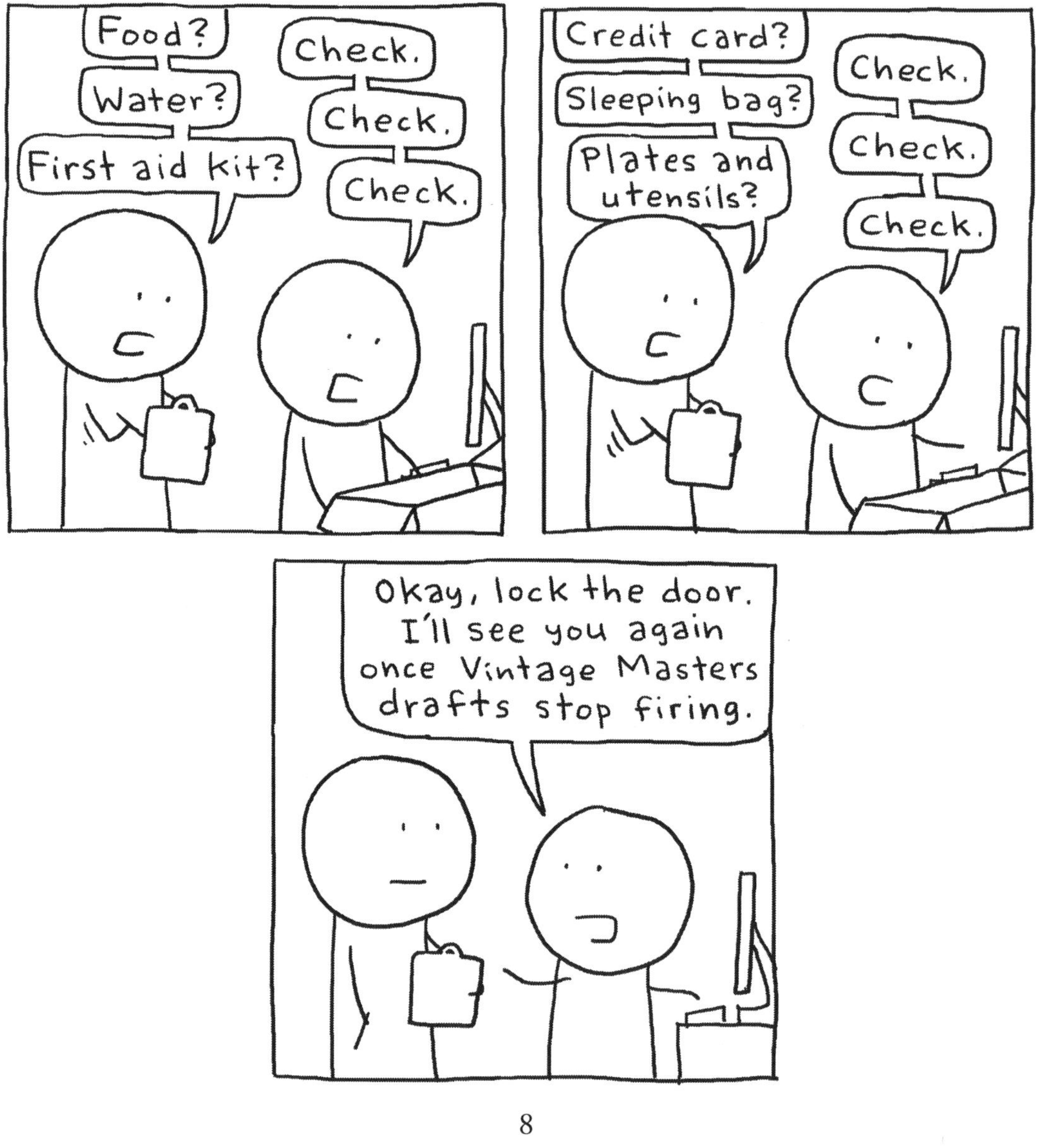
Food?
Water?
First aid kit?
Check.
Check.
Check.
Credit card?
Sleeping bag?
Plates and utensils?
Check.
Check.
Check.
Okay, lock the door. I'll see you again once Vintage Masters drafts stop firing.

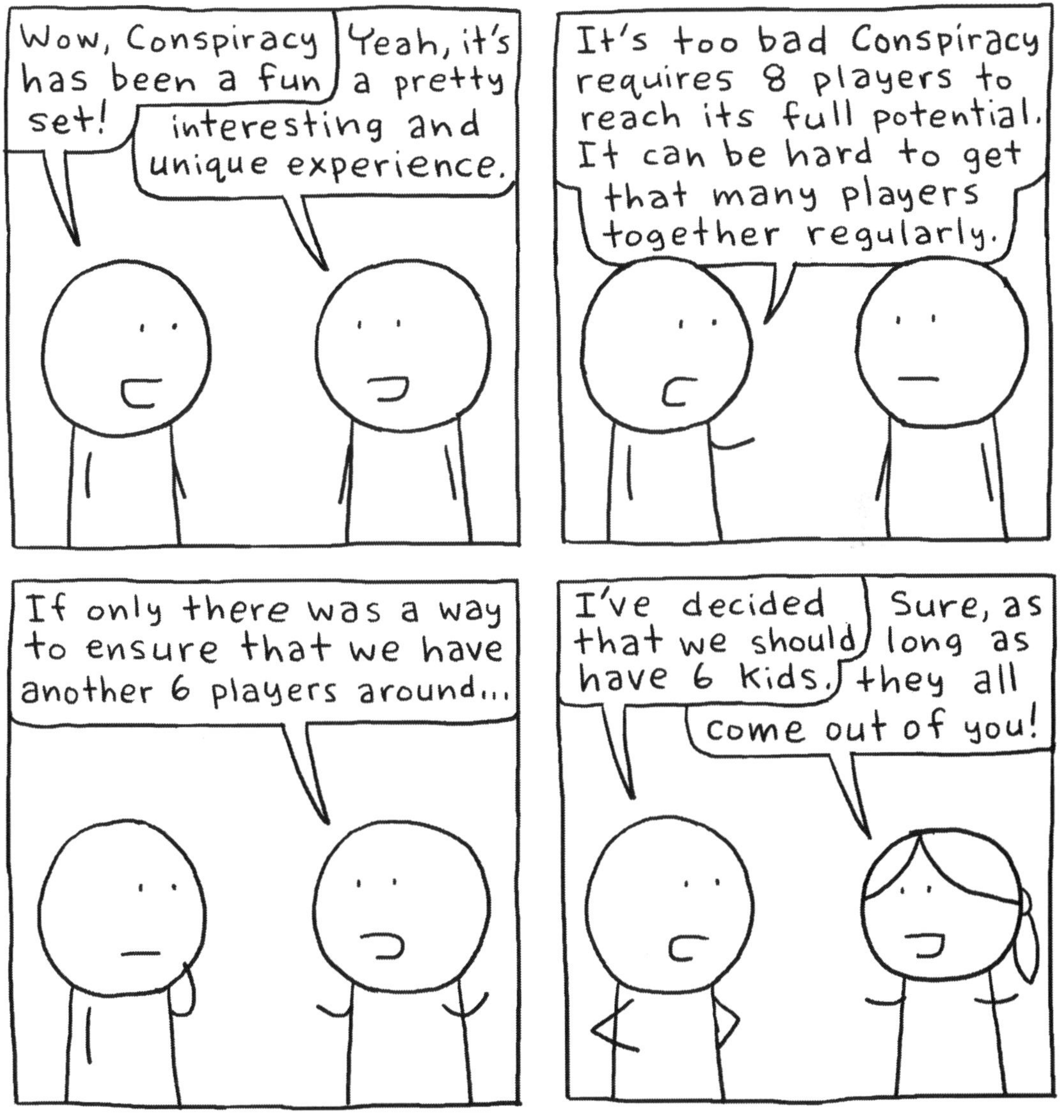
Wow, Conspiracy has been a fun set!
Yeah, it's a pretty interesting and unique experience.
It's too bad Conspiracy requires 8 players to reach its full potential. It can be hard to get that many players together regularly.
If only there was a way to ensure that we have another 6 players around...
I've decided that we should have 6 kids.
Sure, as long as they all come out of you!

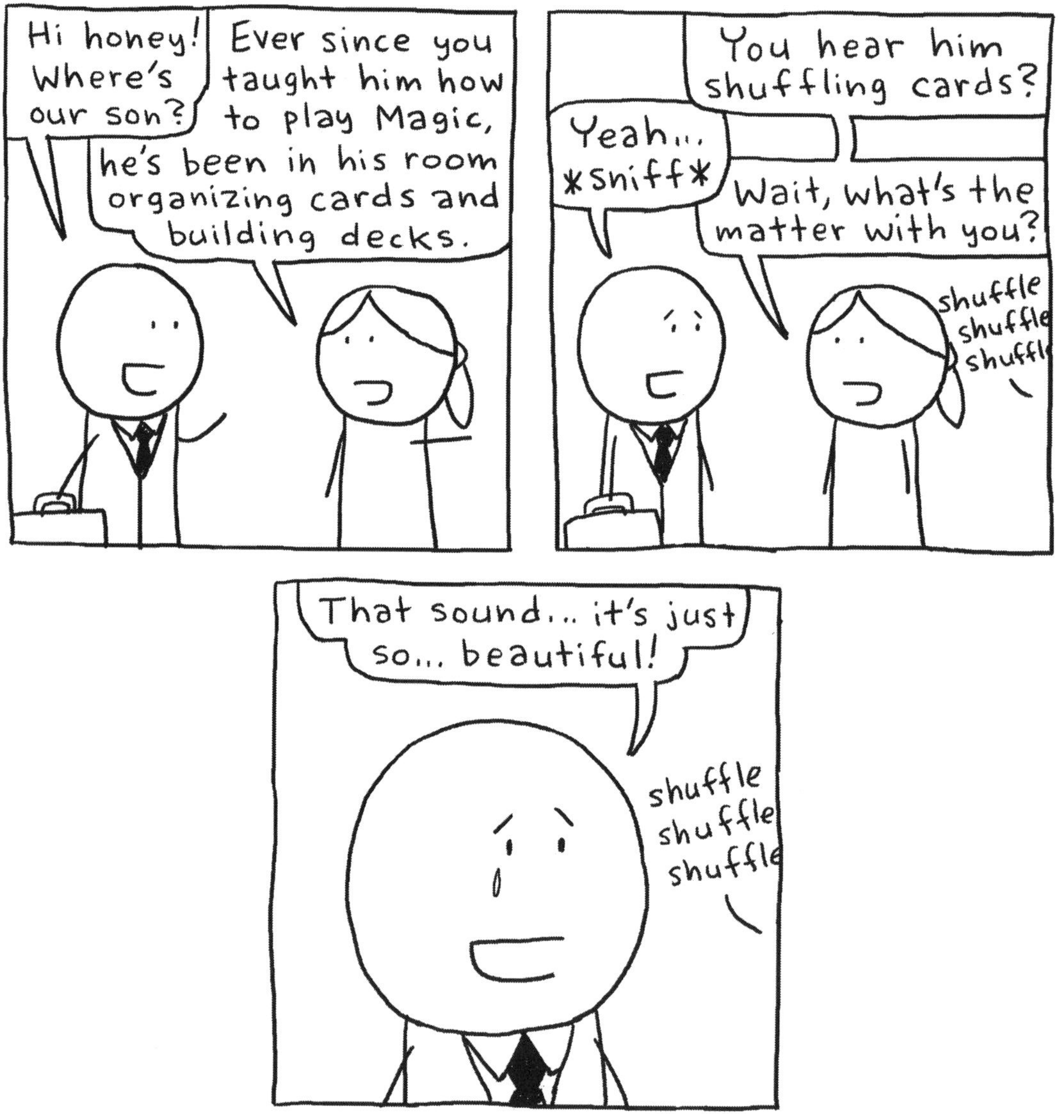
Hi honey! Where's our son?
Ever since you taught him how to play Magic,
he's been in his room organizing cards and building decks.
You hear him shuffling cards?
Yeah... *sniff*
Wait, what's the matter with you?
shuffle shuffle
That sound... it's just so... beautiful!
shuffle shuffle shuffle

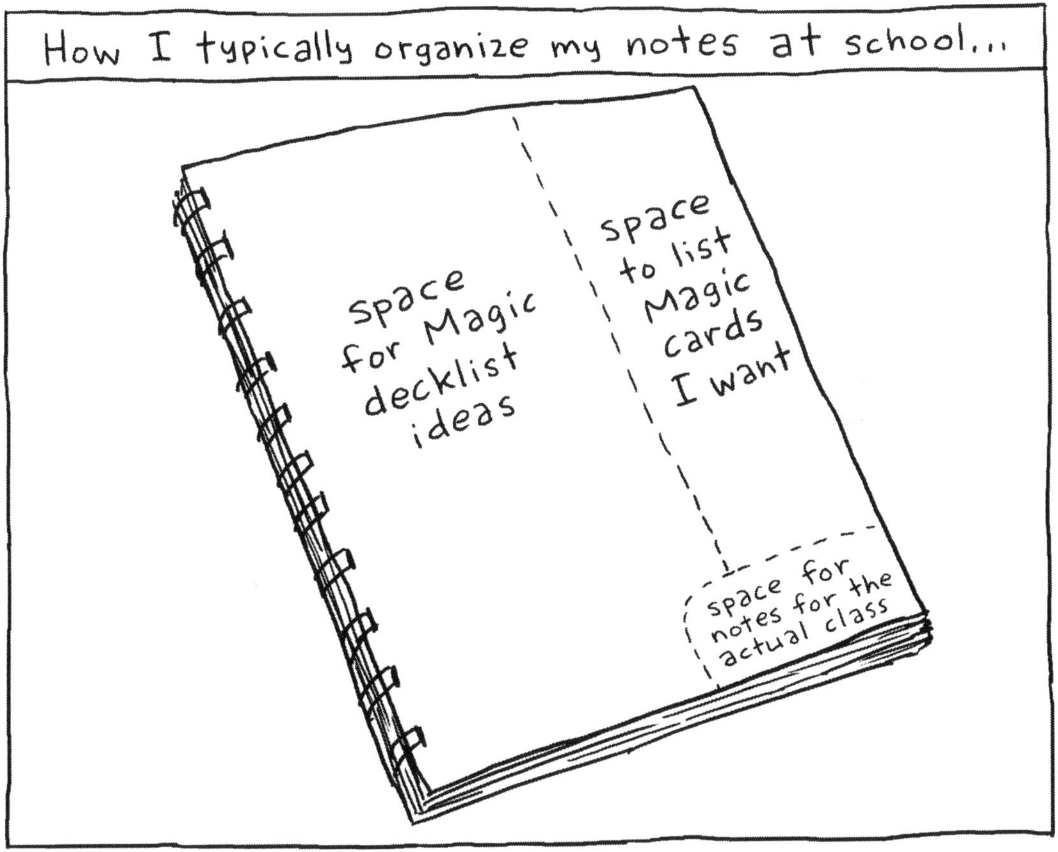
How I typically organize my notes at school...
space for Magic decklist ideas
space to list Magic cards I want
space for notes for the actual class

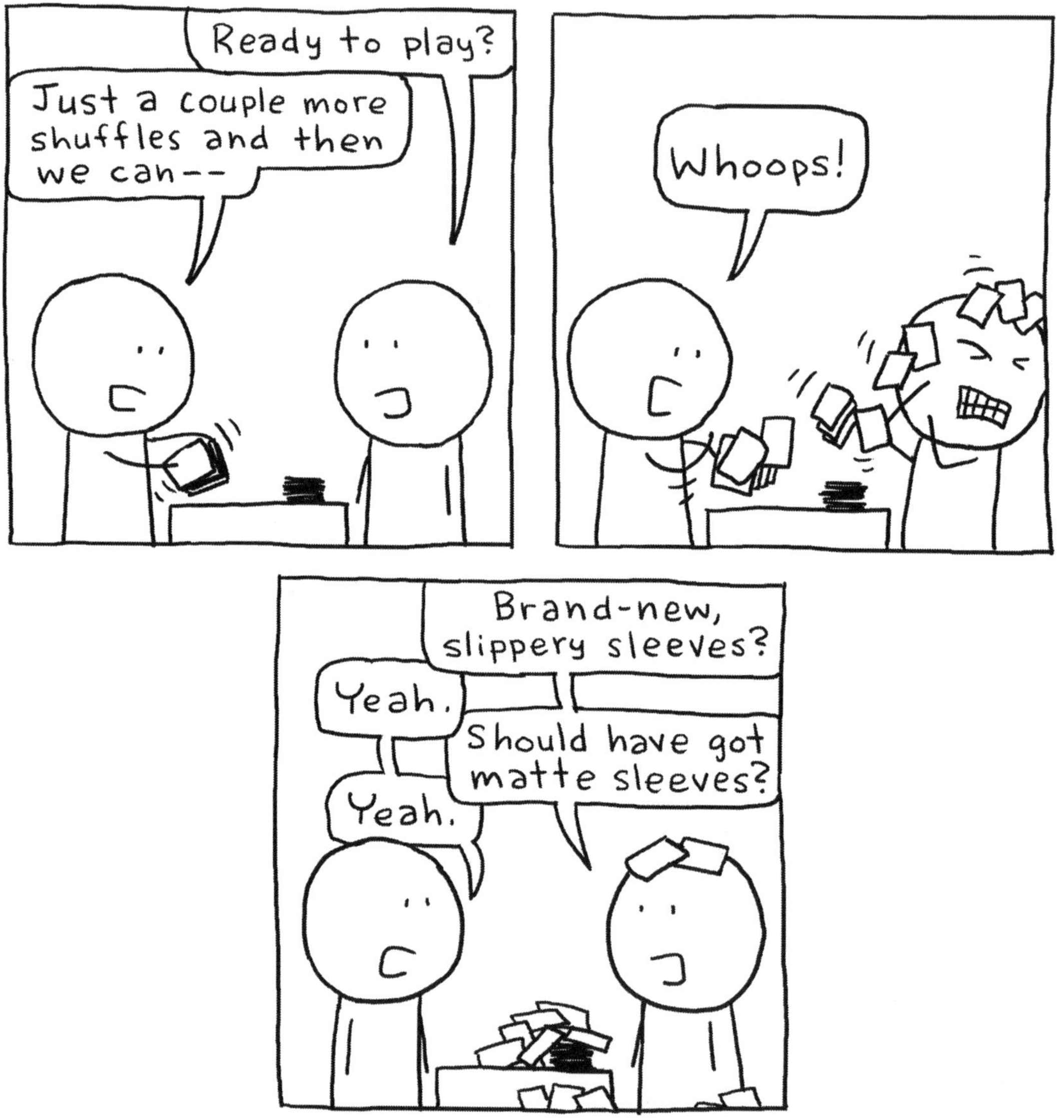
Ready to play?
Just a couple more shuffles and then we can--
Whoops!
Brand-new, slippery sleeves?
Yeah.
Should have got matte sleeves?
Yeah.

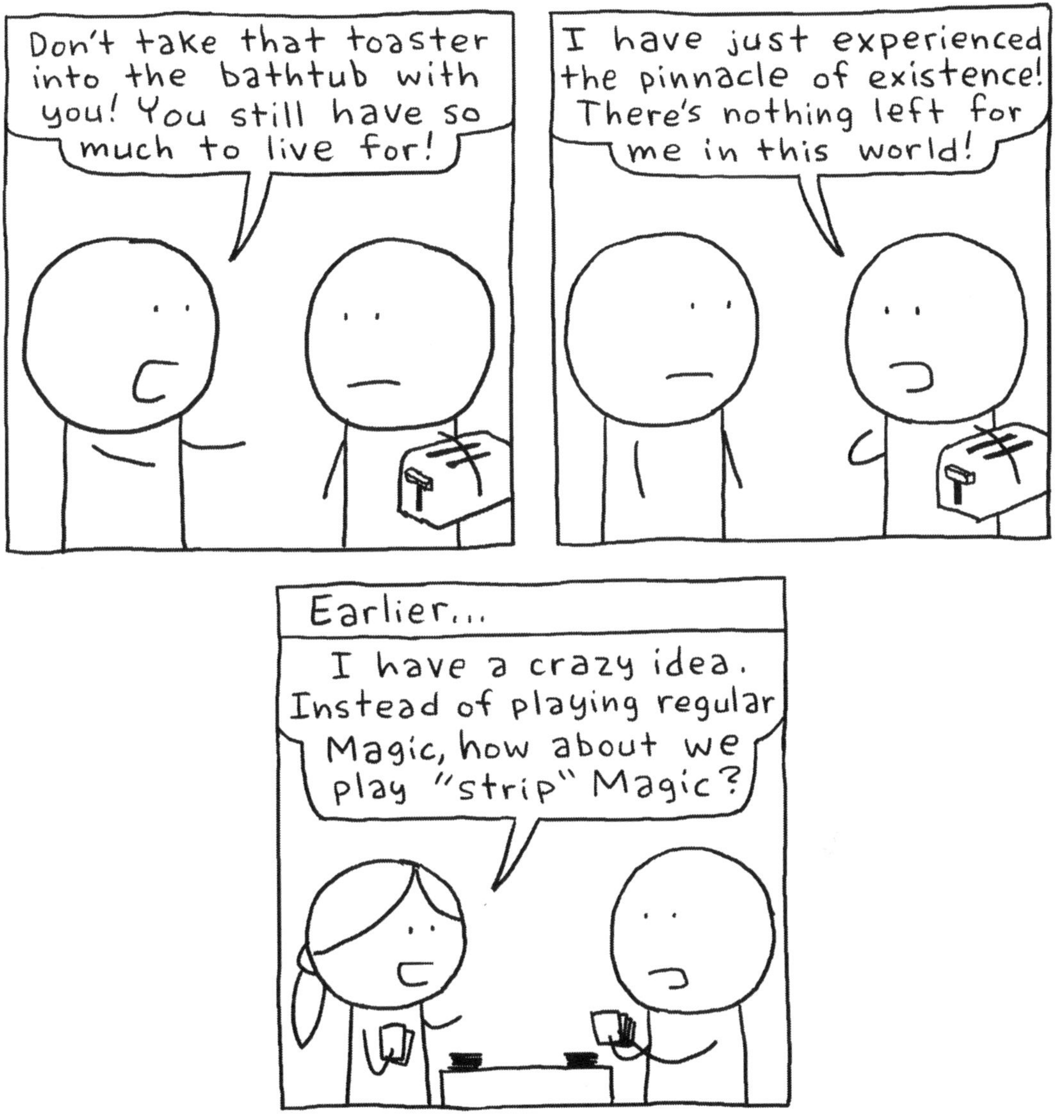
Don't take that toaster into the bathtub with you! You still have so much to live for!
I have just experienced the pinnacle of existence! There's nothing left for me in this world!
Earlier...
I have a crazy idea. Instead of playing regular Magic, how about we play "strip" Magic?

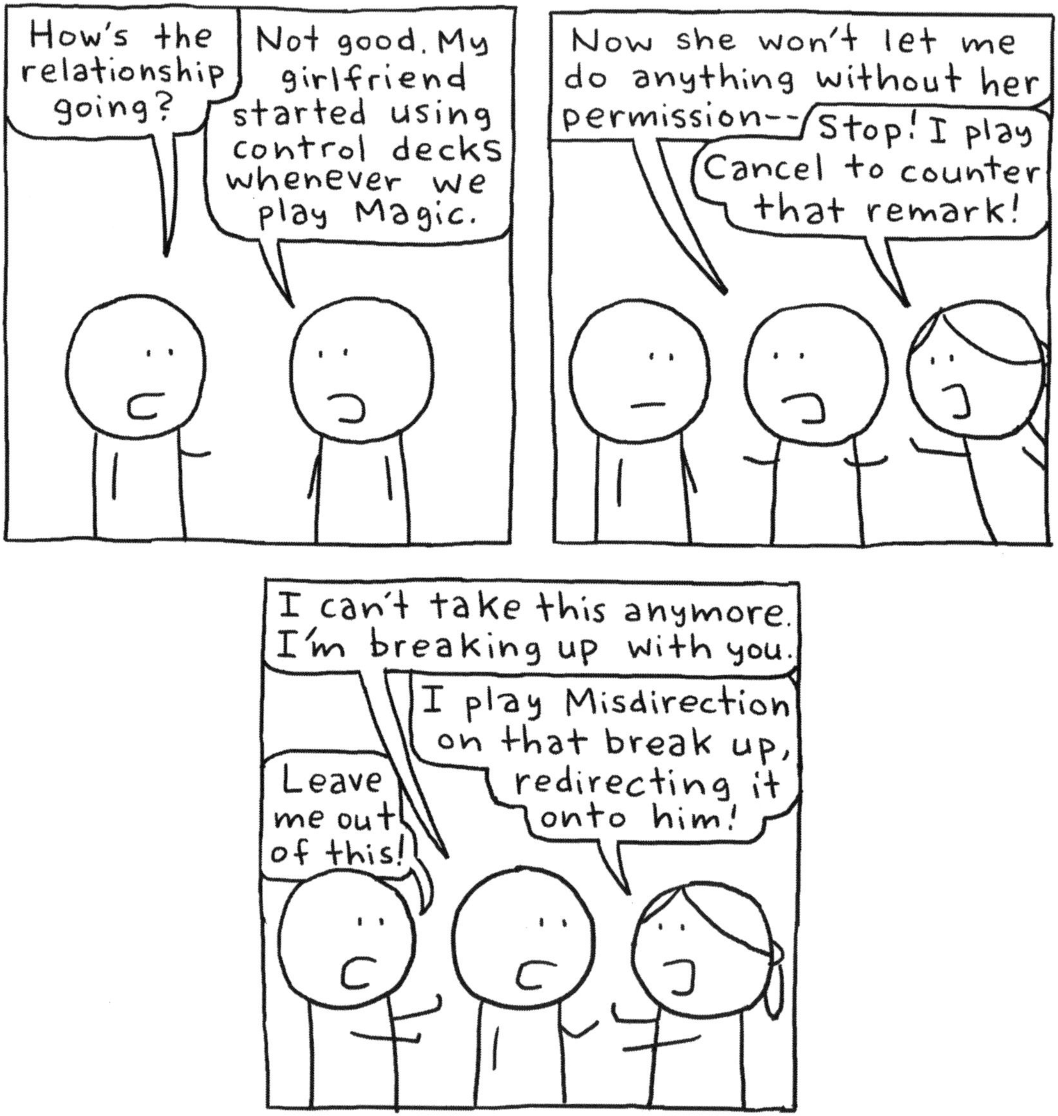
How's the relationship going?
Not good. My girlfriend started using control decks whenever we play Magic.
Now she won't let me do anything without her permission--
Stop! I play Cancel to counter that remark!
I can't take this anymore. I'm breaking up with you.
I play Misdirection on that break up, redirecting it onto him!
Leave me out of this!

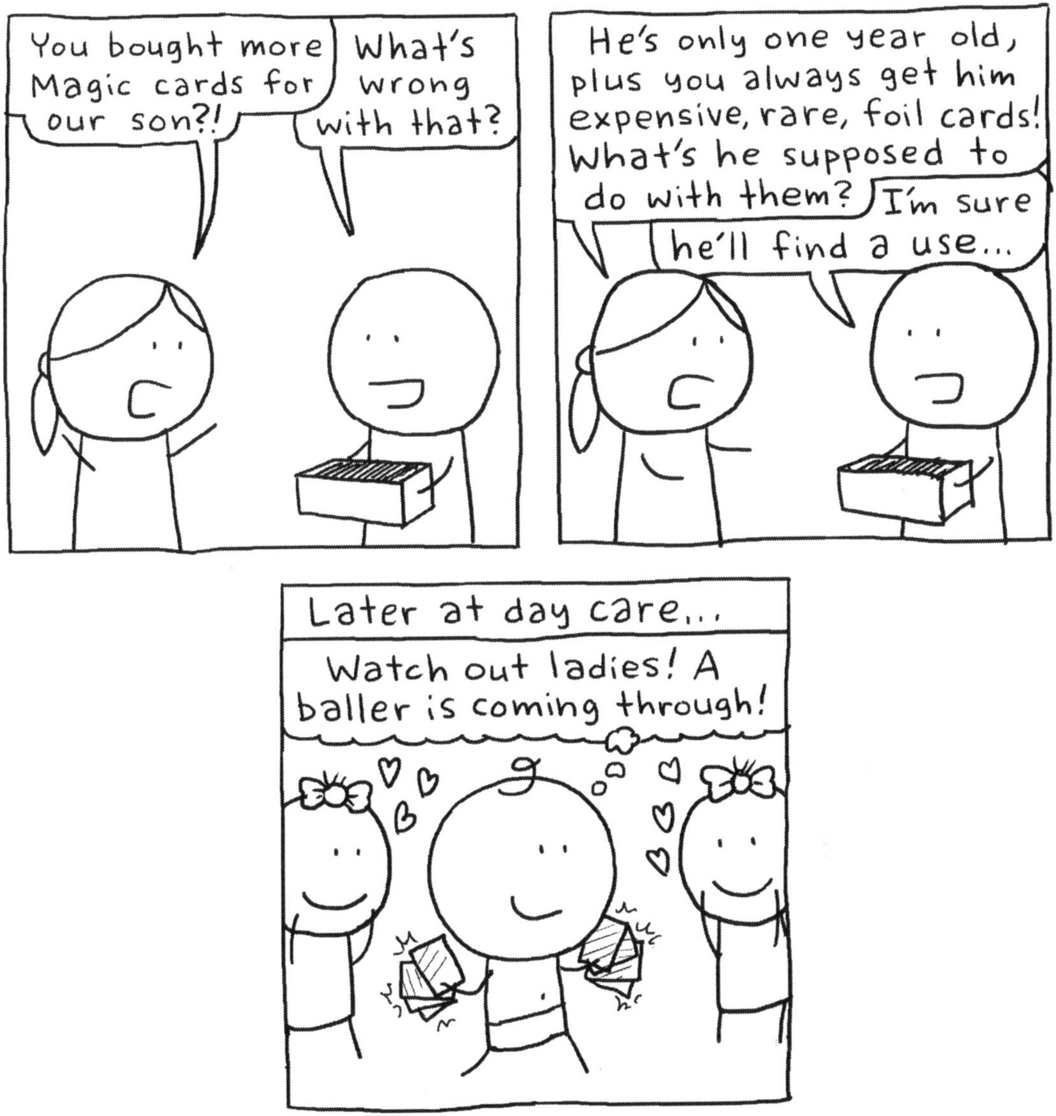
You bought more Magic cards for our son?!
What's wrong with that?
He's only one year old, plus you always get him expensive, rare, foil cards! What's he supposed to do with them?
I'm sure he'll find a use...
Later at day care...
Watch out ladies! A baller is coming through!

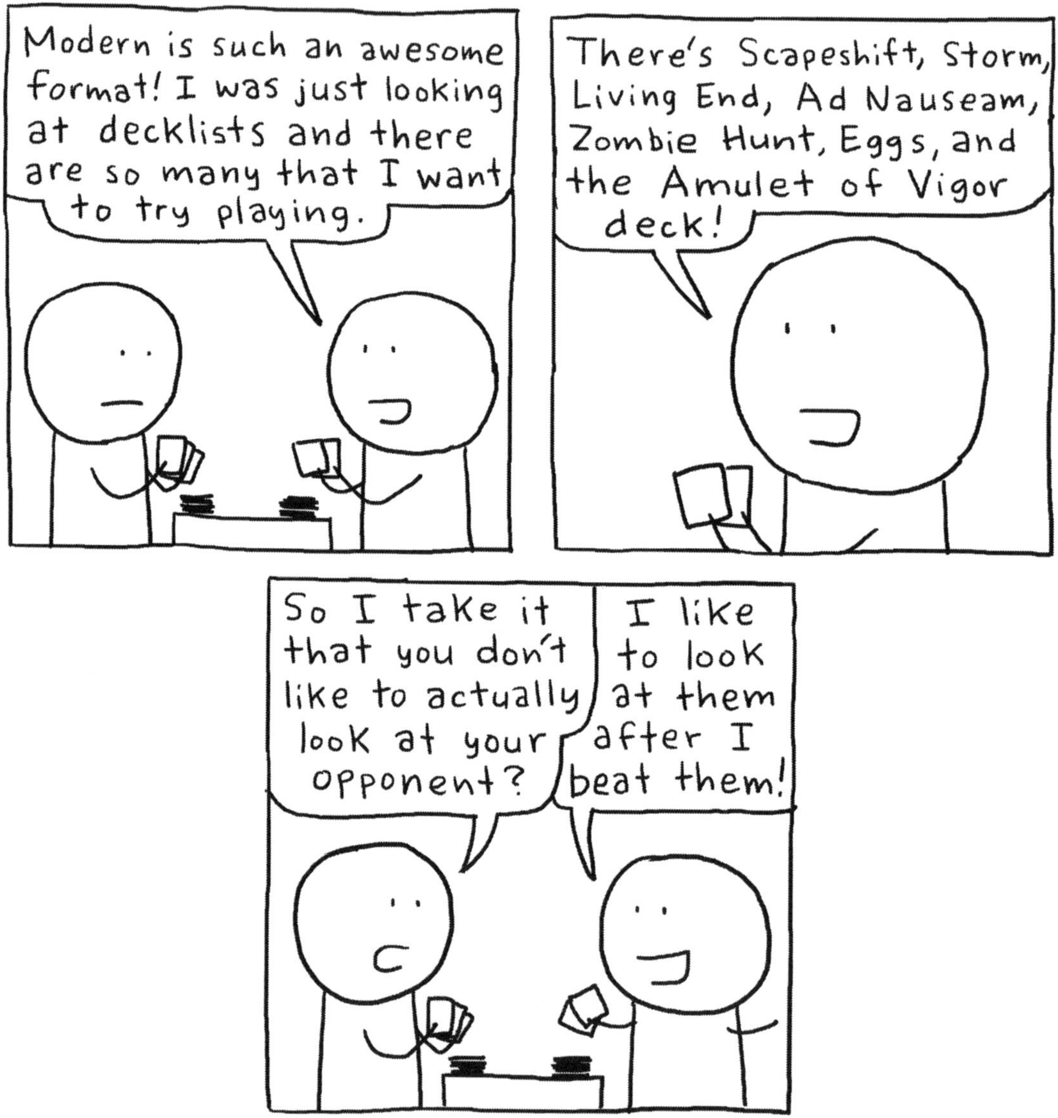
Modern is such an awesome format! I was just looking at decklists and there are so many that I want to try playing.
There's Scapeshift, Storm, Living End, Ad Nauseam, Zombie Hunt, Eggs, and the Amulet of Vigor deck!
So I take it that you don't like to actually look at your opponent?
I like to look at them after I beat them!

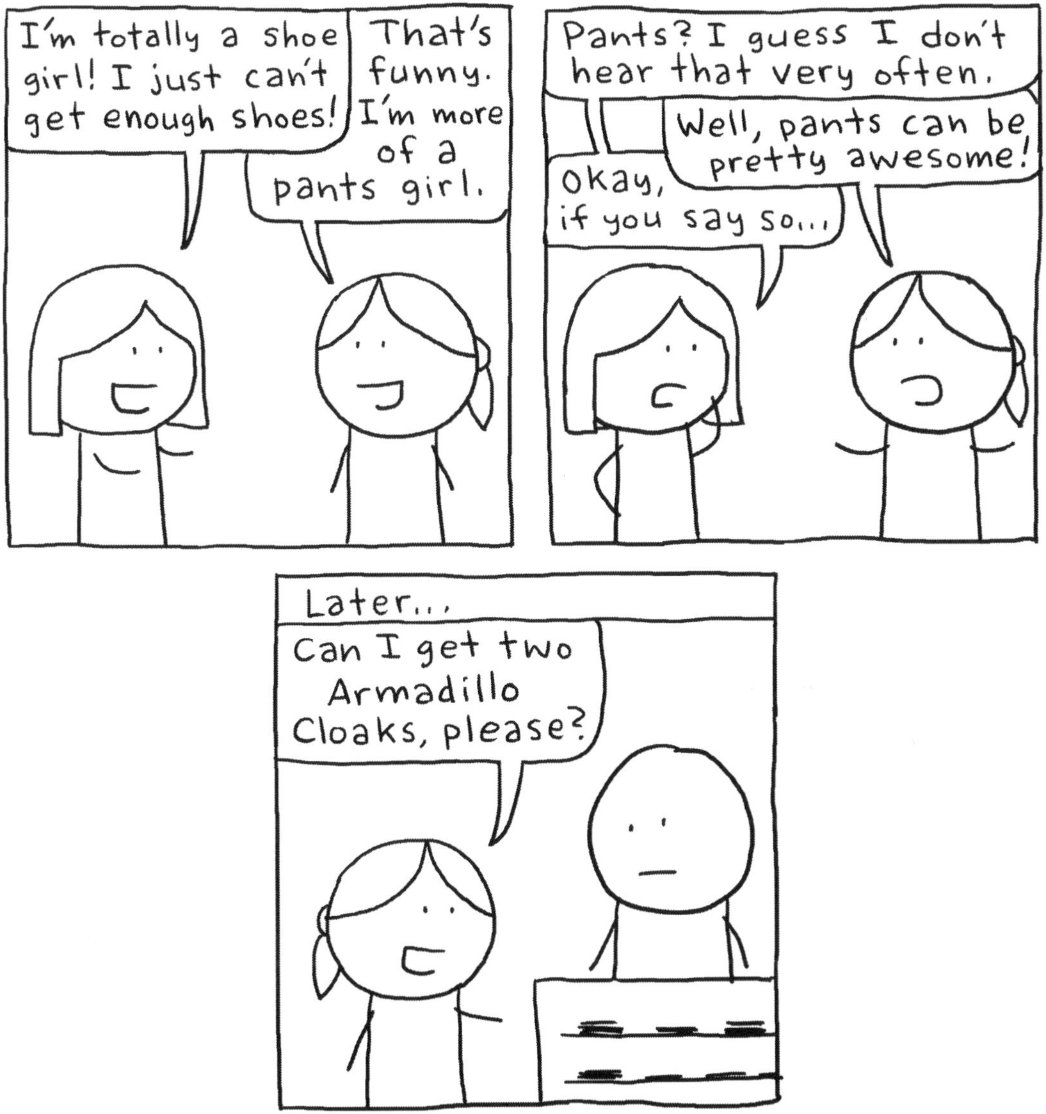
I'm totally a shoe girl! I just can't get enough shoes!
That's funny. I'm more of a pants girl.
Pants? I guess I don't hear that very often.
Well, pants can be pretty awesome!
Okay, if you say so...
Later...
Can I get two Armadillo Cloaks, please?

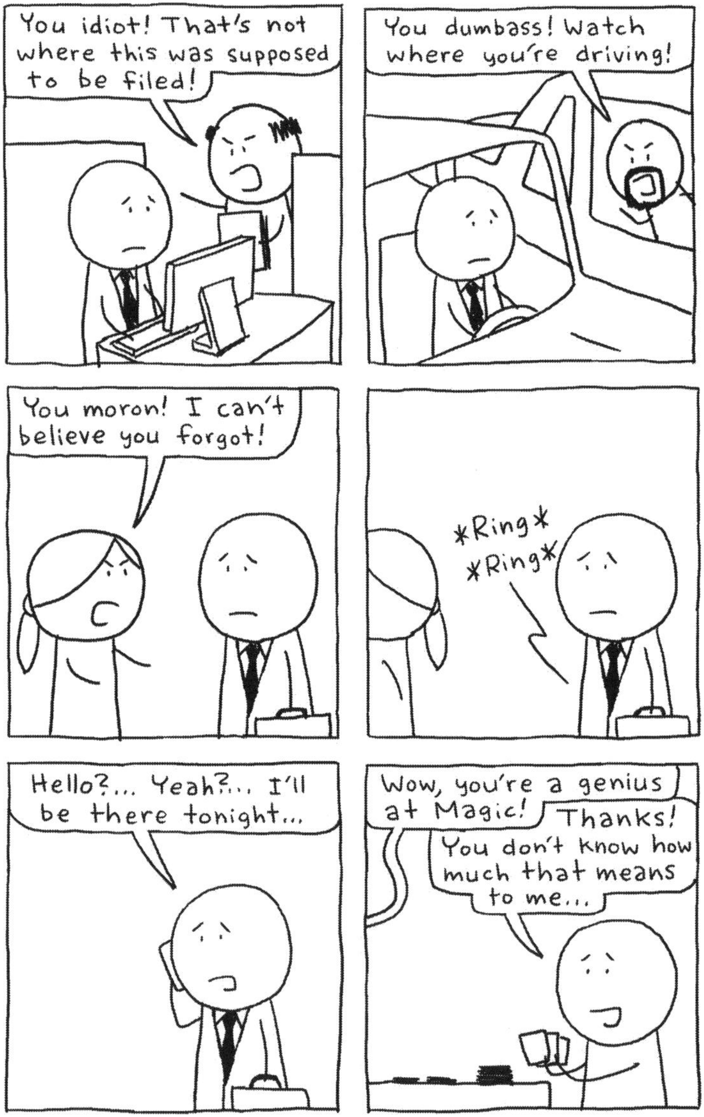
You idiot! That's not where this was supposed to be filed!
You dumbass! Watch where you're driving!
You moron! I can't believe you forgot!
Ring
Ring
Hello?... Yeah?... I'll be there tonight...
Wow, you're a genius at Magic!
Thanks! You don't know how much that means to me...

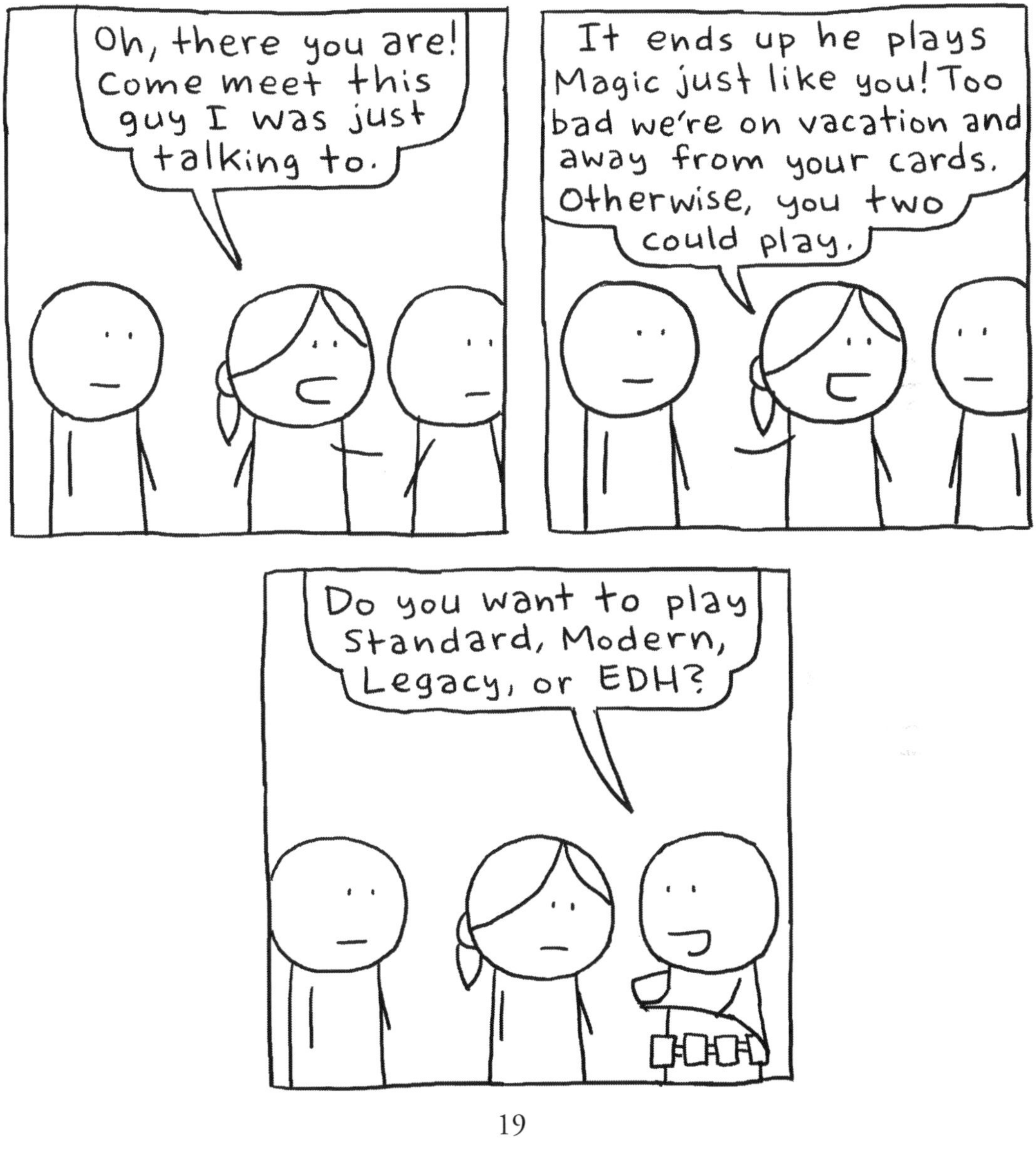
Oh, there you are! Come meet this guy I was just talking to.
It ends up he plays Magic just like you! Too bad we're on vacation and away from your cards. Otherwise, you two could play.
Do you want to play Standard, Modern, Legacy, or EDH?

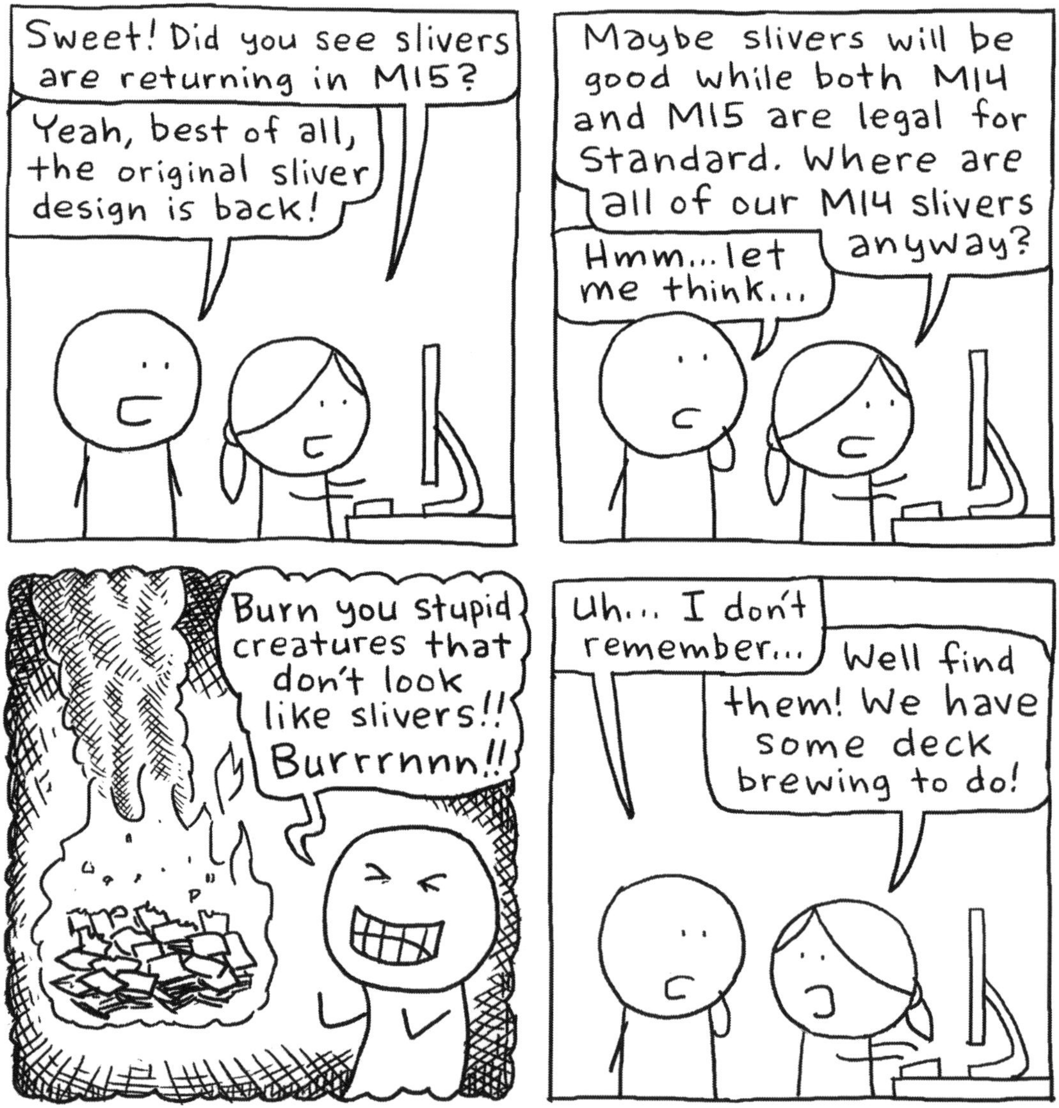
Sweet! Did you see slivers are returning in M15?
Yeah, best of all, the original sliver design is back!
Maybe slivers will be good while both M14 and M15 are legal for Standard. Where are all of our M14 slivers anyway?
Hmm... let me think...
Burn you stupid creatures that don't look like slivers!! Burrrnnn!!
Uh... I don't remember...
Well find them! We have some deck brewing to do!

15 years ago...
I can't wait until I'm older and have a real job. Then I'll be able to buy all the Magic cards I want now, no matter the cost!
Yeah, me too!
Me too!
Now...
Why the hell do these old Magic cards cost so much money?!

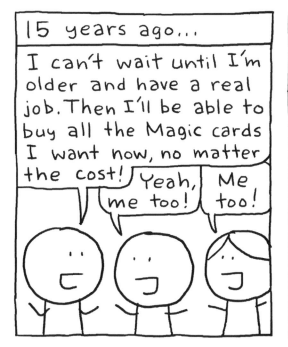

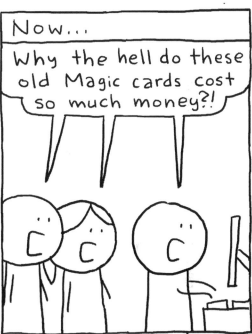

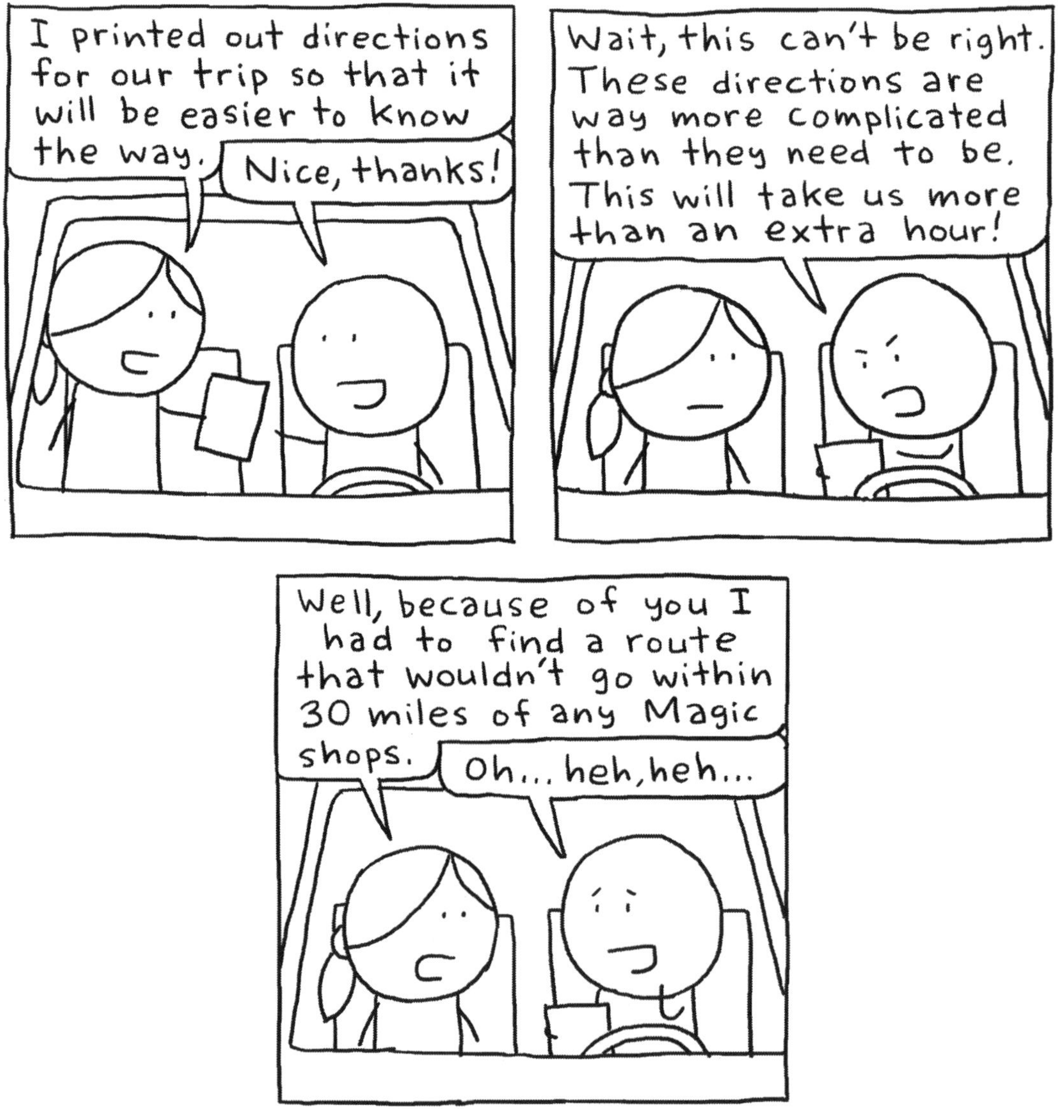
I printed out directions for our trip so that it will be easier to know the way.
Nice, thanks!
Wait, this can't be right. These directions are way more complicated than they need to be. This will take us more than an extra hour!
Well, because of you I had to find a route that wouldn't go within 30 miles of any Magic shops.
Oh... heh, heh...

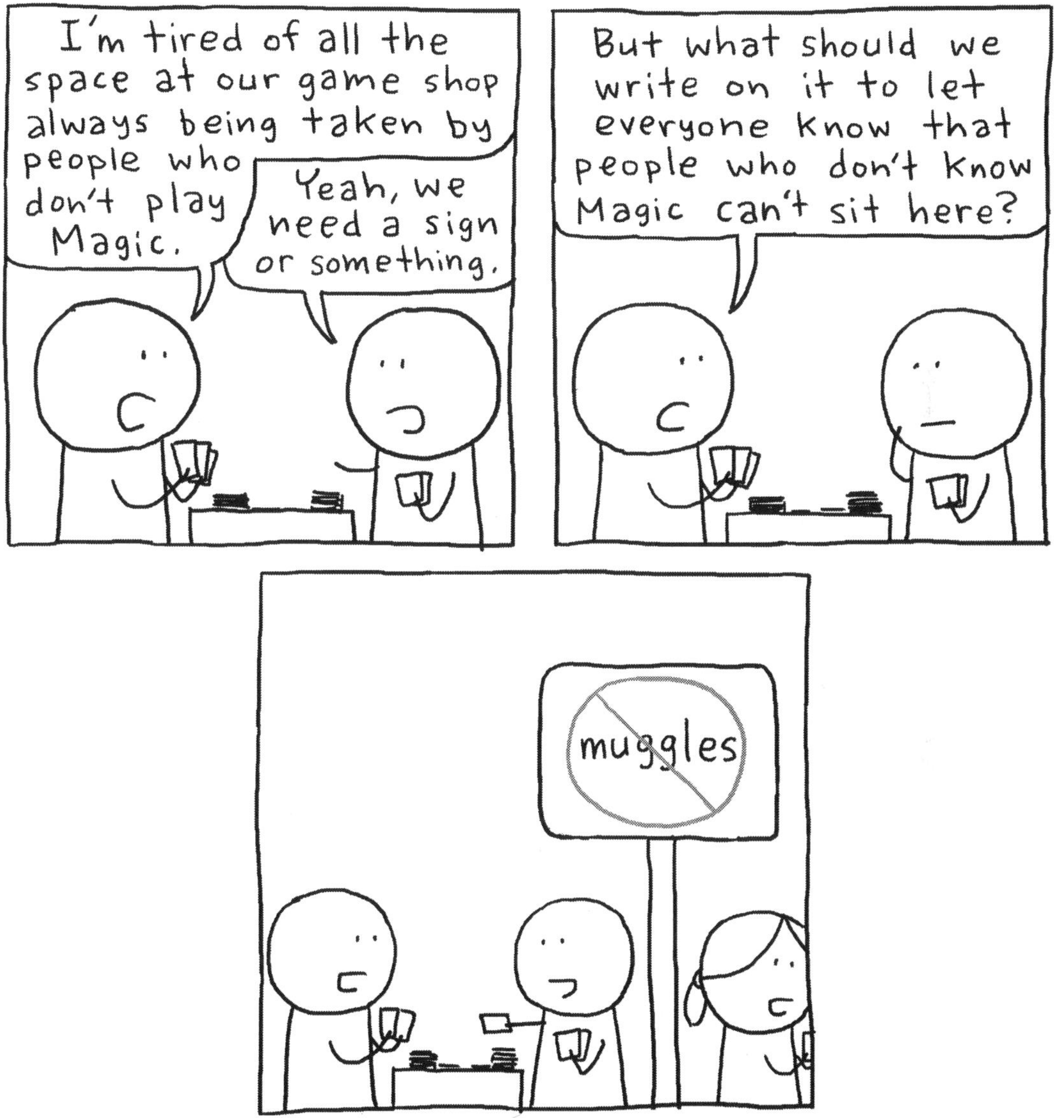
I'm tired of all the space at our game shop always being taken by people who don't play Magic.
Yeah, we need a sign or something.
But what should we write on it to let everyone know that people who don't know Magic can't sit here?
muggles

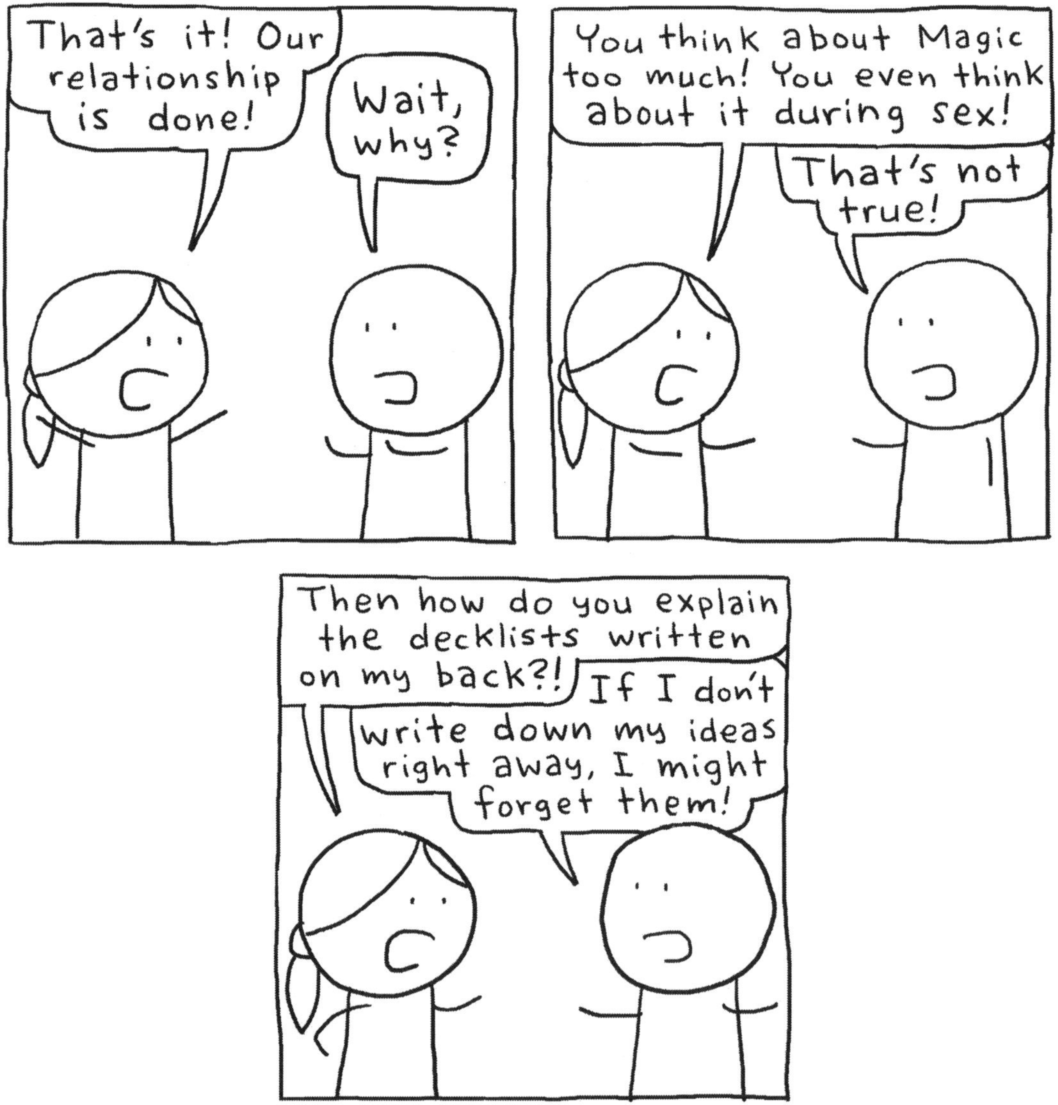
That's it! Our relationship is done!
Wait, why?
You think about Magic too much! You even think about it during sex!
That's not true!
Then how do you explain the decklists written on my back?!
If I don't write down my ideas right away, I might forget them!

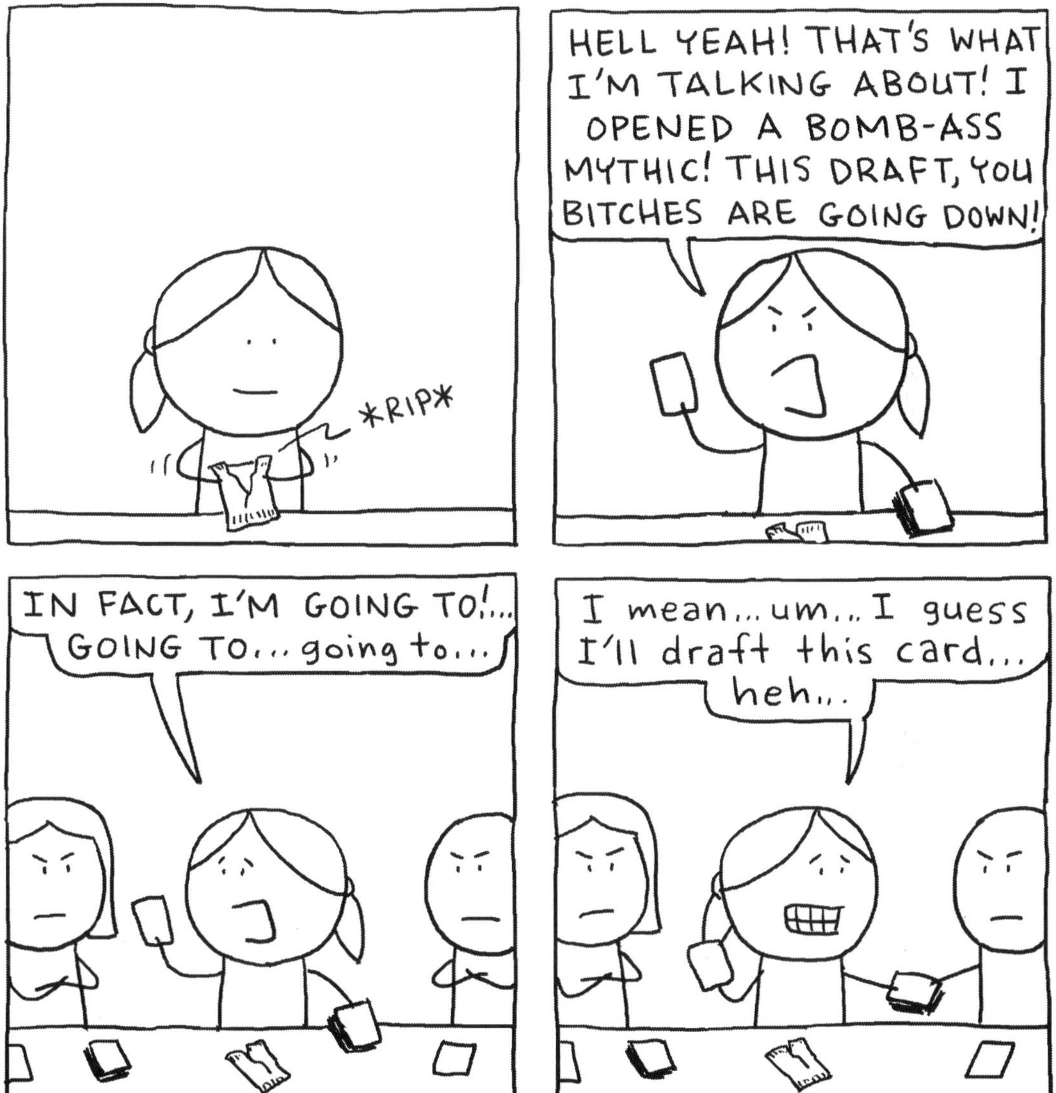
RIP
HELL YEAH! THAT'S WHAT I'M TALKING ABOUT! I OPENED A BOMB-ASS MYTHIC! THIS DRAFT, YOU BITCHES ARE GOING DOWN!
IN FACT, I'M GOING TO!... GOING TO... going to...
I mean... um... I guess I'll draft this card... heh...

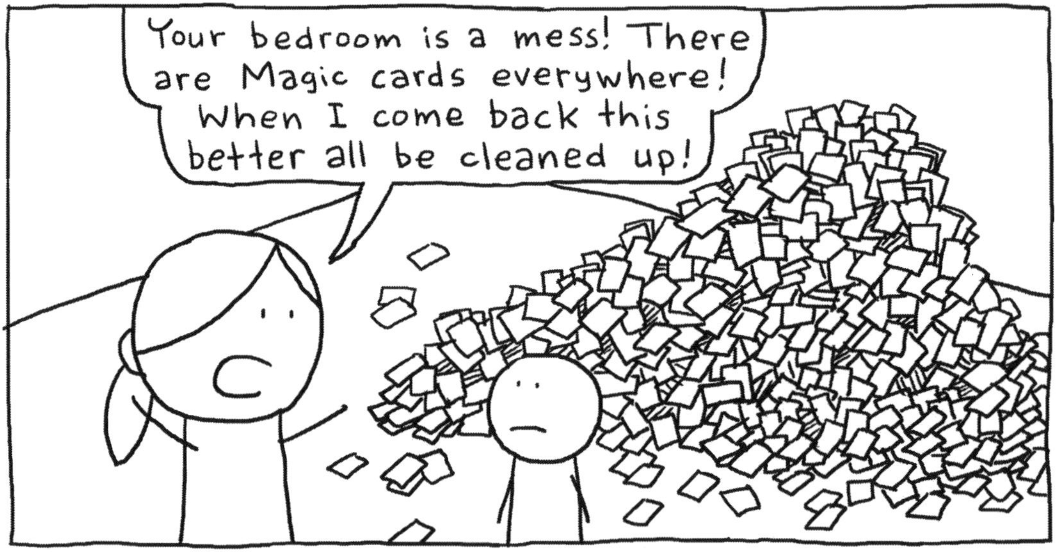
Your bedroom is a mess! There are Magic cards everywhere! When I come back this better all be cleaned up!

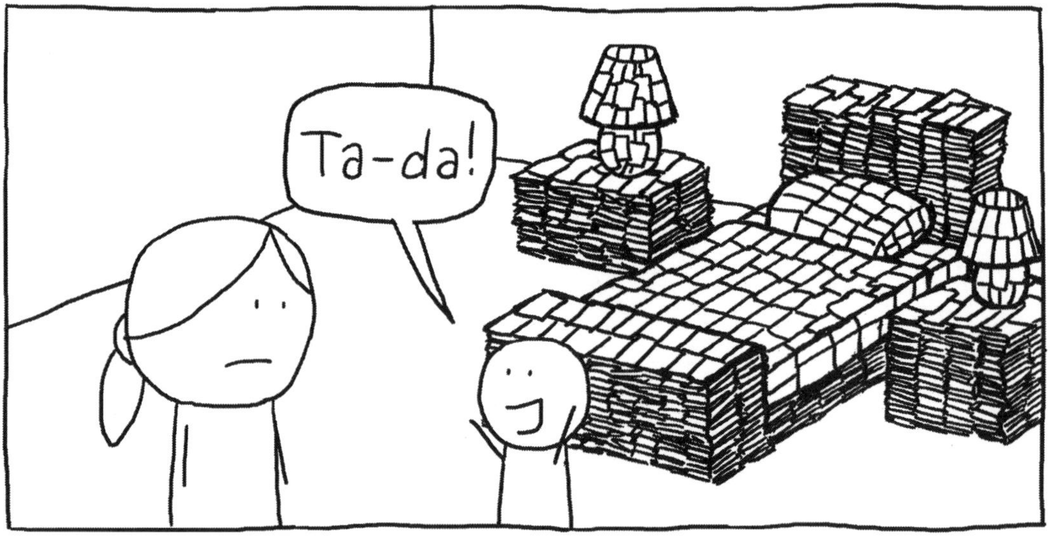
Ta-da!

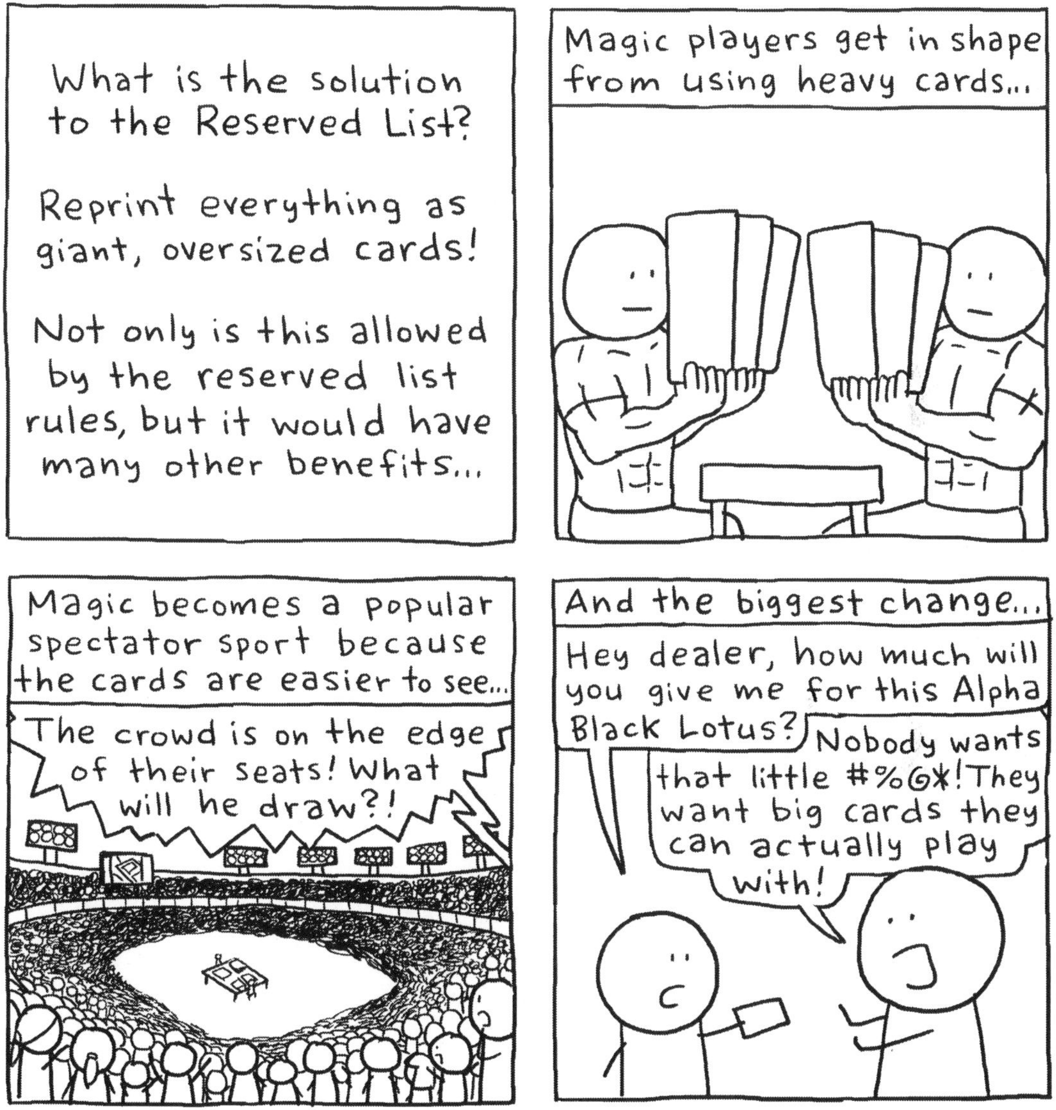
What is the solution to the Reserved List?
Reprint everything as giant, oversized cards!
Not only is this allowed by the reserved list rules, but it would have many other benefits...
Magic players get in shape from using heavy cards...
Magic becomes a popular spectator sport because the cards are easier to see...
The crowd is on the edge of their seats! What will he draw?!
And the biggest change...
Hey dealer, how much will you give me for this Alpha Black Lotus?
Nobody wants that little #%@*! They want big cards they can actually play with!

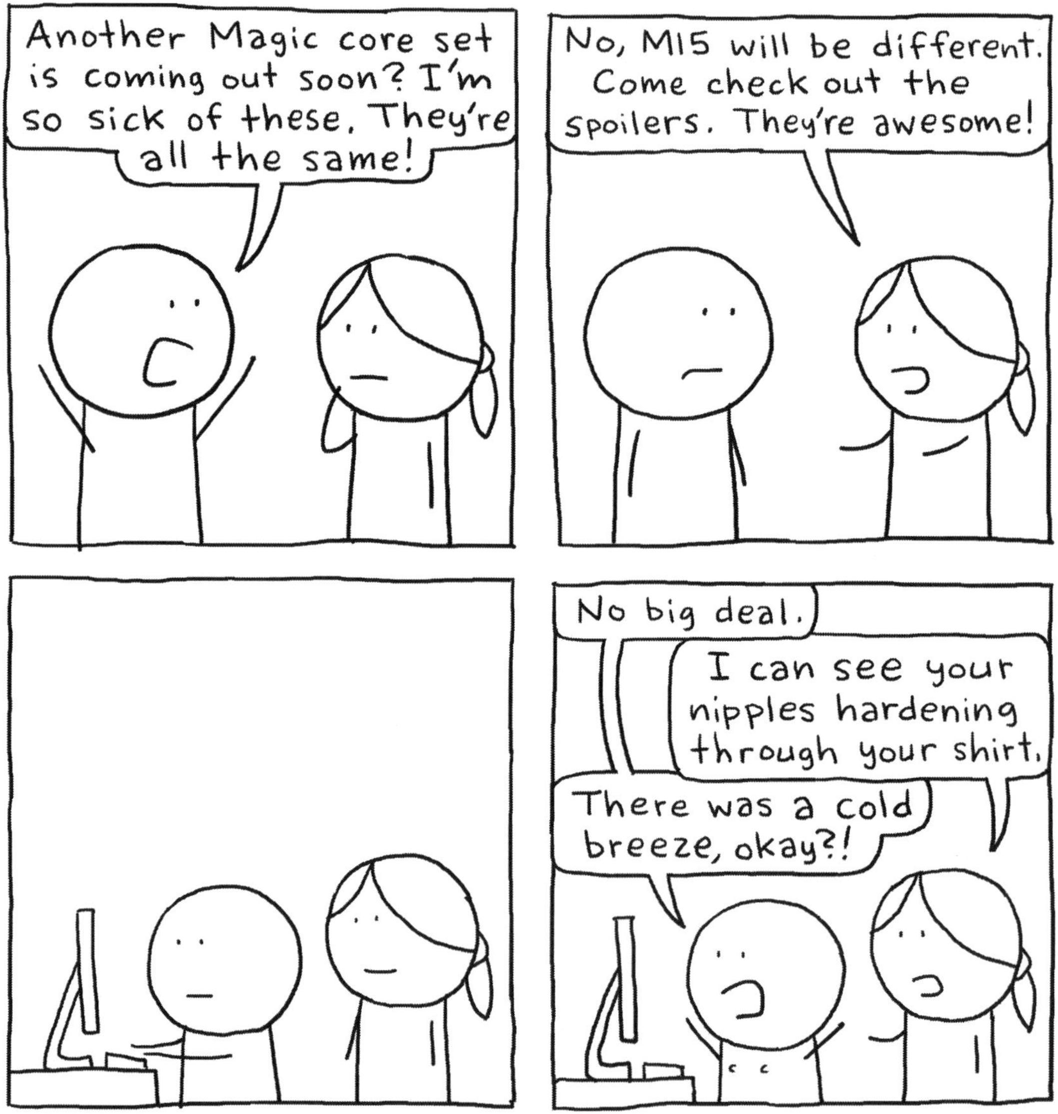
Another Magic core set is coming out soon? I'm so sick of these. They're all the same!
No, M15 will be different. Come check out the spoilers. They're awesome!
No big deal.
I can see your nipples hardening through your shirt.
There was a cold breeze, okay?!

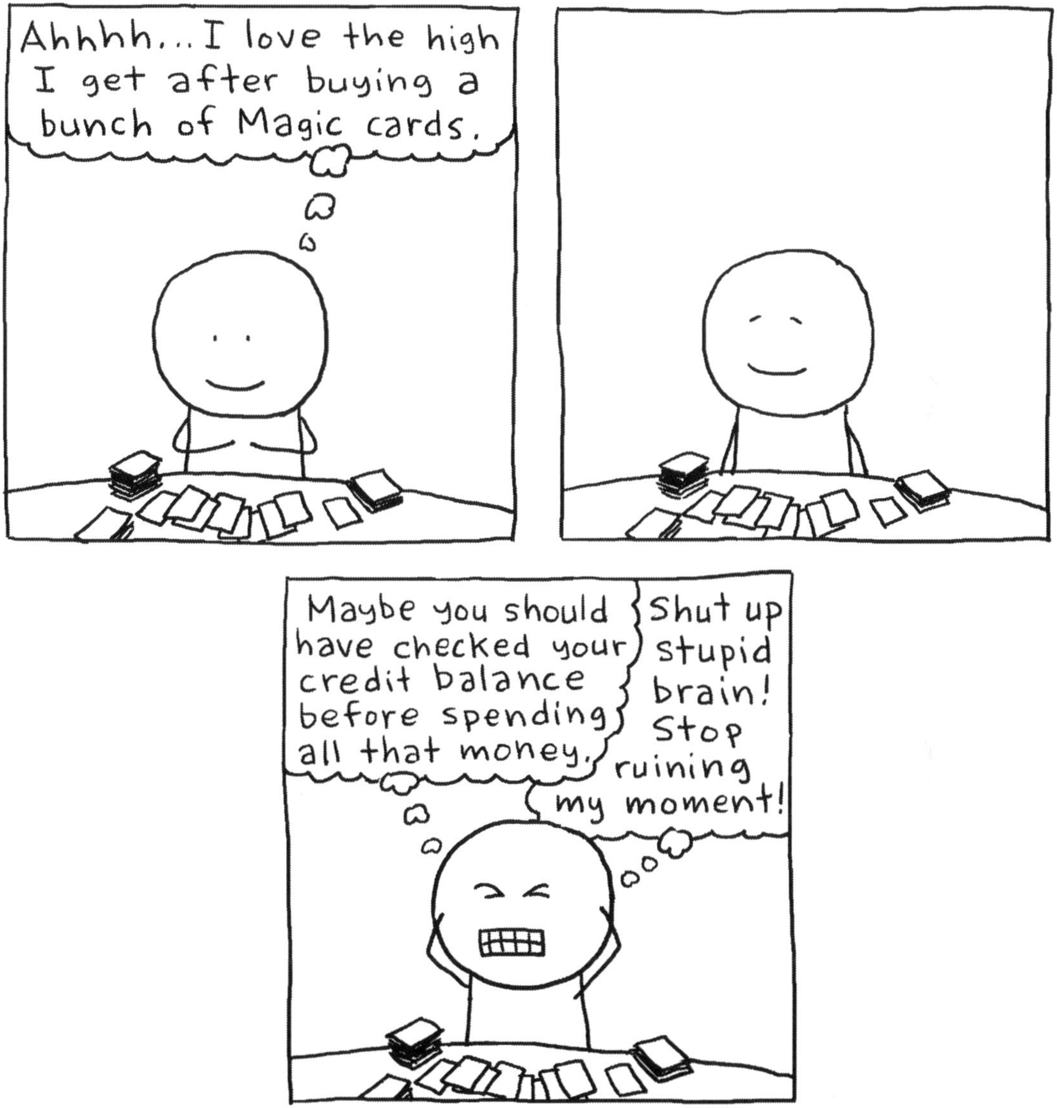
Ahhhh... I love the high I get after buying a bunch of Magic cards.
Maybe you should have checked your credit balance before spending all that money.
Shut up stupid brain! Stop ruining my moment!

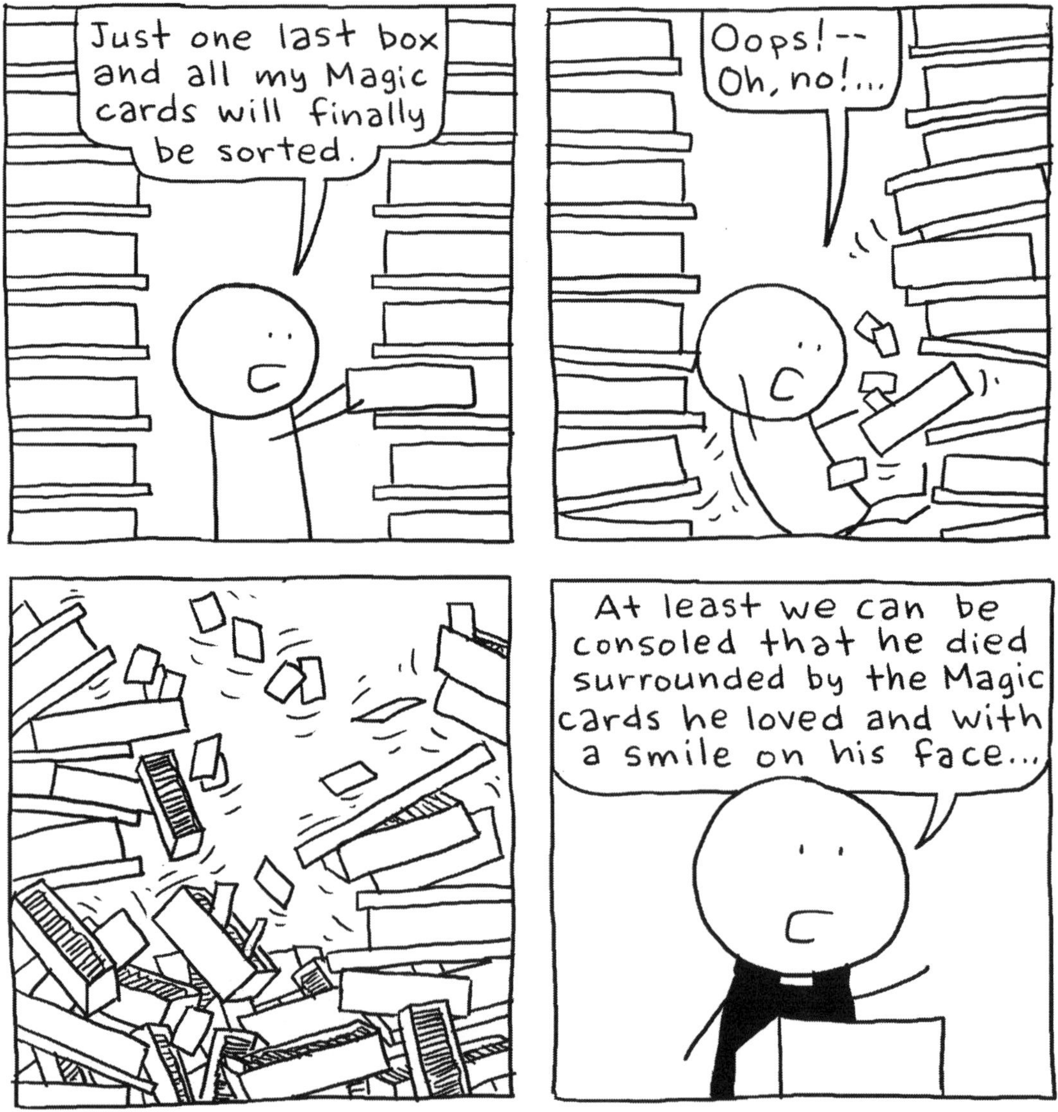
Just one last box and all my Magic cards will finally be sorted.
Oops!-- Oh, no!...
At least we can be consoled that he died surrounded by the Magic cards he loved and with a smile on his face...

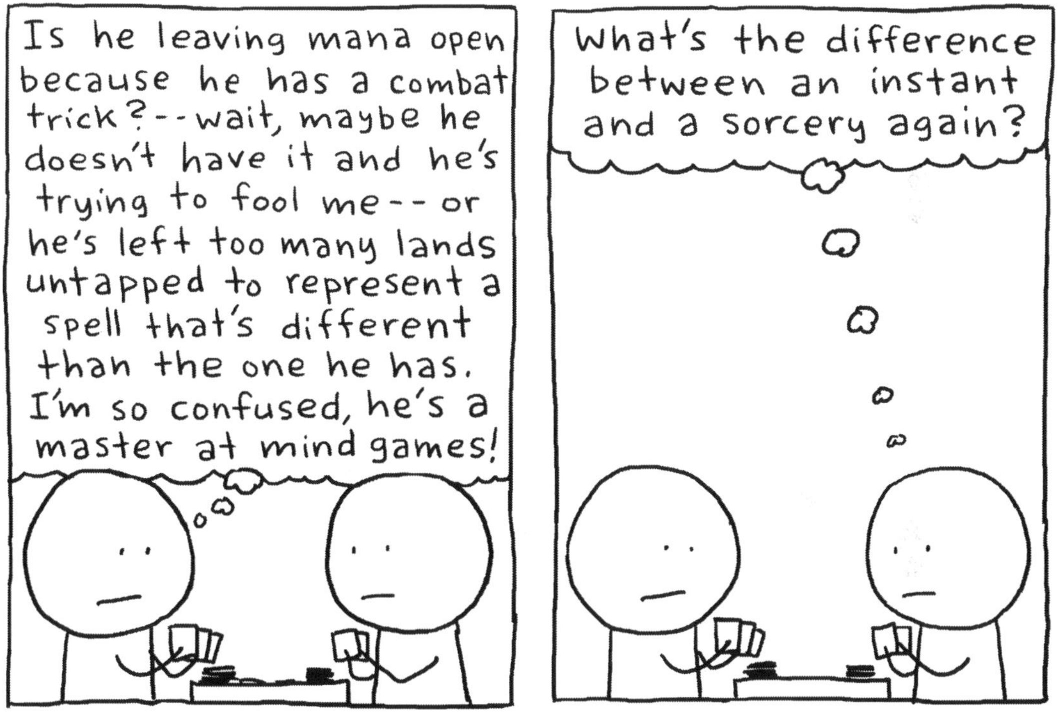
Is he leaving mana open because he has a combat trick?--wait, maybe he doesn't have it and he's trying to fool me--or he's left too many lands untapped to represent a spell that's different than the one he has. I'm so confused, he's a master at mind games!
What's the difference between an instant and a sorcery again?

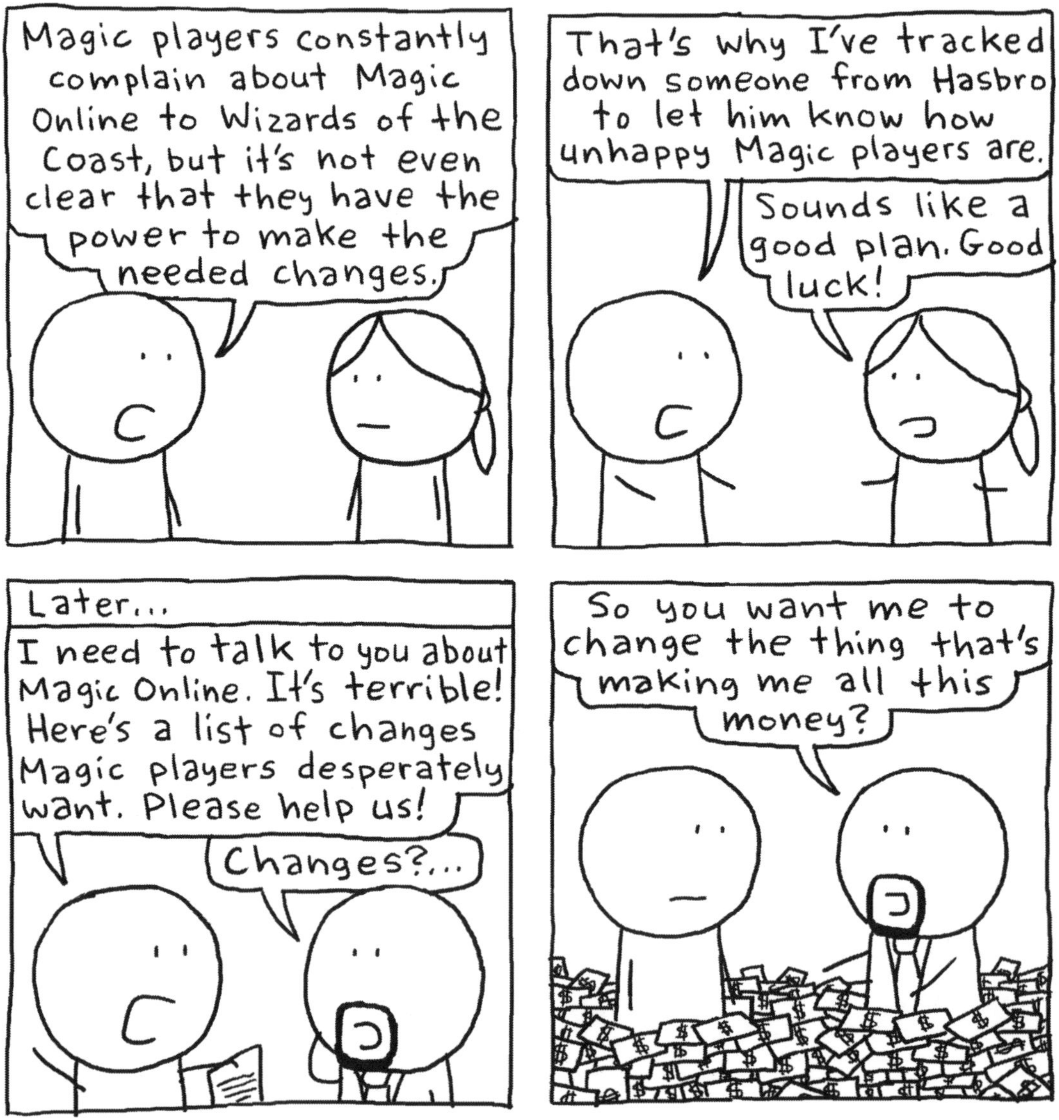
Magic players constantly complain about Magic Online to Wizards of the Coast, but it's not even clear that they have the power to make the needed changes.
That's why I've tracked down someone from Hasbro to let him know how unhappy Magic players are.
Sounds like a good plan. Good luck!
Later...
I need to talk to you about Magic Online. It's terrible! Here's a list of changes Magic players desperately want. Please help us!
Changes?...
So you want me to change the thing that's making me all this money?

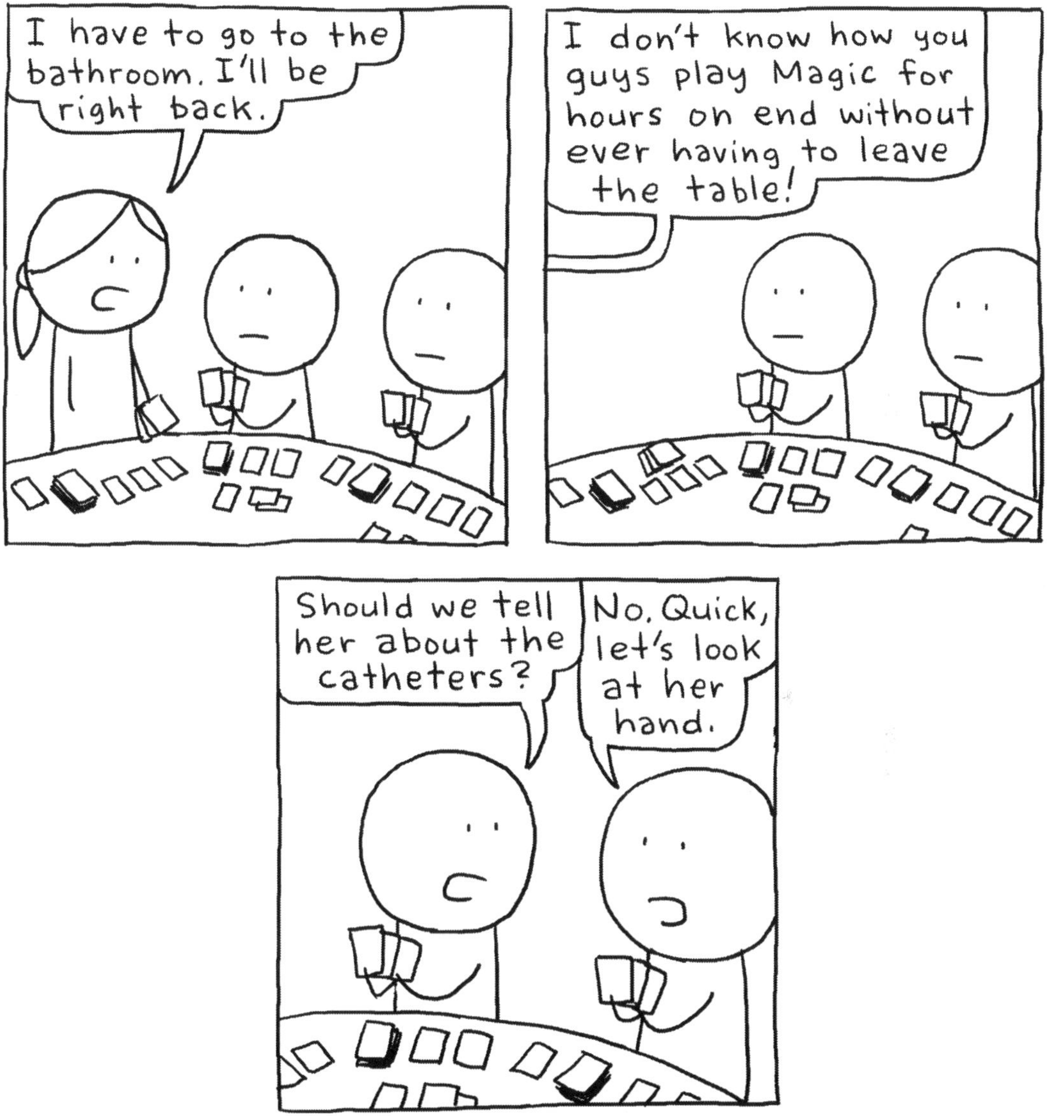
I have to go to the bathroom. I'll be right back.
I don't know how you guys play Magic for hours on end without ever having to leave the table!
Should we tell her about the catheters?
No. Quick, let's look at her hand.

I'm going to go on a run and listen to the latest Limited Resources podcast.
Okay, see you later.
5 1/2 hours later...
It looks like he died from running for too long.
Why did he have to run during a set review show?!

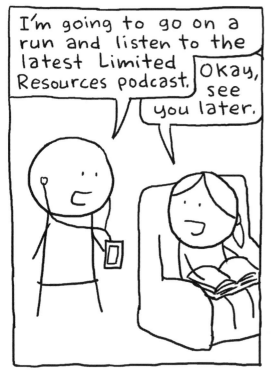

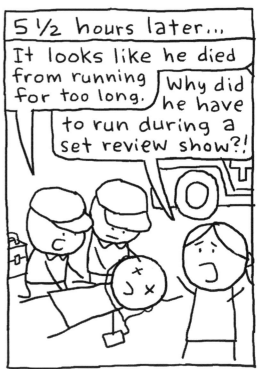

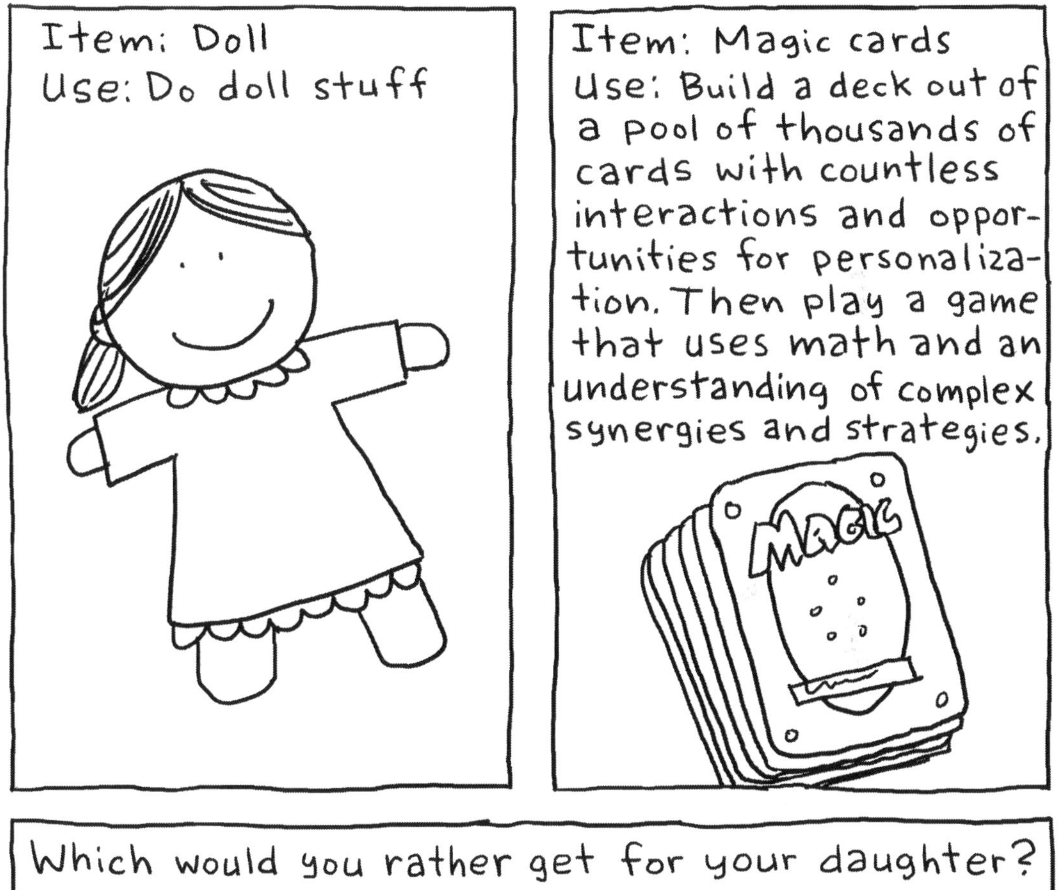
Item: Doll
Use: Do doll stuff
Item: Magic cards
Use: Build a deck out of a pool of thousands of cards with countless interactions and opportunities for personalization. Then play a game that uses math and an understanding of complex synergies and strategies.
MAGIC
Which would you rather get for your daughter?

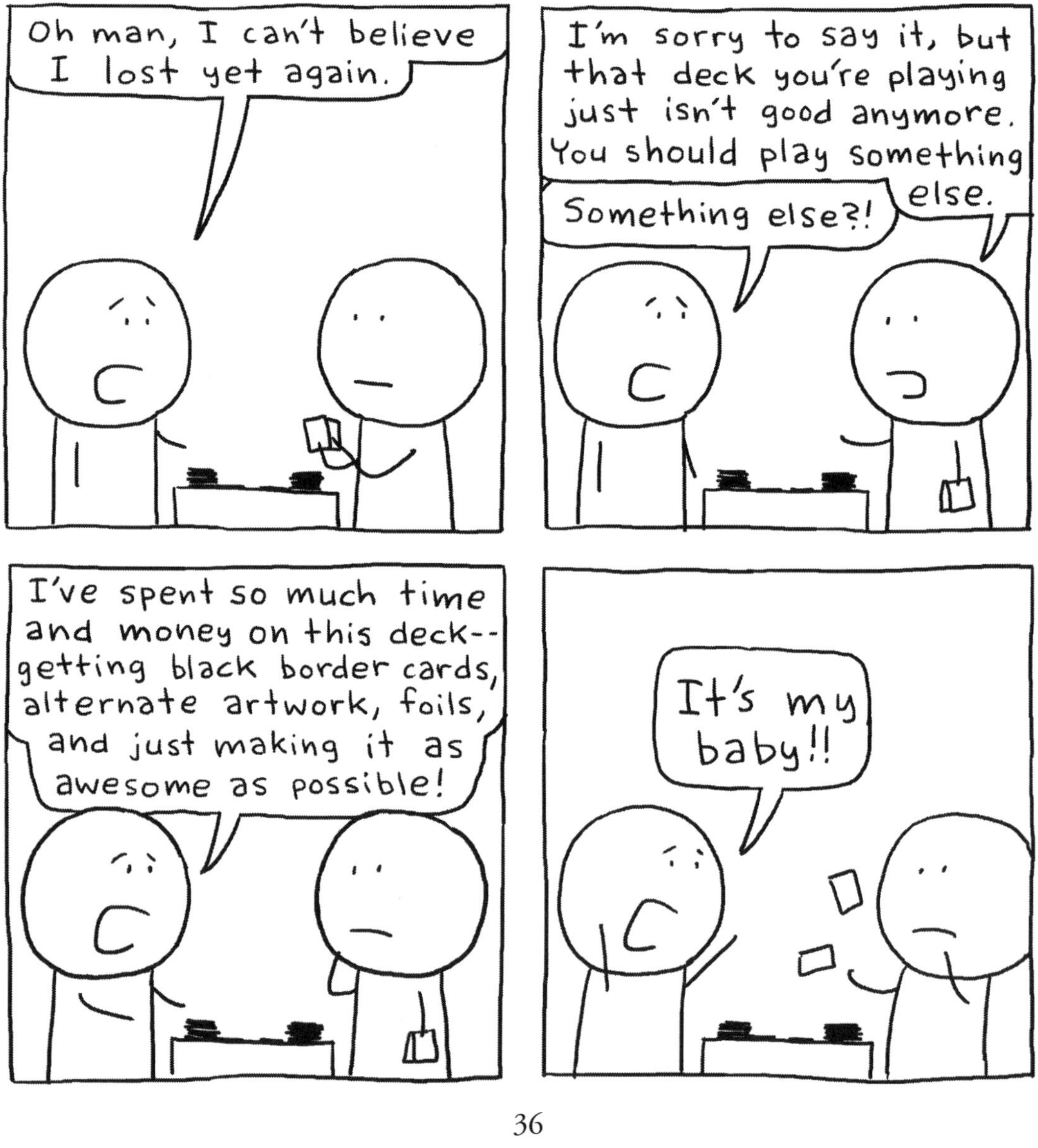
Oh man, I can't believe I lost yet again.
I'm sorry to say it, but that deck you're playing just isn't good anymore. You should play something else.
Something else?!
I've spent so much time and money on this deck--getting black border cards, alternate artwork, foils, and just making it as awesome as possible!
It's my baby!!

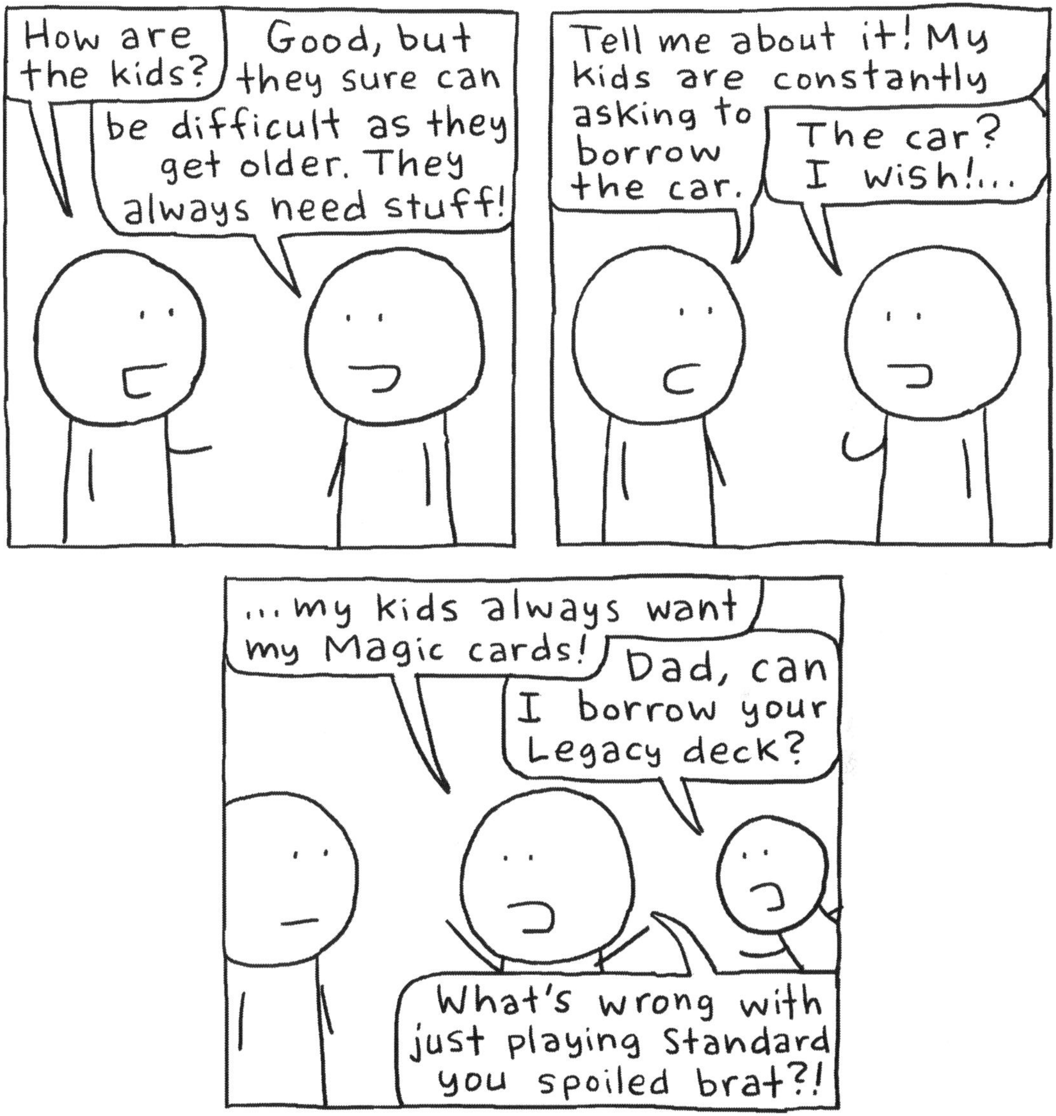
How are the kids?
Good, but they sure can be difficult as they get older. They always need stuff!
Tell me about it! My kids are constantly asking to borrow the car.
The car? I wish!...
...my kids always want my Magic cards!
Dad, can I borrow your Legacy deck?
What's wrong with just playing Standard you spoiled brat?!

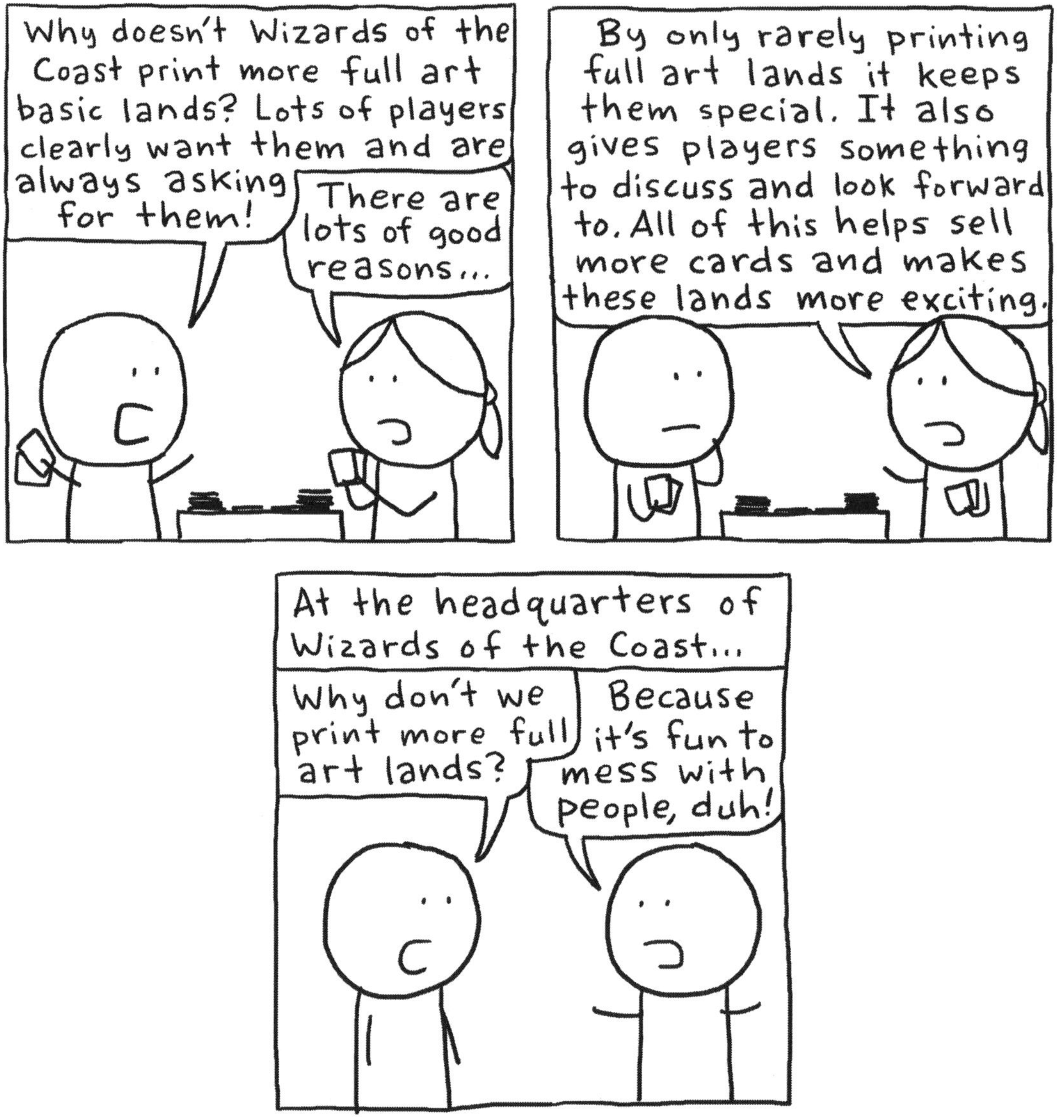
Why doesn't Wizards of the Coast print more full art basic lands? Lots of players clearly want them and are always asking for them!
There are lots of good reasons...
By only rarely printing full art lands it keeps them special. It also gives players something to discuss and look forward to. All of this helps sell more cards and makes these lands more exciting.
At the headquarters of Wizards of the Coast...
Why don't we print more full art lands?
Because it's fun to mess with people, duh!

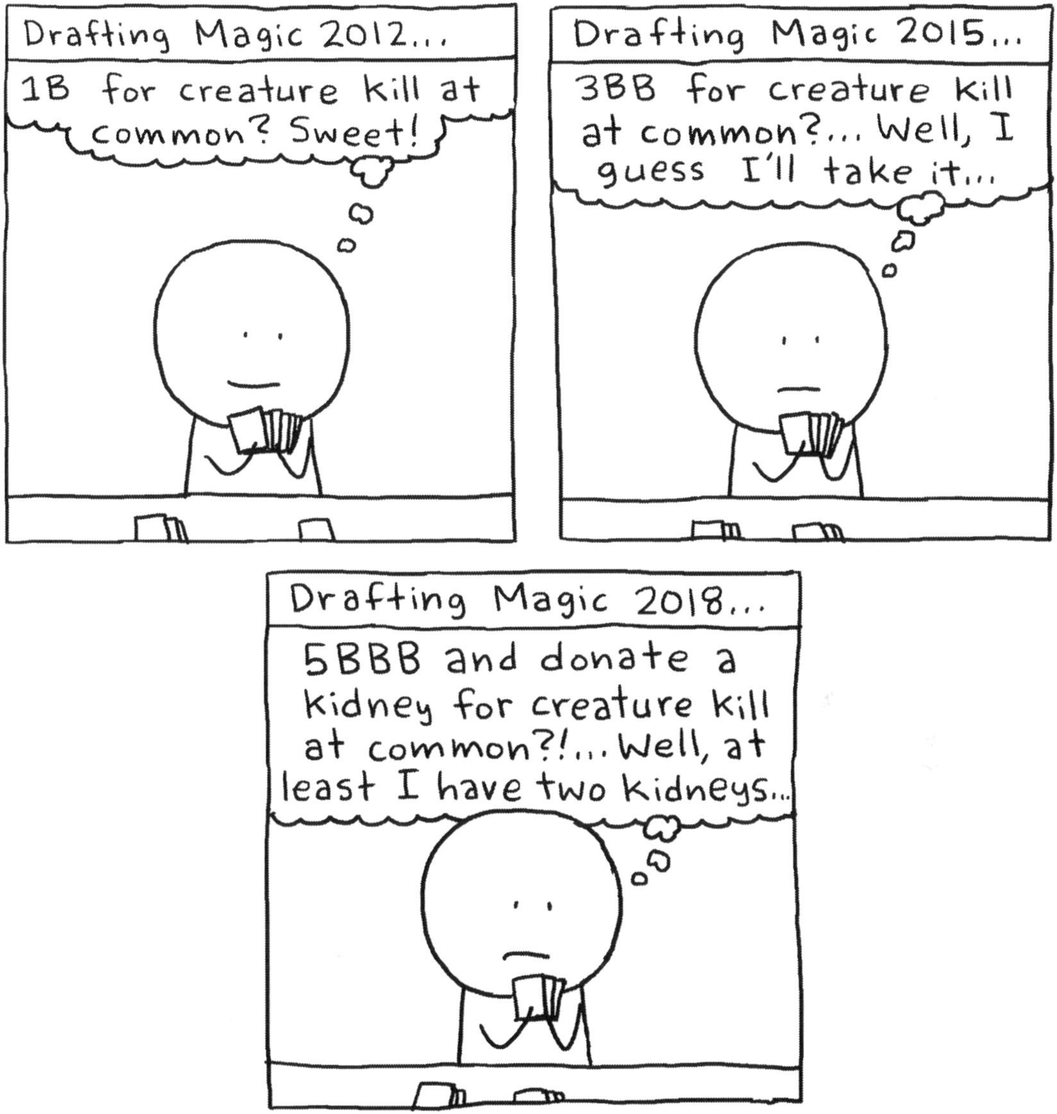
Drafting Magic 2012...
1B for creature kill at common? Sweet!
Drafting Magic 2015...
3BB for creature kill at common?... Well, I guess I'll take it...
Drafting Magic 2018...
5BBB and donate a kidney for creature kill at common?!... Well, at least I have two kidneys...

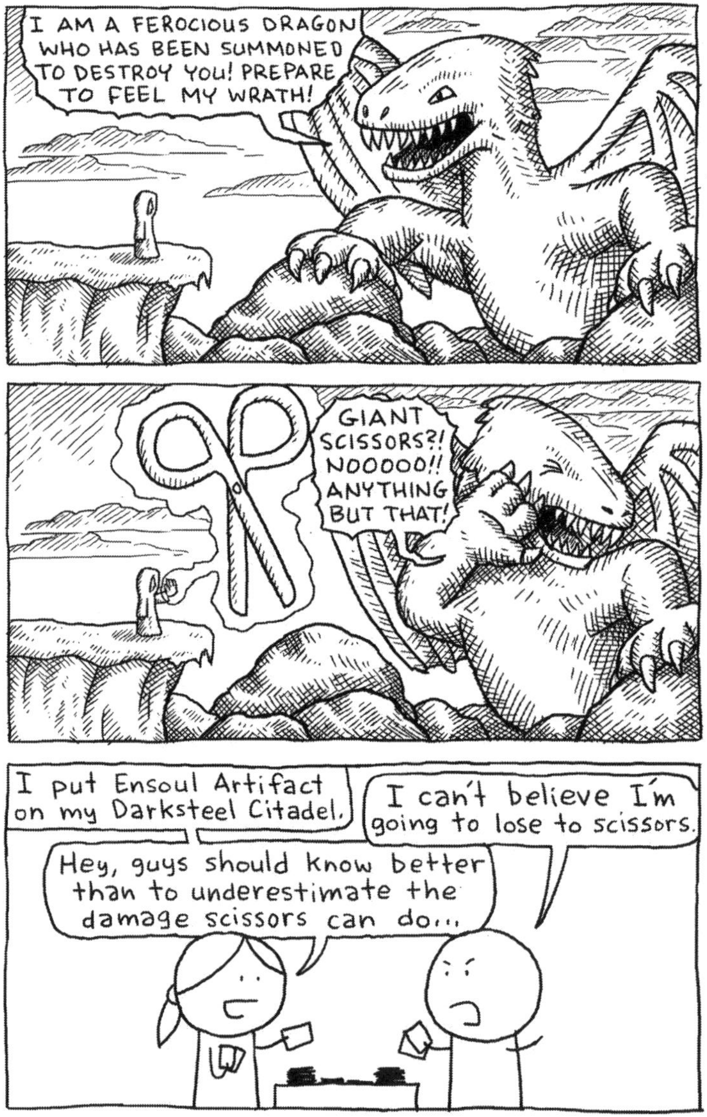
I AM A FEROCIOUS DRAGON WHO HAS BEEN SUMMONED TO DESTROY YOU! PREPARE TO FEEL MY WRATH!
GIANT SCISSORS?! NOOOOO!! ANYTHING BUT THAT!
I put Ensoul Artifact on my Darksteel Citadel.
I can't believe I'm going to lose to scissors.
Hey, guys should know better than to underestimate the damage scissors can do...

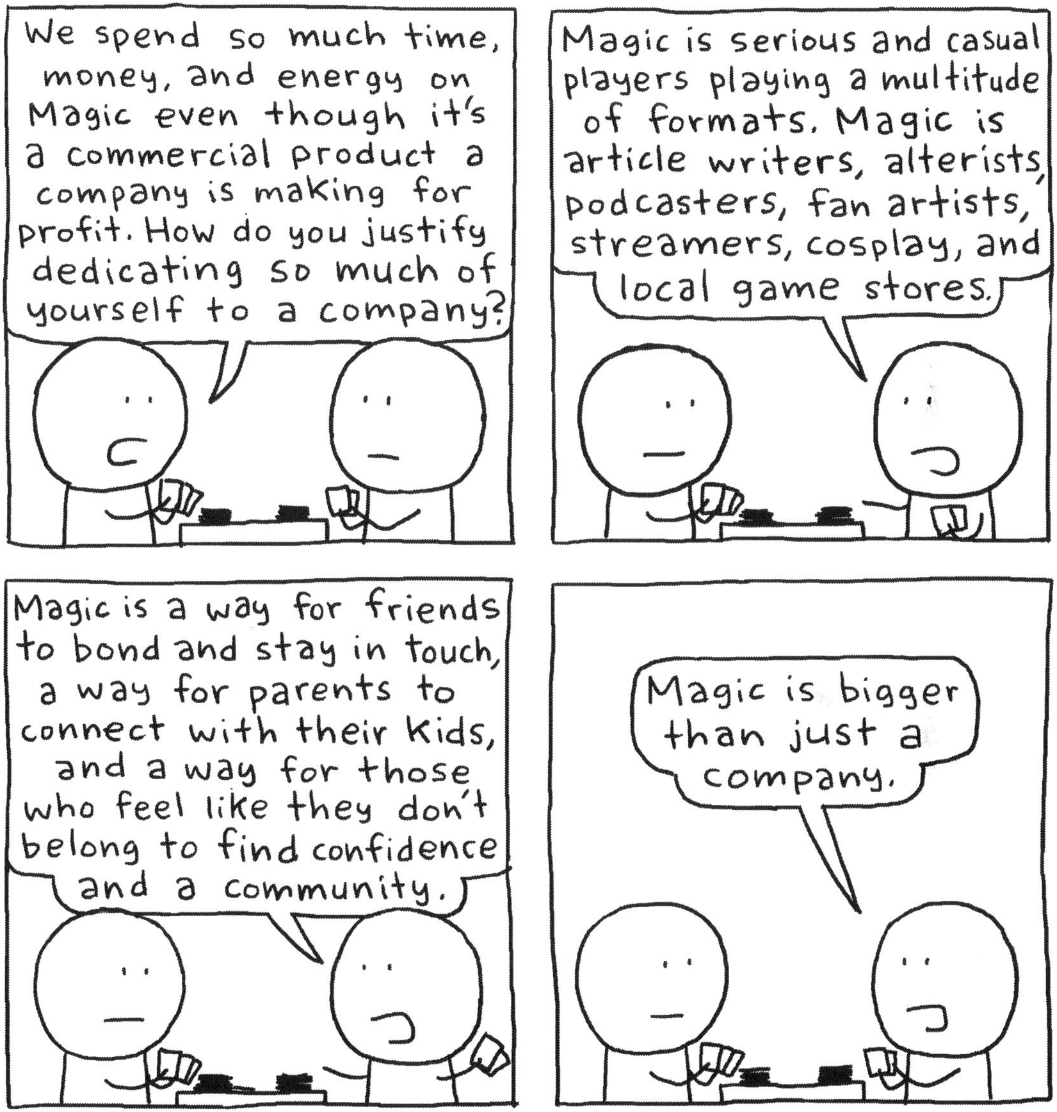
We spend so much time, money, and energy on Magic even though it's a commercial product a company is making for profit. How do you justify dedicating so much of yourself to a company?
Magic is serious and casual players playing a multitude of formats. Magic is article writers, alterists, podcasters, fan artists, streamers, cosplay, and local game stores.
Magic is a way for friends to bond and stay in touch, a way for parents to connect with their kids, and a way for those who feel like they don't belong to find confidence and a community.
Magic is bigger than just a company.

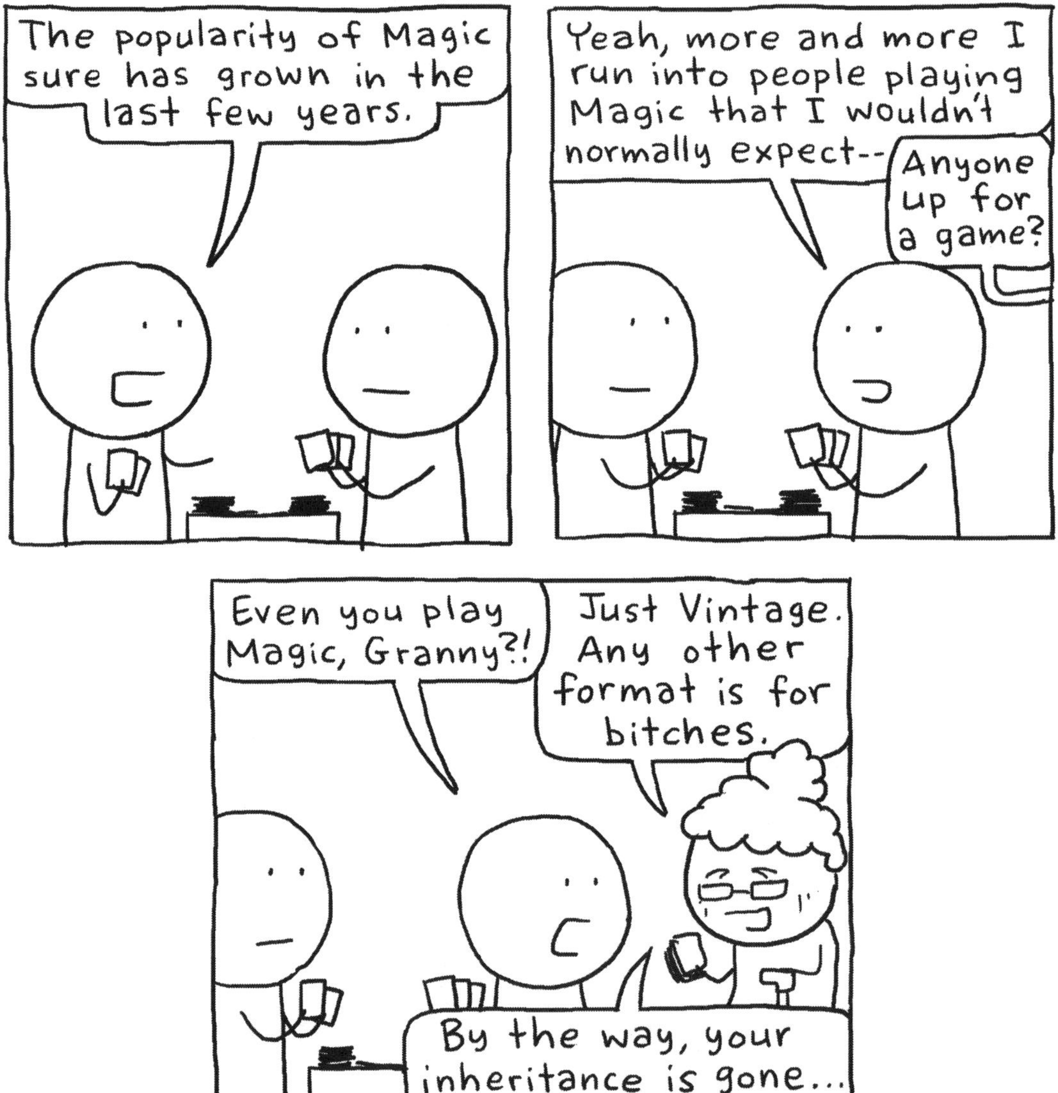
The popularity of Magic sure has grown in the last few years.
Yeah, more and more I run into people playing Magic that I wouldn't normally expect--
Anyone up for a game?
Even you play Magic, Granny?!
Just Vintage. Any other format is for bitches.
By the way, your inheritance is gone...

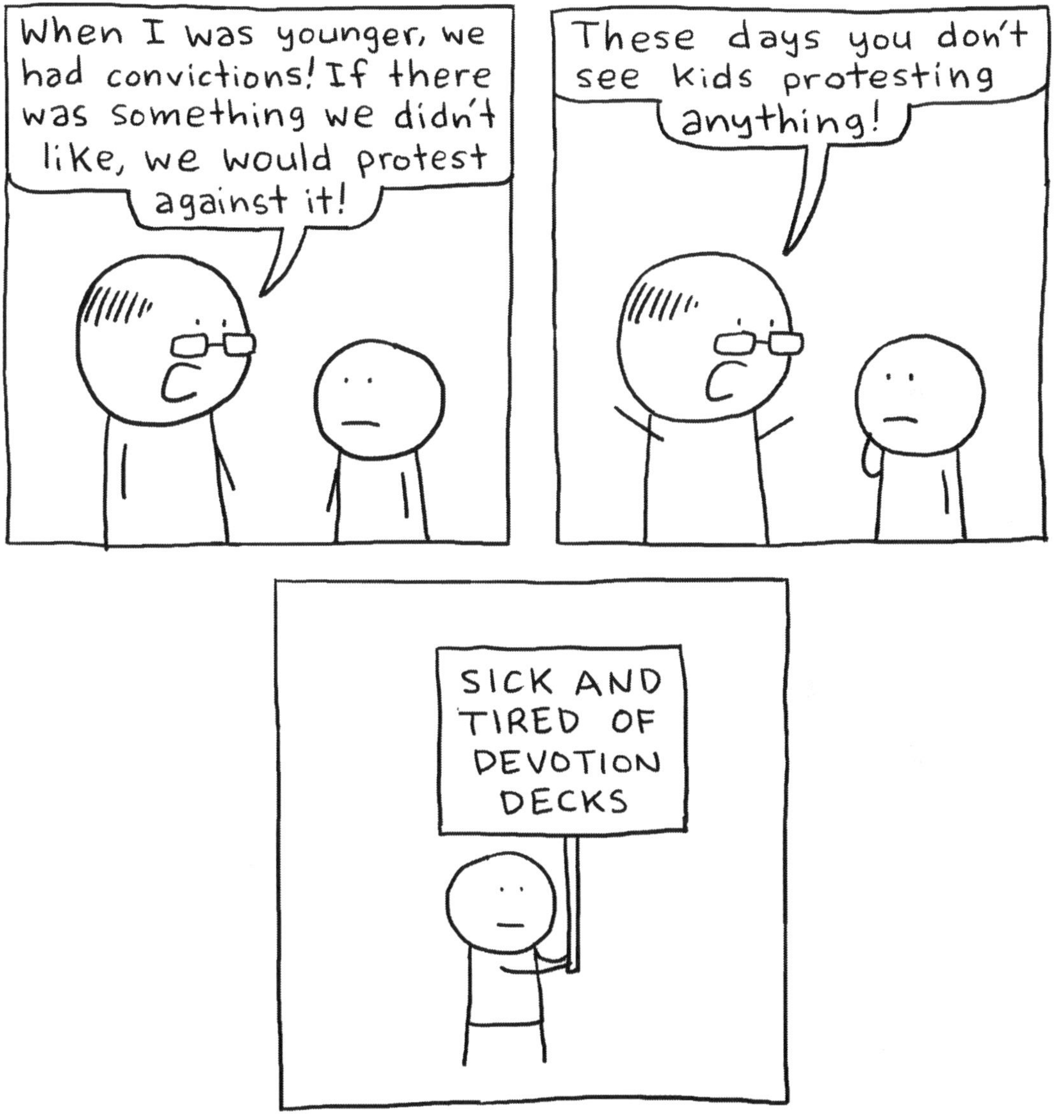
When I was younger, we had convictions! If there was something we didn't like, we would protest against it!
These days you don't see kids protesting anything!
SICK AND TIRED OF DEVOTION DECKS

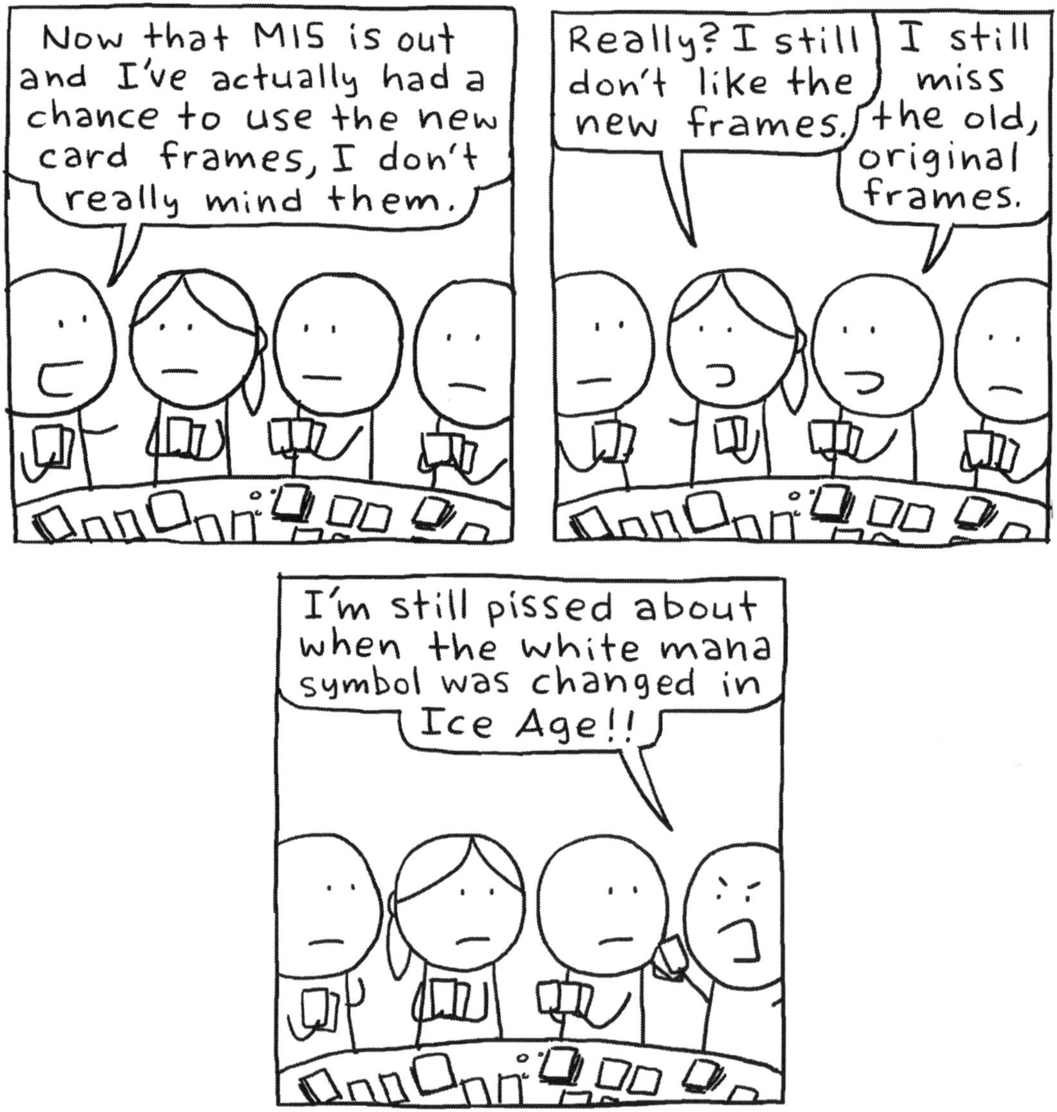
Now that M15 is out and I've actually had a chance to use the new card frames, I don't really mind them.
Really? I still don't like the new frames.
I still miss the old, original frames.
I'm still pissed about when the white mana symbol was changed in Ice Age!!

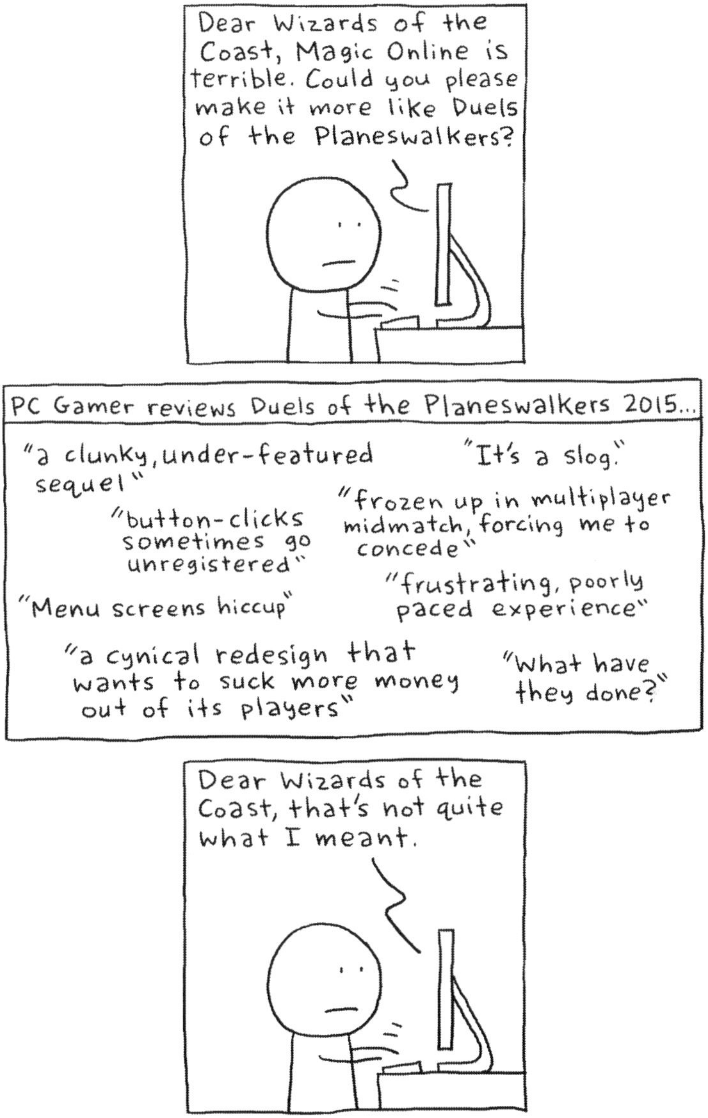
Dear Wizards of the Coast, Magic Online is terrible. Could you please make it more like Duels of the Planeswalkers?
PC Gamer reviews Duels of the Planeswalkers 2015...
"a clunky, under-featured sequel"
"It's a slog."
"button-clicks sometimes go unregistered"
"frozen up in multiplayer midmatch, forcing me to concede"
"Menu screens hiccup"
"frustrating, poorly paced experience"
"a cynical redesign that wants to suck more money out of its players"
"What have they done?"
Dear Wizards of the Coast, that's not quite what I meant.

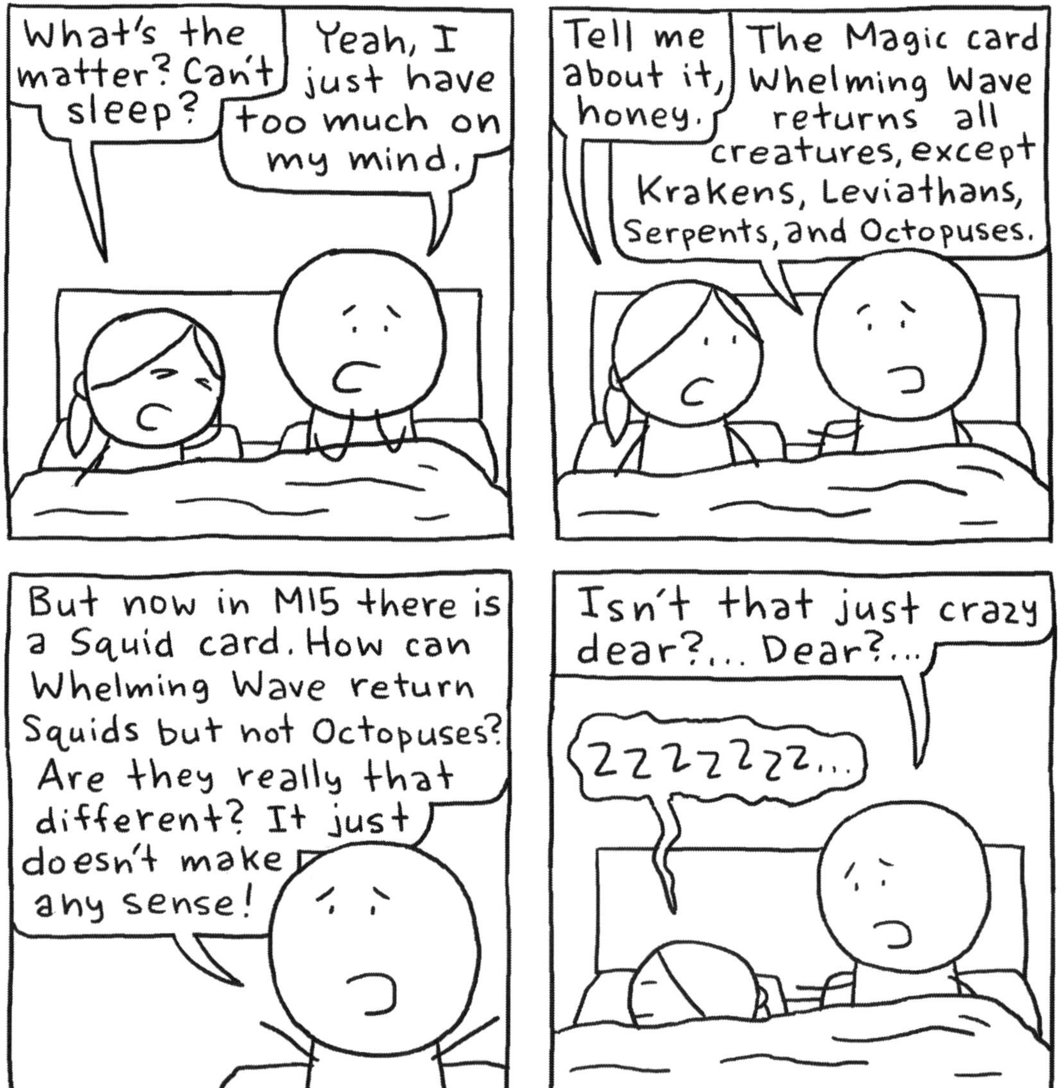
What's the matter? Can't sleep?
Yeah, I just have too much on my mind.
Tell me about it, honey.
The Magic card Whelming Wave returns all creatures, except Krakens, Leviathans, Serpents, and Octopuses.
But now in M15 there is a Squid card. How can Whelming Wave return Squids but not Octopuses? Are they really that different? It just doesn't make any sense!
Isn't that just crazy dear?... Dear?...
ZZZZZZZ...

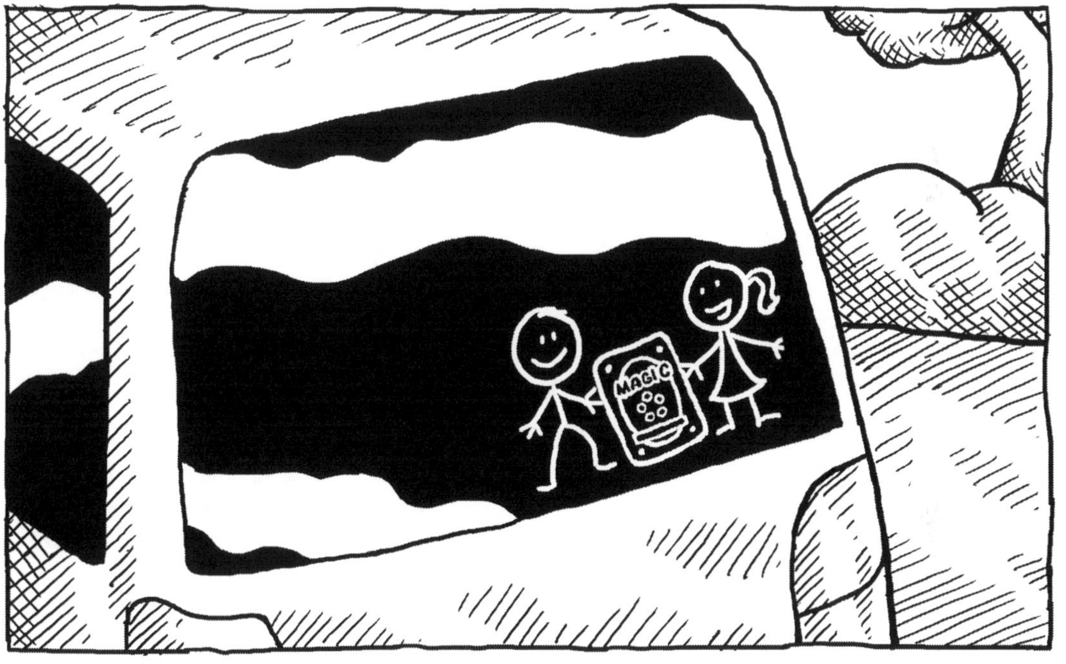
MAGIC

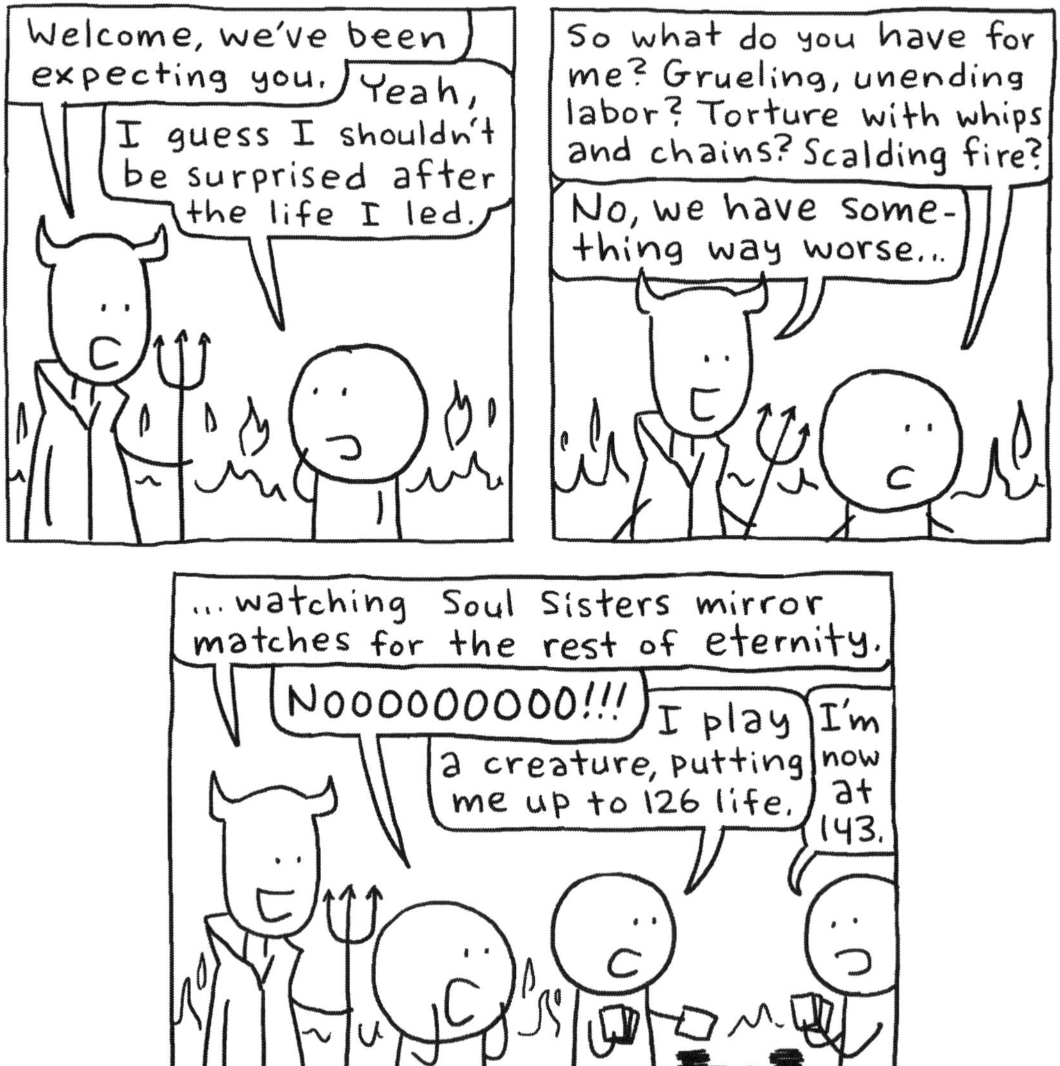
Welcome, we've been expecting you.
Yeah, I guess I shouldn't be surprised after the life I led.
So what do you have for me? Grueling, unending labor? Torture with whips and chains? Scalding fire?
No, we have something way worse...
...watching Soul Sisters mirror matches for the rest of eternity.
Noooooooooo!!!
I play a creature, putting me up to 126 life.
I'm now at 143.

Can I buy a lottery ticket?
Of course not! You're way too young!
Can I buy a pack of Modern Masters?
Sure!

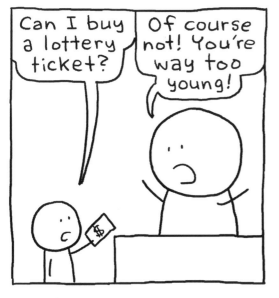

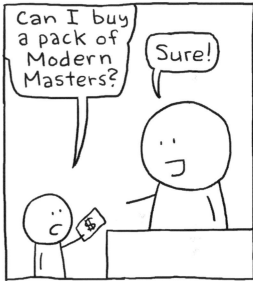

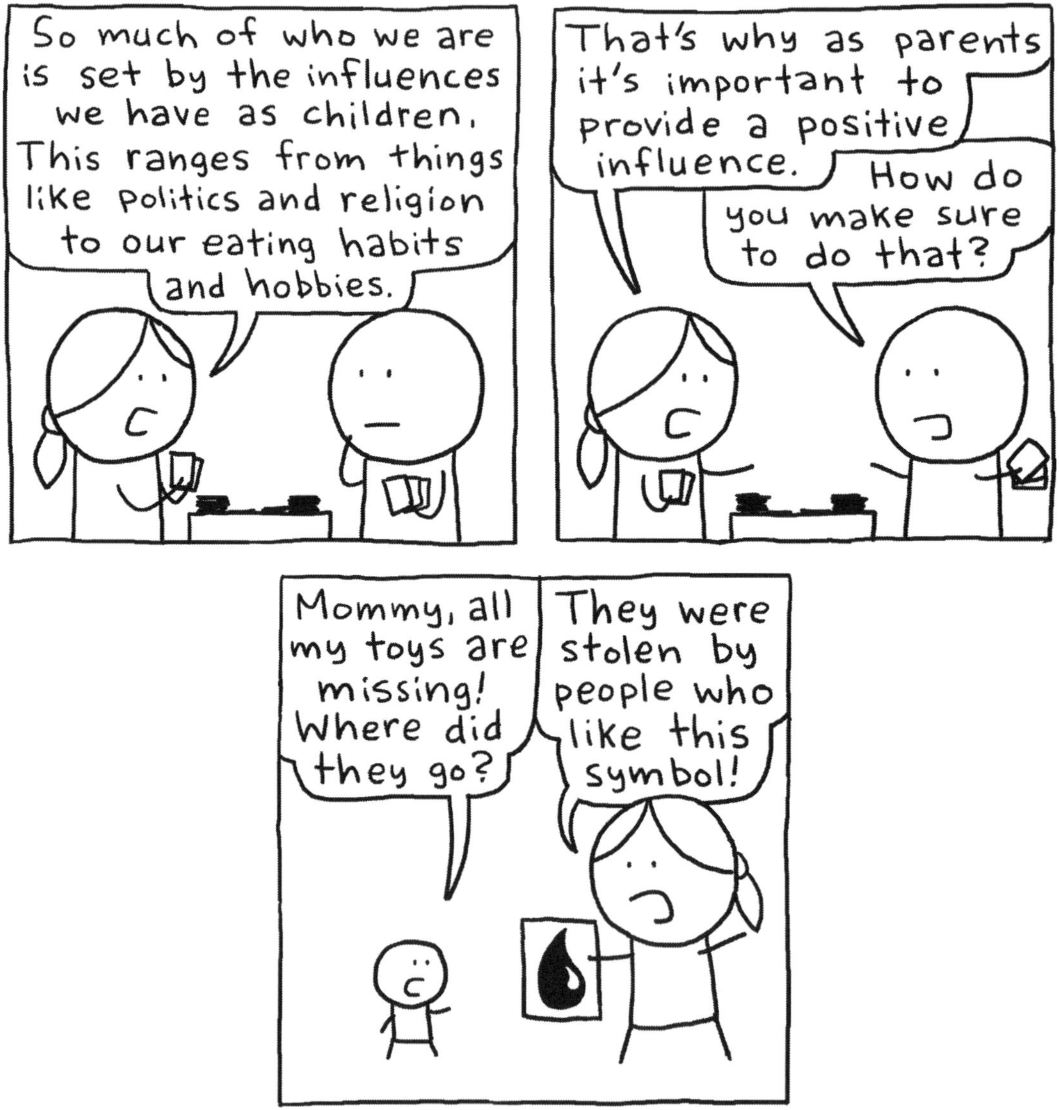
So much of who we are is set by the influences we have as children. This ranges from things like politics and religion to our eating habits and hobbies.
That's why as parents it's important to provide a positive influence.
How do you make sure to do that?
Mommy, all my toys are missing! Where did they go?
They were stolen by people who like this symbol!

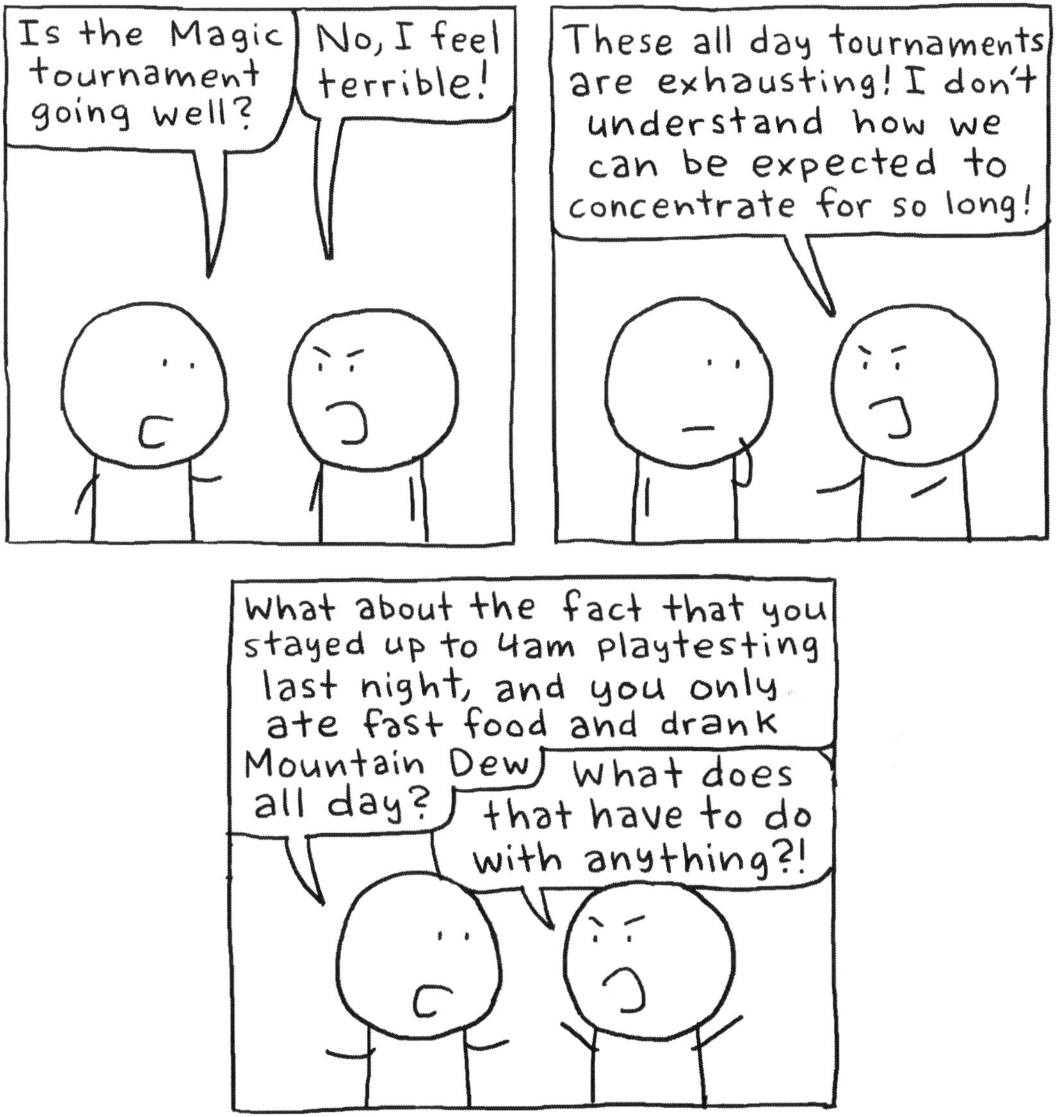
Is the Magic tournament going well?
No, I feel terrible!
These all day tournaments are exhausting! I don't understand how we can be expected to concentrate for so long!
What about the fact that you stayed up to 4am playtesting last night, and you only ate fast food and drank Mountain Dew all day?
What does that have to do with anything?!

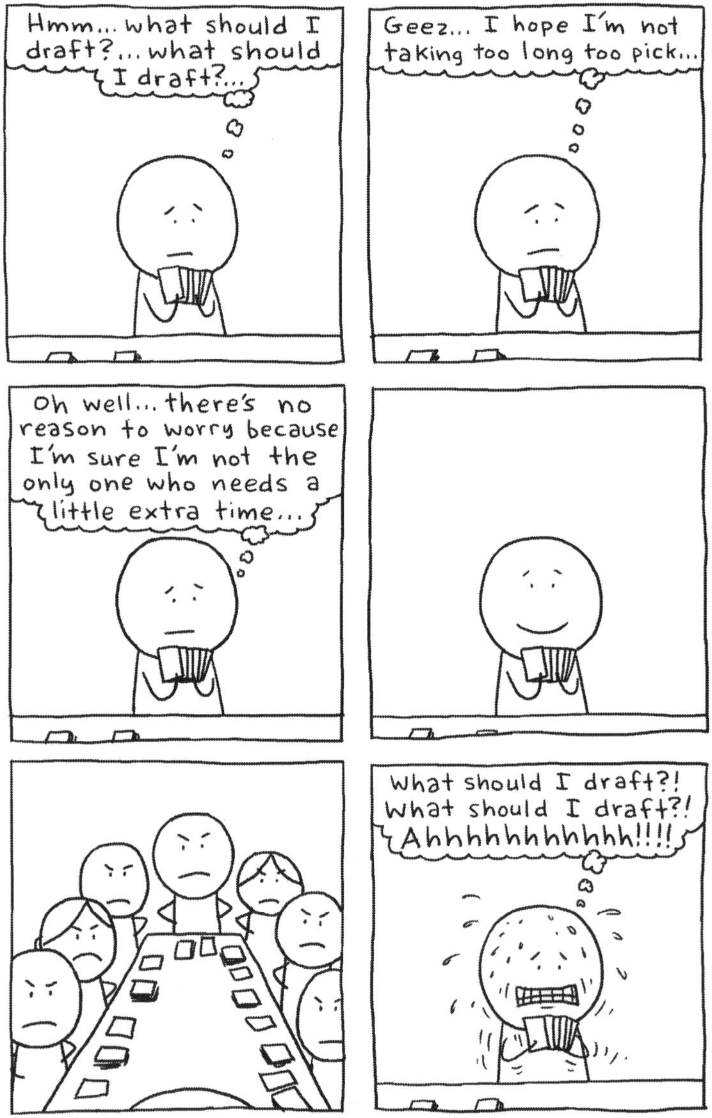
Hmm... what should I draft?... what should I draft?...
Geez... I hope I'm not taking too long too pick...
Oh well... there's no reason to worry because I'm sure I'm not the only one who needs a little extra time...
What should I draft?! What should I draft?! Ahhhhhhhhhh!!!!

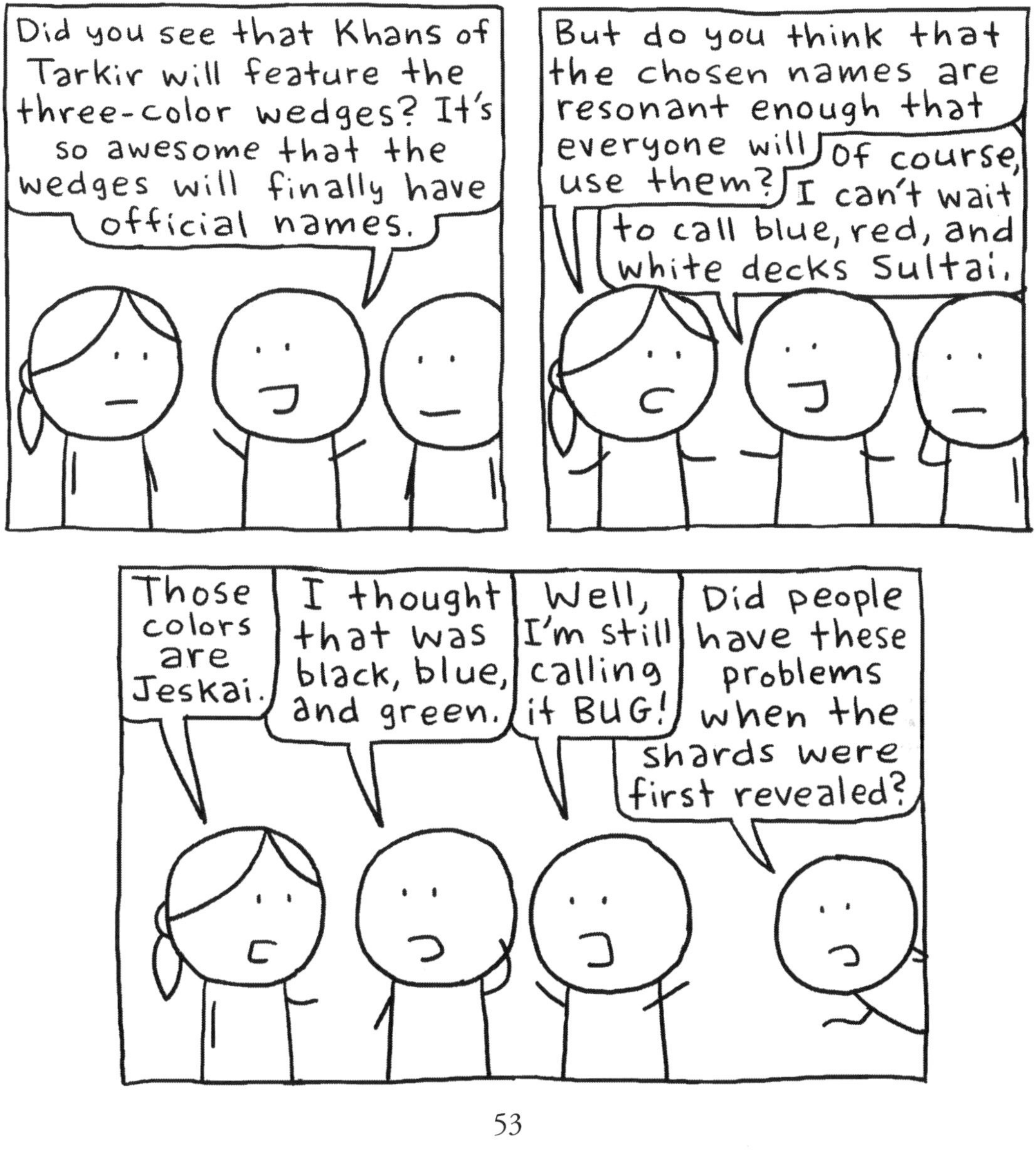
Did you see that Khans of Tarkir will feature the three-color wedges? It's so awesome that the wedges will finally have official names.
But do you think that the chosen names are resonant enough that everyone will use them?
Of course, I can't wait to call blue, red, and white decks Sultai.
Those colors are Jeskai.
I thought that was black, blue, and green.
Well, I'm still calling it BUG!
Did people have these problems when the shards were first revealed?

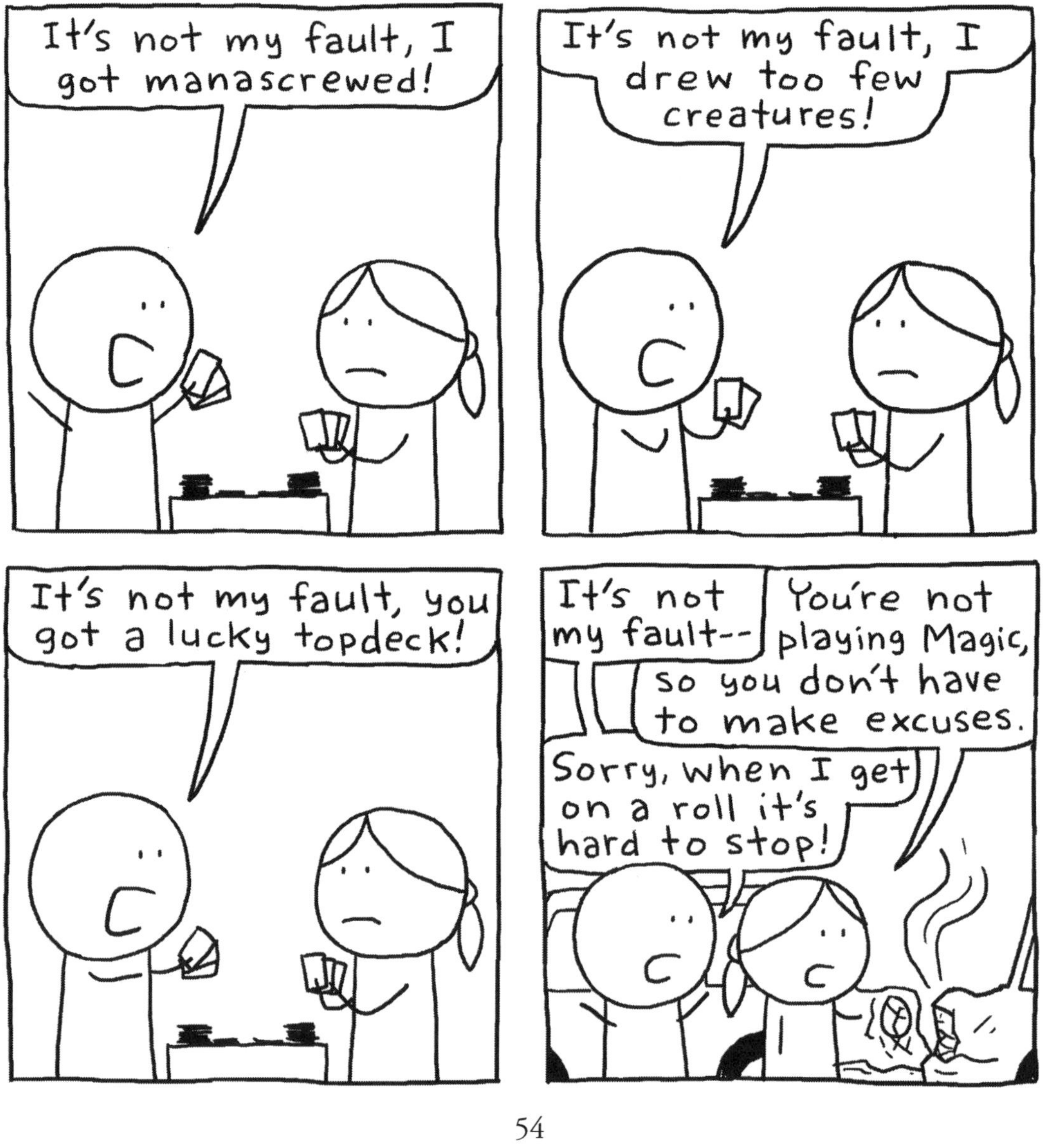
It's not my fault, I got manascrewed!
It's not my fault, I drew too few creatures!
It's not my fault, you got a lucky topdeck!
It's not my fault--
You're not playing Magic, so you don't have to make excuses.
Sorry, when I get on a roll it's hard to stop!

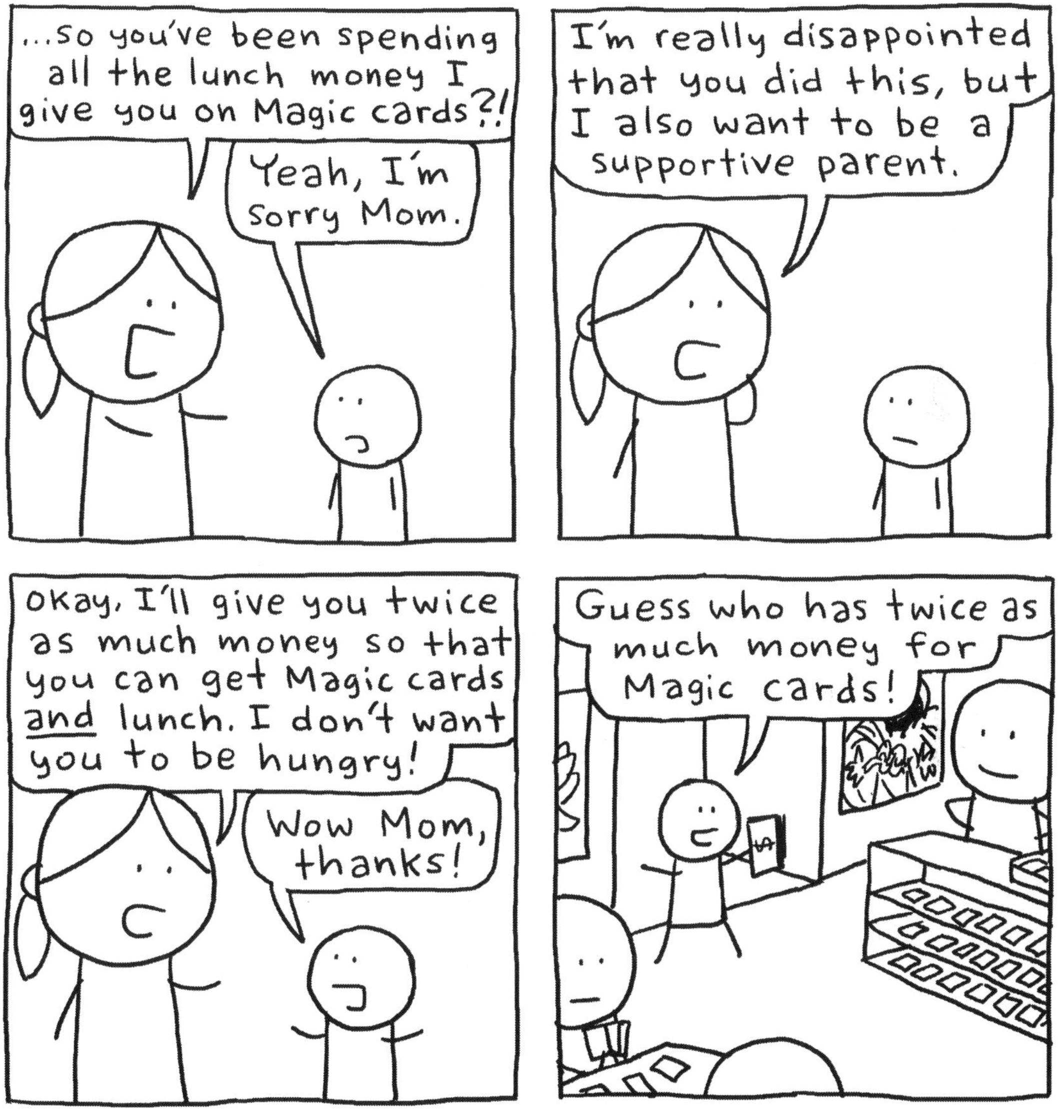
...so you've been spending all the lunch money I give you on Magic cards?!
Yeah, I'm sorry Mom.
I'm really disappointed that you did this, but I also want to be a supportive parent.
Okay, I'll give you twice as much money so that you can get Magic cards and lunch. I don't want you to be hungry!
Wow Mom, thanks!
Guess who has twice as much money for Magic cards!

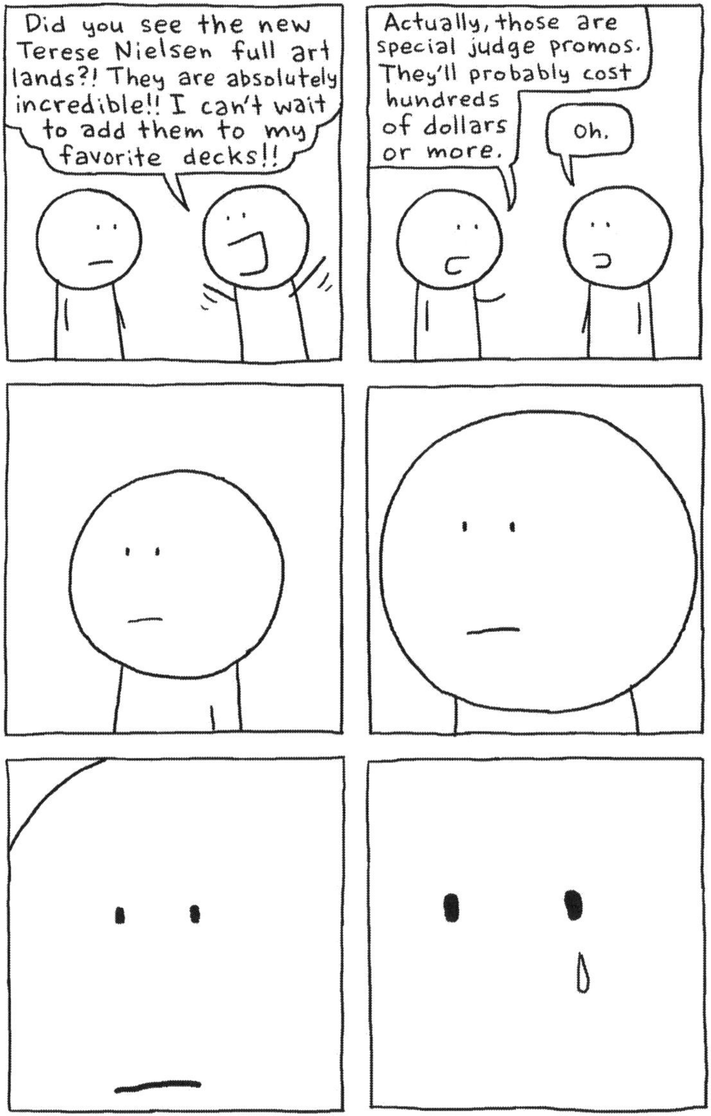
Did you see the new Terese Nielsen full art lands?! They are absolutely incredible!! I can't wait to add them to my favorite decks!!
Actually, those are special judge promos. They'll probably cost hundreds of dollars or more.
Oh.

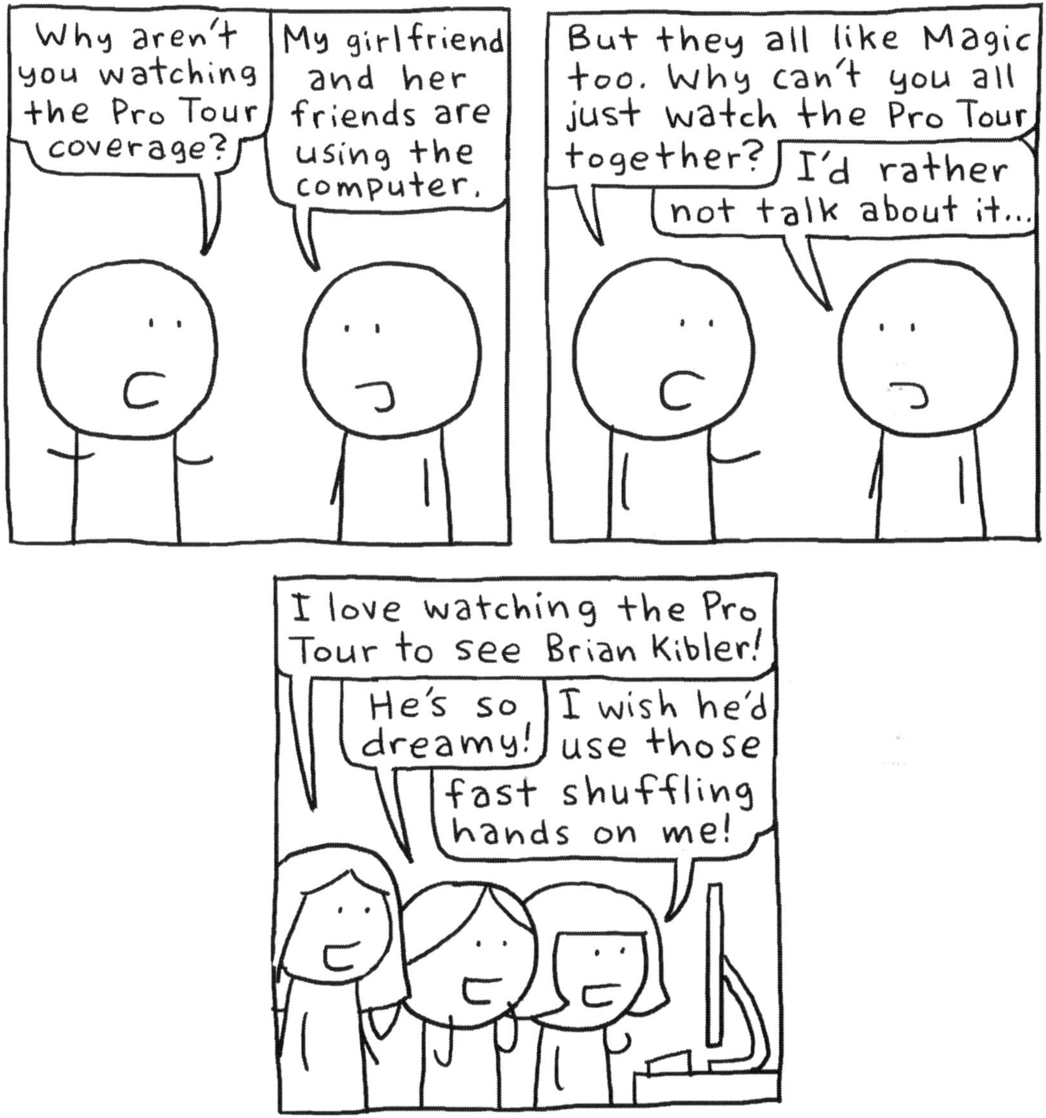
Why aren't you watching the Pro Tour coverage?
My girlfriend and her friends are using the computer.
But they all like Magic too. Why can't you all just watch the Pro Tour together?
I'd rather not talk about it...
I love watching the Pro Tour to see Brian Kibler!
He's so dreamy!
I wish he'd use those fast shuffling hands on me!

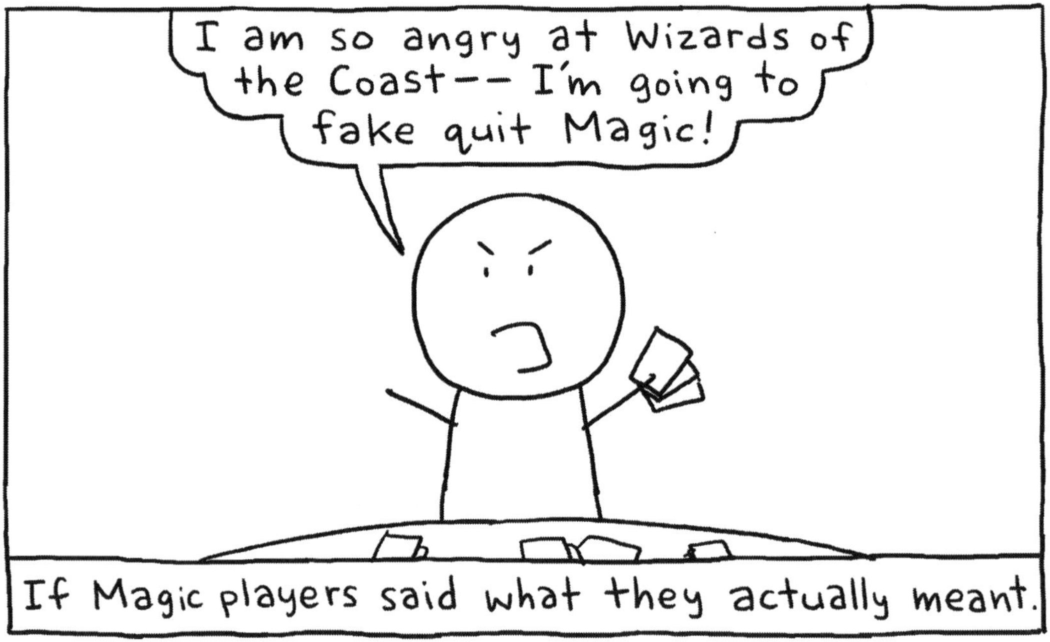
I am so angry at Wizards of the Coast-- I'm going to fake quit Magic!
If Magic players said what they actually meant.

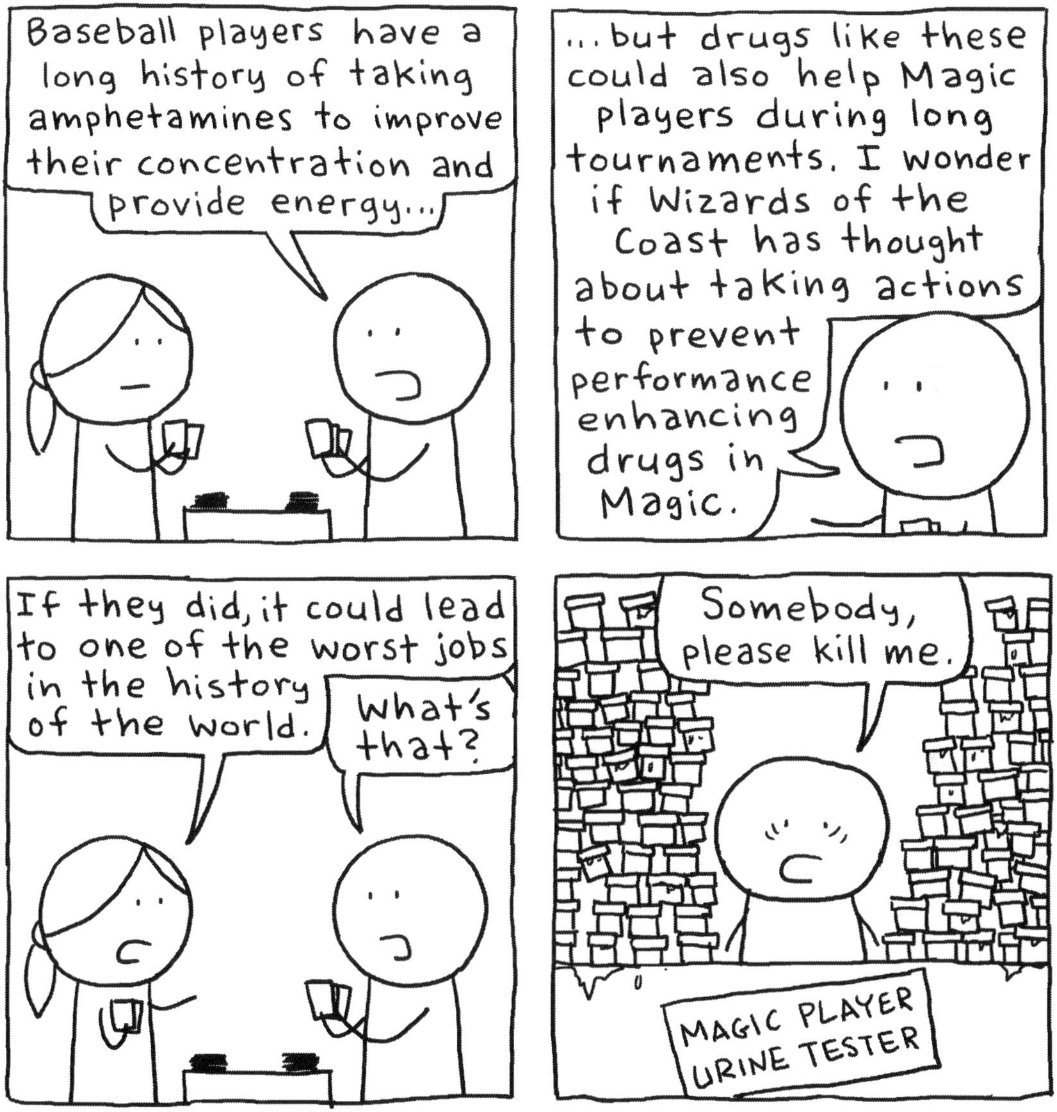
Baseball players have a long history of taking amphetamines to improve their concentration and provide energy...
...but drugs like these could also help Magic players during long tournaments. I wonder if Wizards of the Coast has thought about taking actions to prevent performance enhancing drugs in Magic.
If they did, it could lead to one of the worst jobs in the history of the world.
What's that?
Somebody, please kill me.
MAGIC PLAYER URINE TESTER

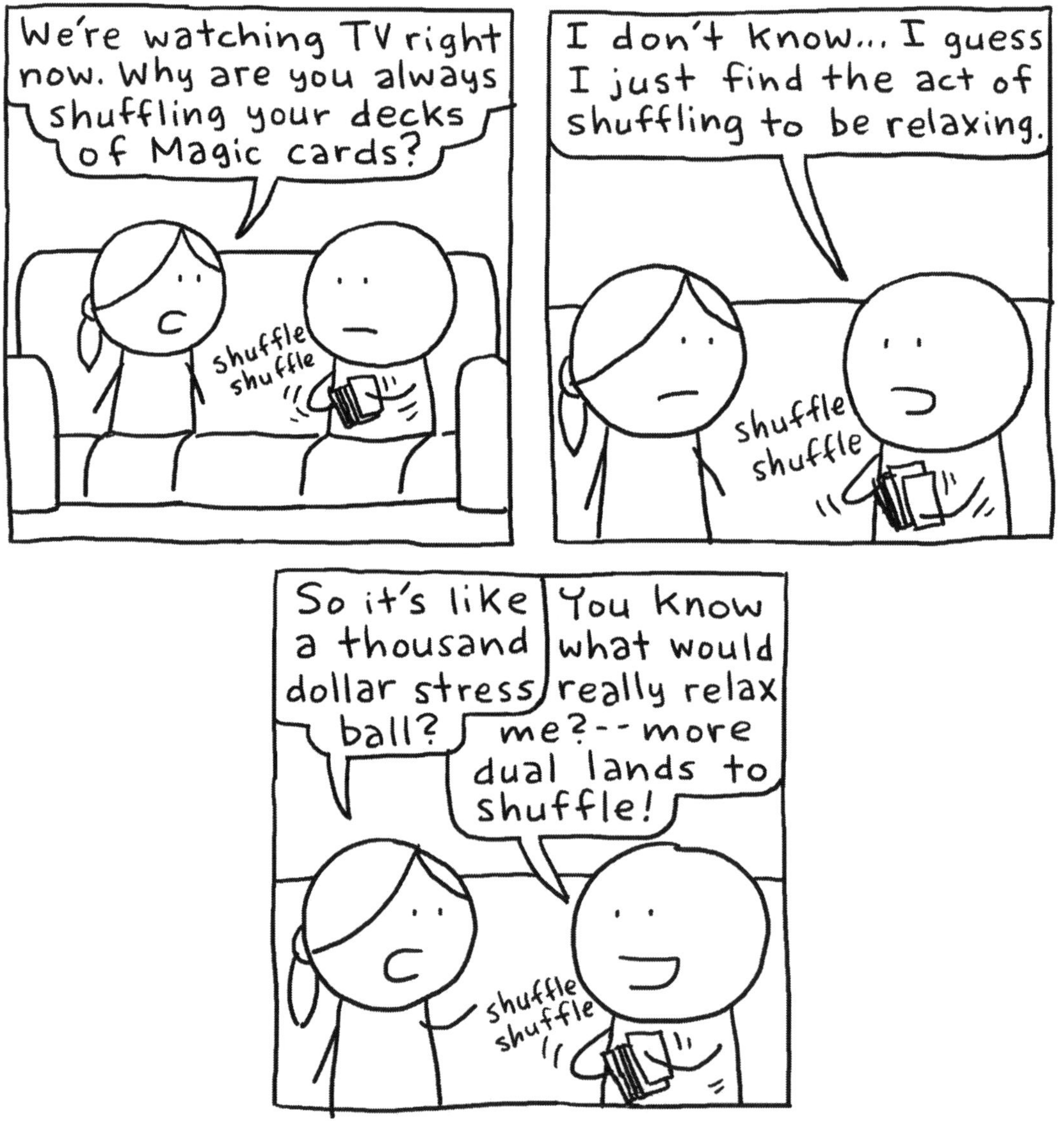
We're watching TV right now. Why are you always shuffling your decks of Magic cards?
shuffle shuffle
I don't know... I guess I just find the act of shuffling to be relaxing.
shuffle shuffle
So it's like a thousand dollar stress ball?
You know what would really relax me?-- more dual lands to shuffle!
shuffle shuffle

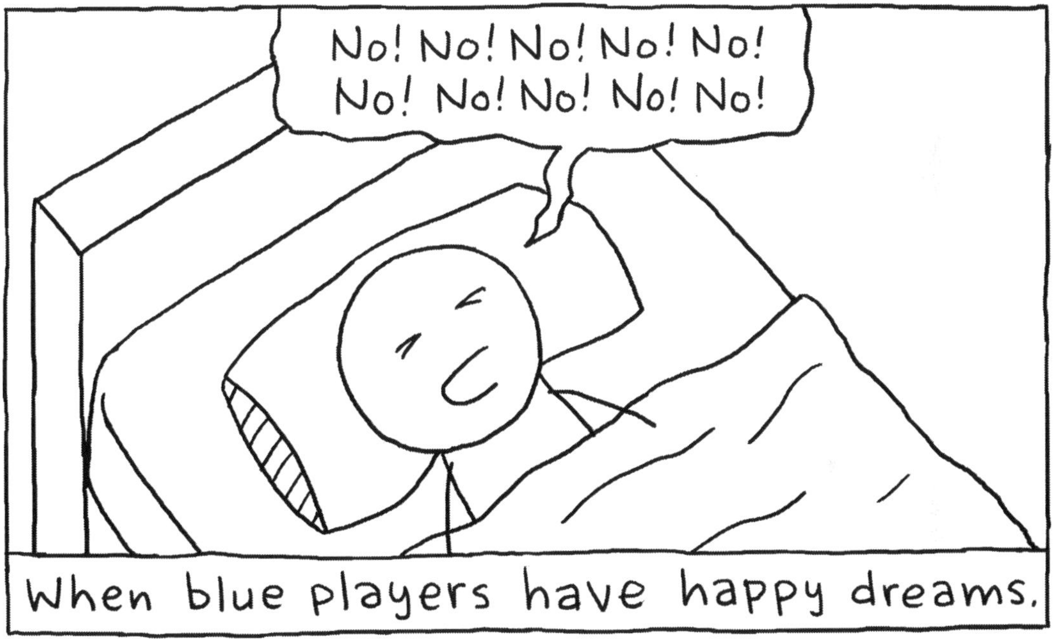
No! No! No! No! No!
No! No! No! No! No!
When blue players have happy dreams.

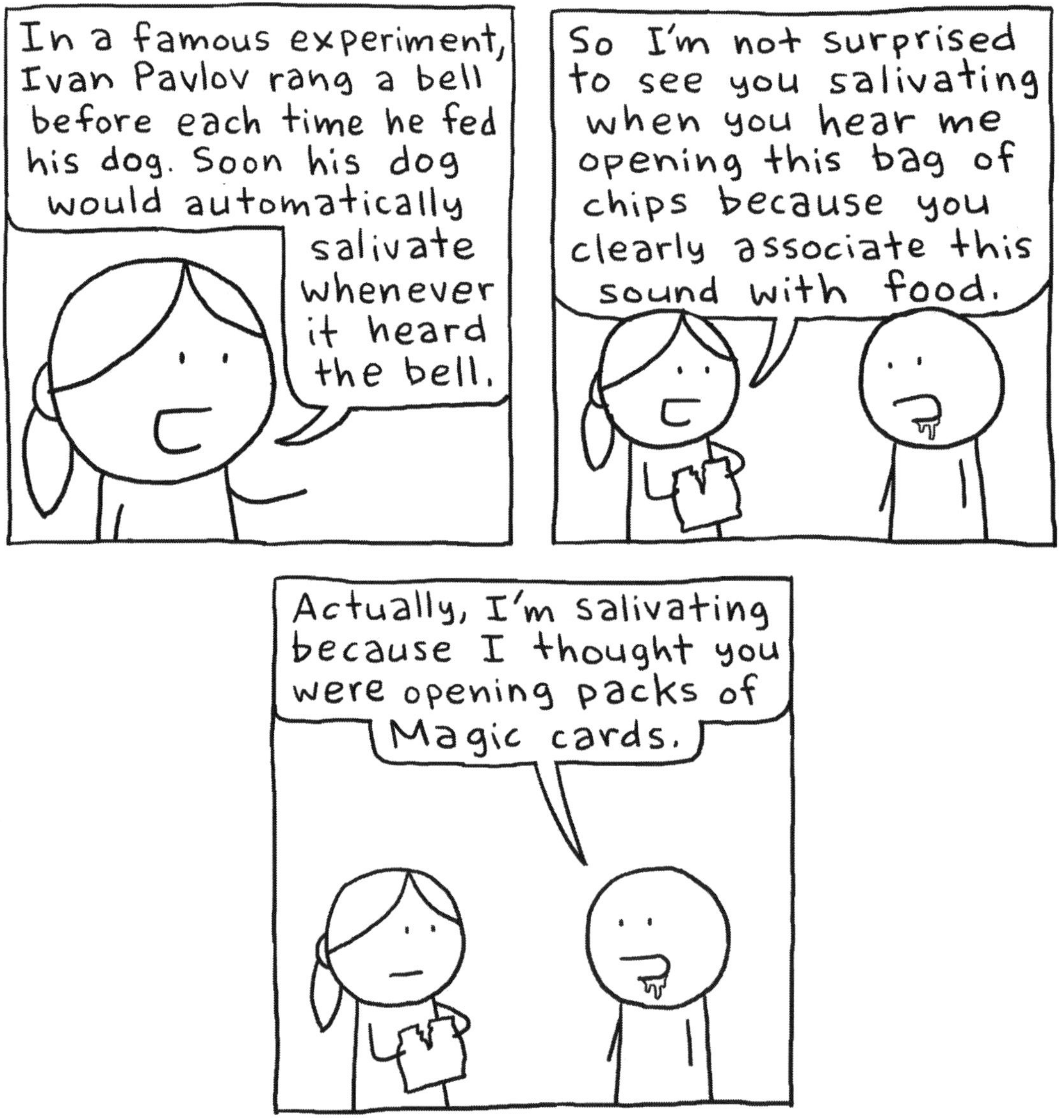
In a famous experiment, Ivan Pavlov rang a bell before each time he fed his dog. Soon his dog would automatically salivate whenever it heard the bell.
So I'm not surprised to see you salivating when you hear me opening this bag of chips because you clearly associate this sound with food.
Actually, I'm salivating because I thought you were opening packs of Magic cards.

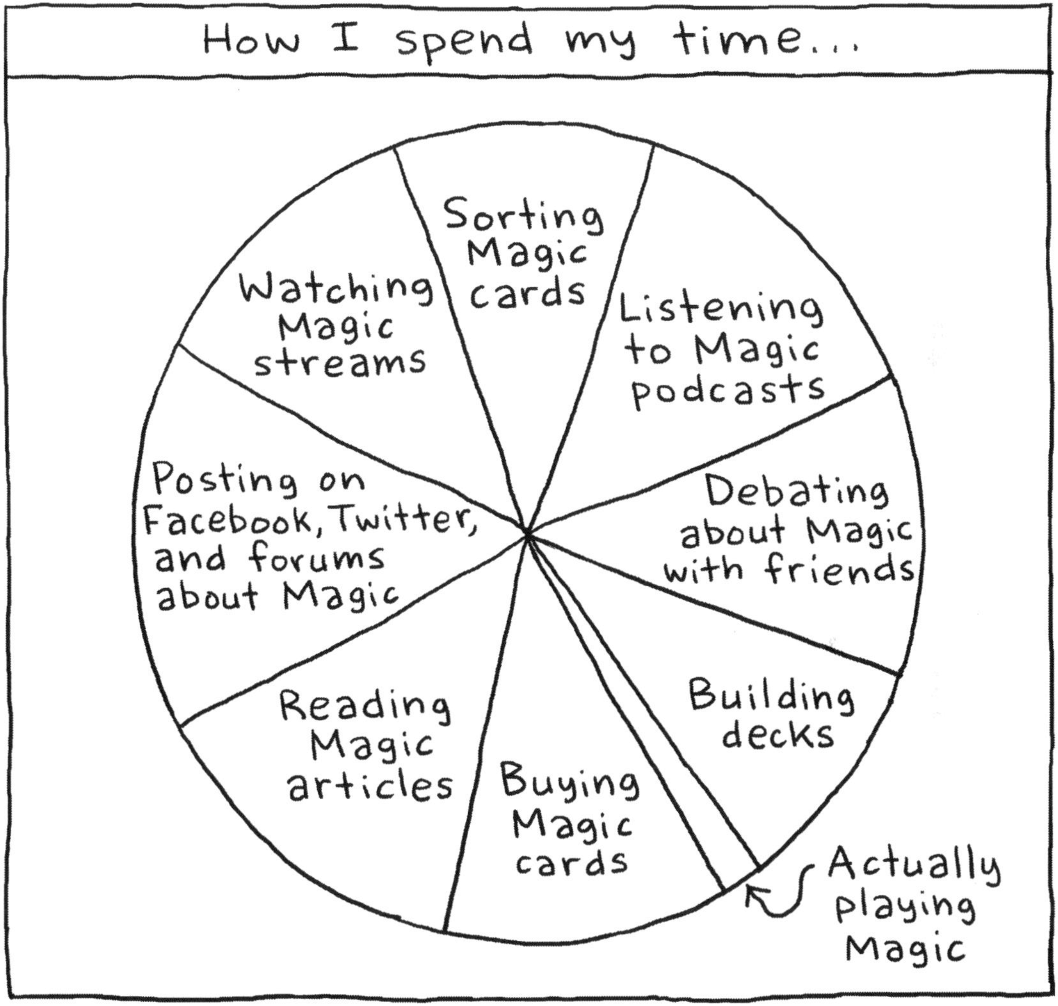
How I spend my time...
Sorting Magic cards
Listening to Magic podcasts
Debating about Magic with friends
Building decks
Actually playing Magic
Buying Magic cards
Reading Magic articles
Posting on Facebook, Twitter, and forums about Magic
Watching Magic streams

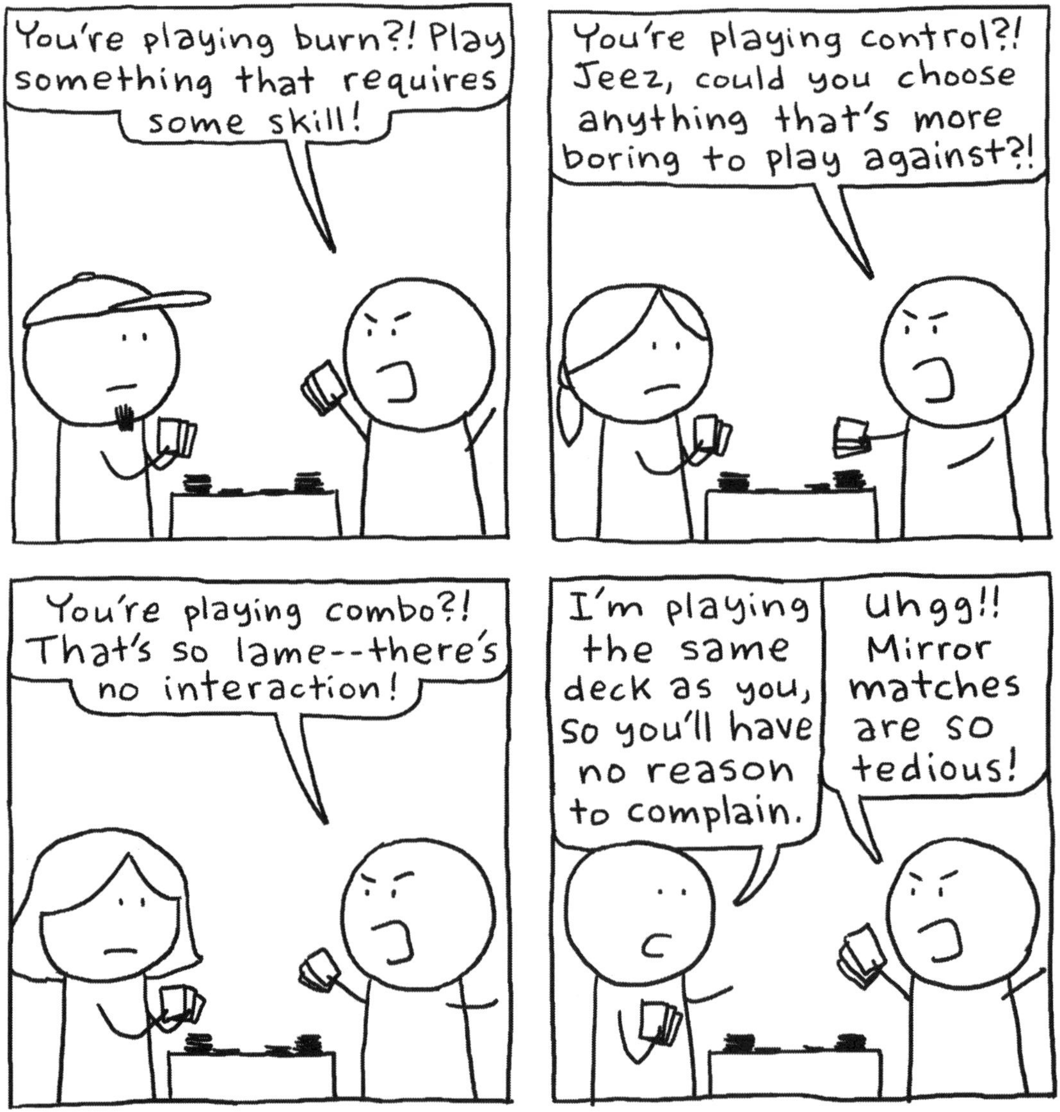
You're playing burn?! Play something that requires some skill!
You're playing control?! Jeez, could you choose anything that's more boring to play against?!
You're playing combo?! That's so lame--there's no interaction!
I'm playing the same deck as you, so you'll have no reason to complain.
Uhgg!! Mirror matches are so tedious!

I can't believe you were drafting Magic cards with another girl behind my back!
Well baby, I did tell you that I was a Magic player.

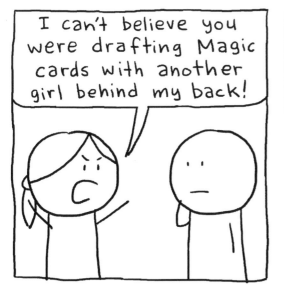

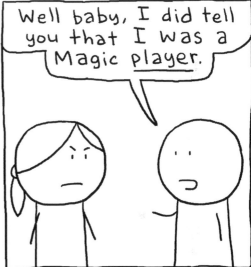

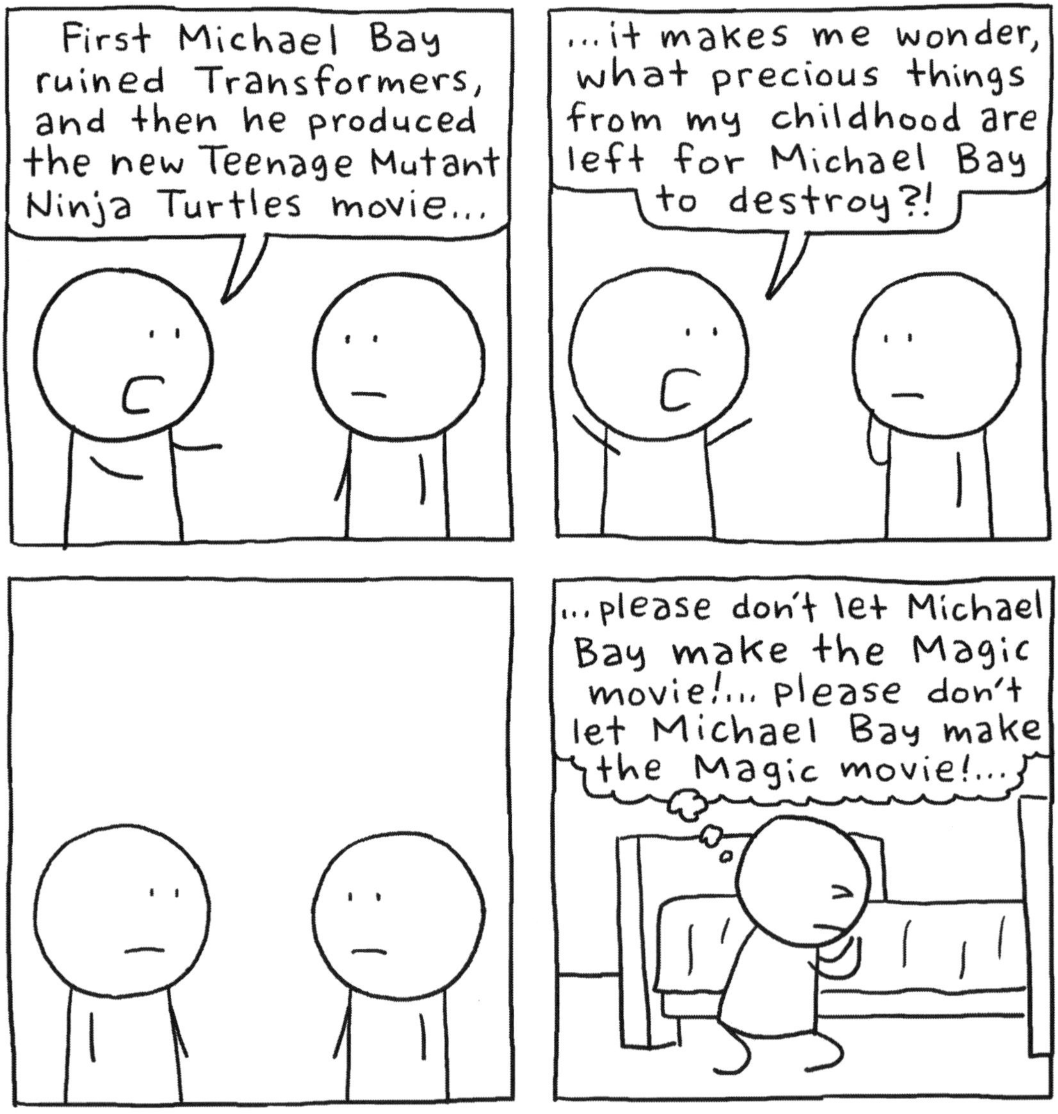
First Michael Bay ruined Transformers, and then he produced the new Teenage Mutant Ninja Turtles movie...
...it makes me wonder, what precious things from my childhood are left for Michael Bay to destroy?!
...please don't let Michael Bay make the Magic movie!... please don't let Michael Bay make the Magic movie!...

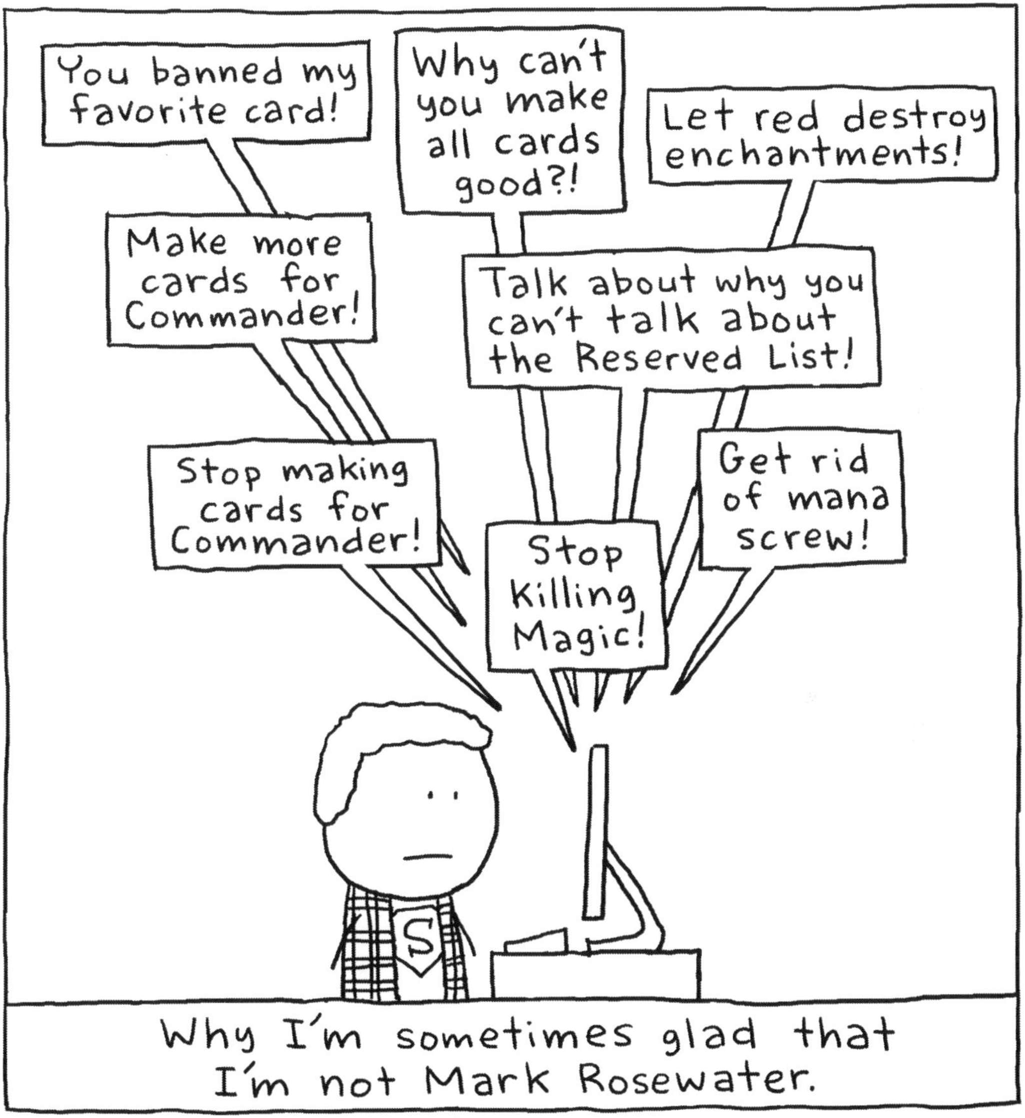
You banned my favorite card!
Why can't you make all cards good?!
Let red destroy enchantments!
Make more cards for Commander!
Talk about why you can't talk about the Reserved List!
Stop making cards for Commander!
Get rid of mana screw!
Stop Killing Magic!
S

Why I'm sometimes glad that I'm not Mark Rosewater.

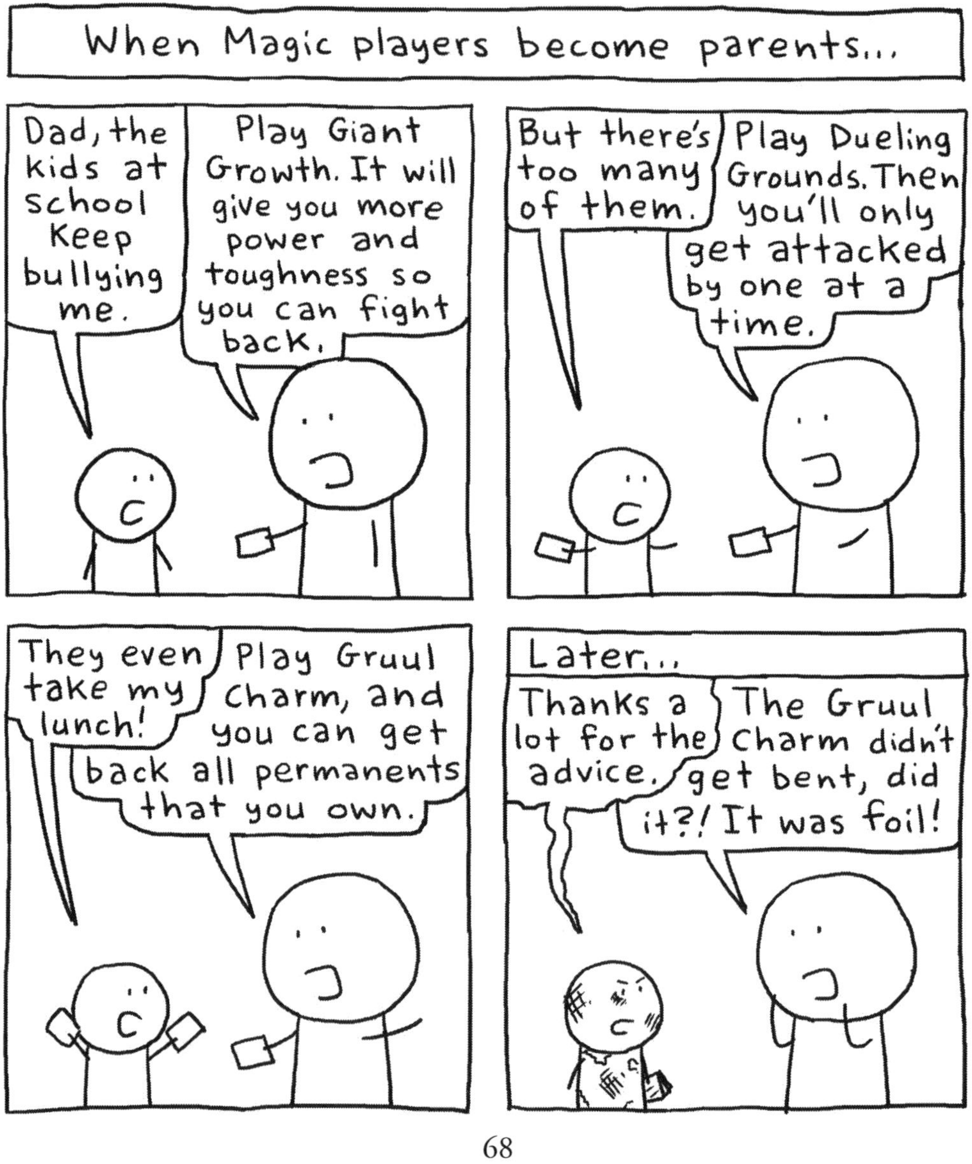
When Magic players become parents...
Dad, the kids at school keep bullying me.
Play Giant Growth. It will give you more power and toughness so you can fight back.
But there's too many of them.
Play Dueling Grounds. Then you'll only get attacked by one at a time.
They even take my lunch!
Play Gruul Charm, and you can get back all permanents that you own.
Later...
Thanks a lot for the advice.
The Gruul Charm didn't get bent, did it?! It was foil!

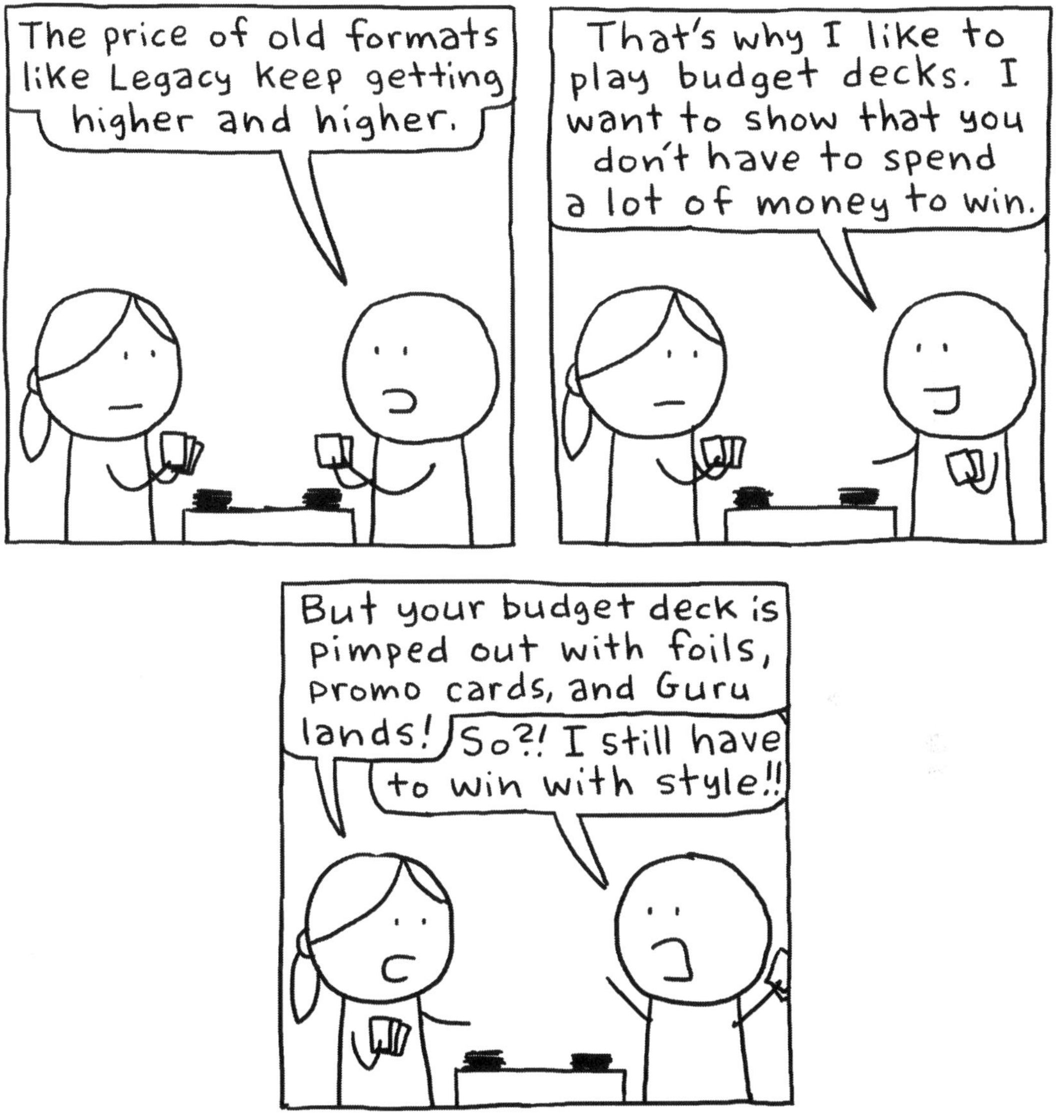
The price of old formats like Legacy keep getting higher and higher.
That's why I like to play budget decks. I want to show that you don't have to spend a lot of money to win.
But your budget deck is pimped out with foils, promo cards, and Guru lands!
So?! I still have to win with style!!

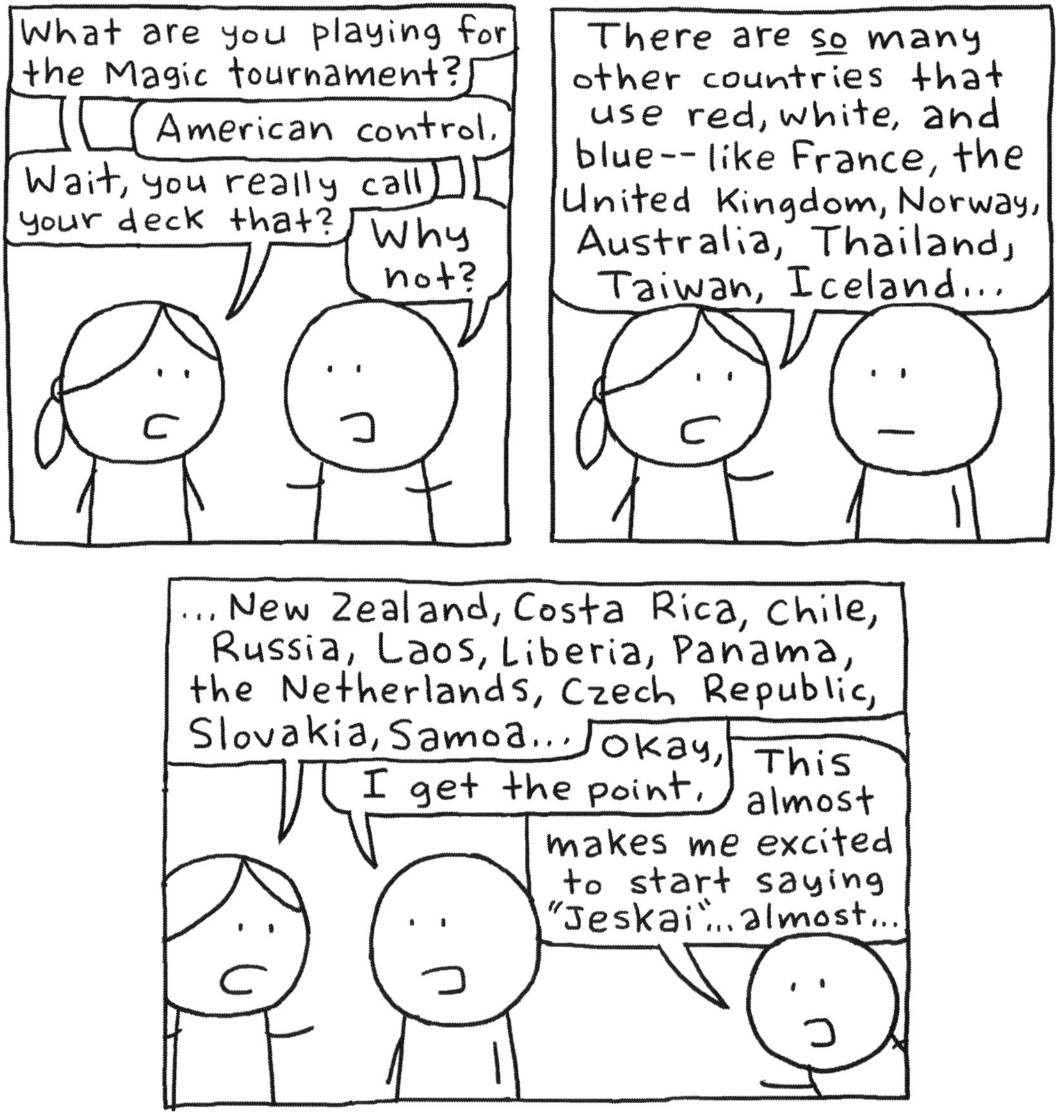
What are you playing for the Magic tournament?
American control.
Wait, you really call your deck that?
Why not?
There are so many other countries that use red, white, and blue--like France, the United Kingdom, Norway, Australia, Thailand, Taiwan, Iceland...
...New Zealand, Costa Rica, Chile, Russia, Laos, Liberia, Panama, the Netherlands, Czech Republic, Slovakia, Samoa...
Okay, I get the point.
This almost makes me excited to start saying "Jeskai"... almost...

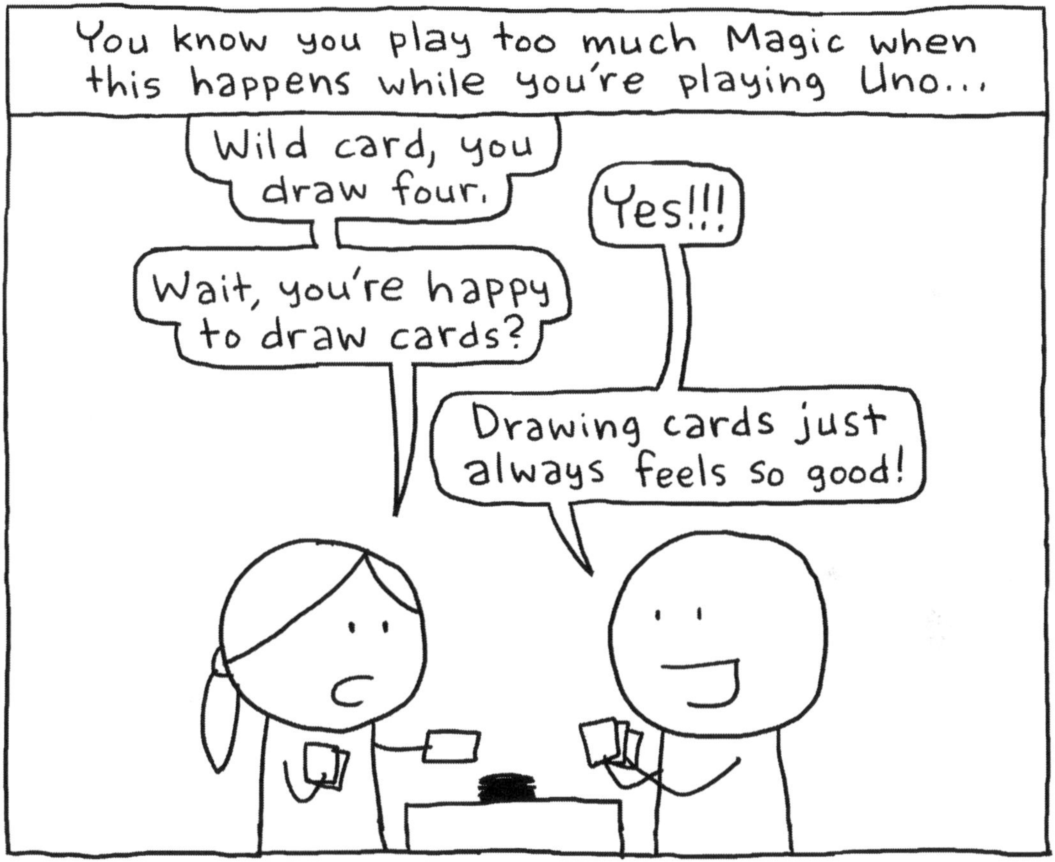
You know you play too much Magic when this happens while you're playing Uno...
Wild card, you draw four.
Wait, you're happy to draw cards?
Yes!!!
Drawing cards just always feels so good!

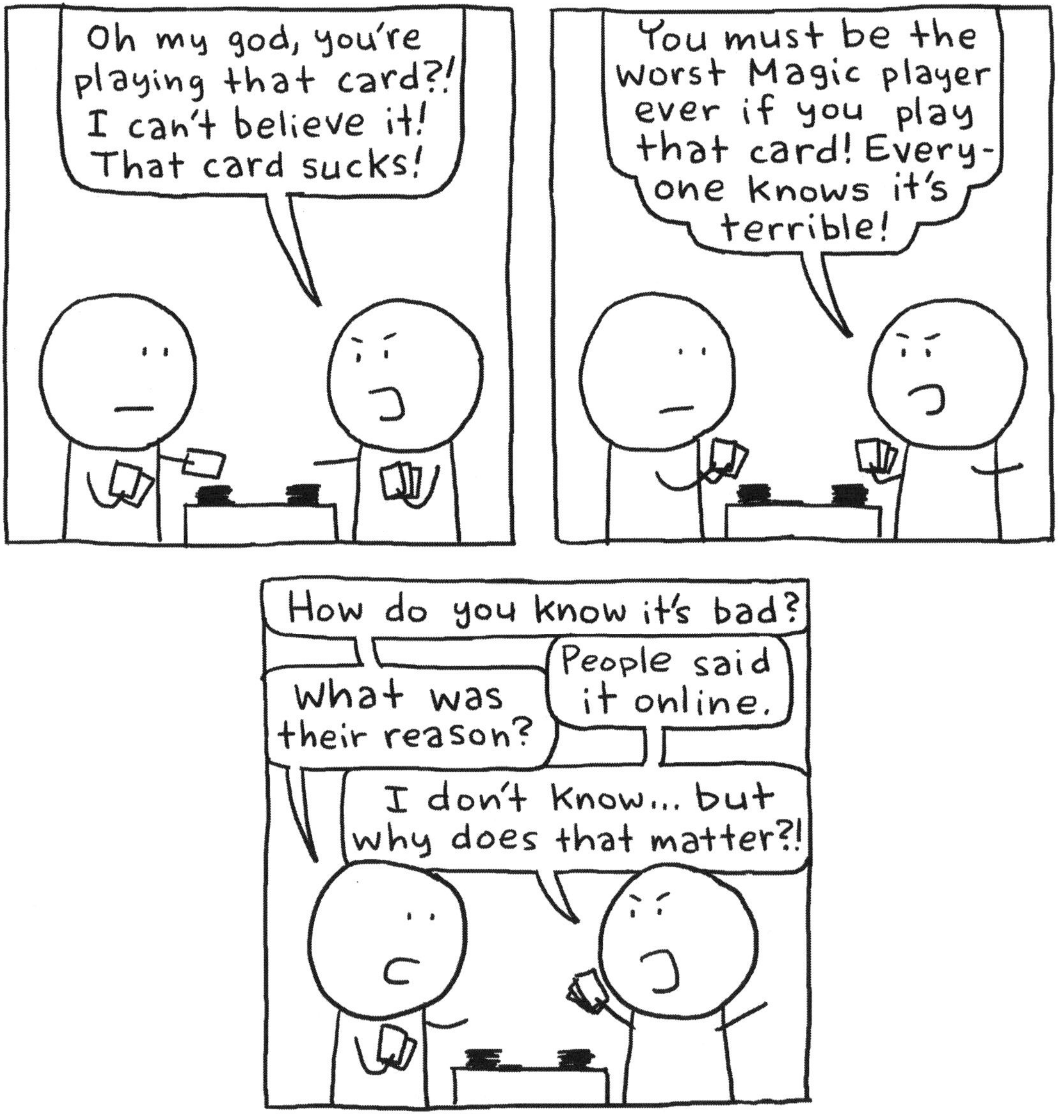
Oh my god, you're playing that card?! I can't believe it! That card sucks!
You must be the worst Magic player ever if you play that card! Every-one knows it's terrible!
How do you know it's bad?
People said it online.
What was their reason?
I don't know... but why does that matter?!

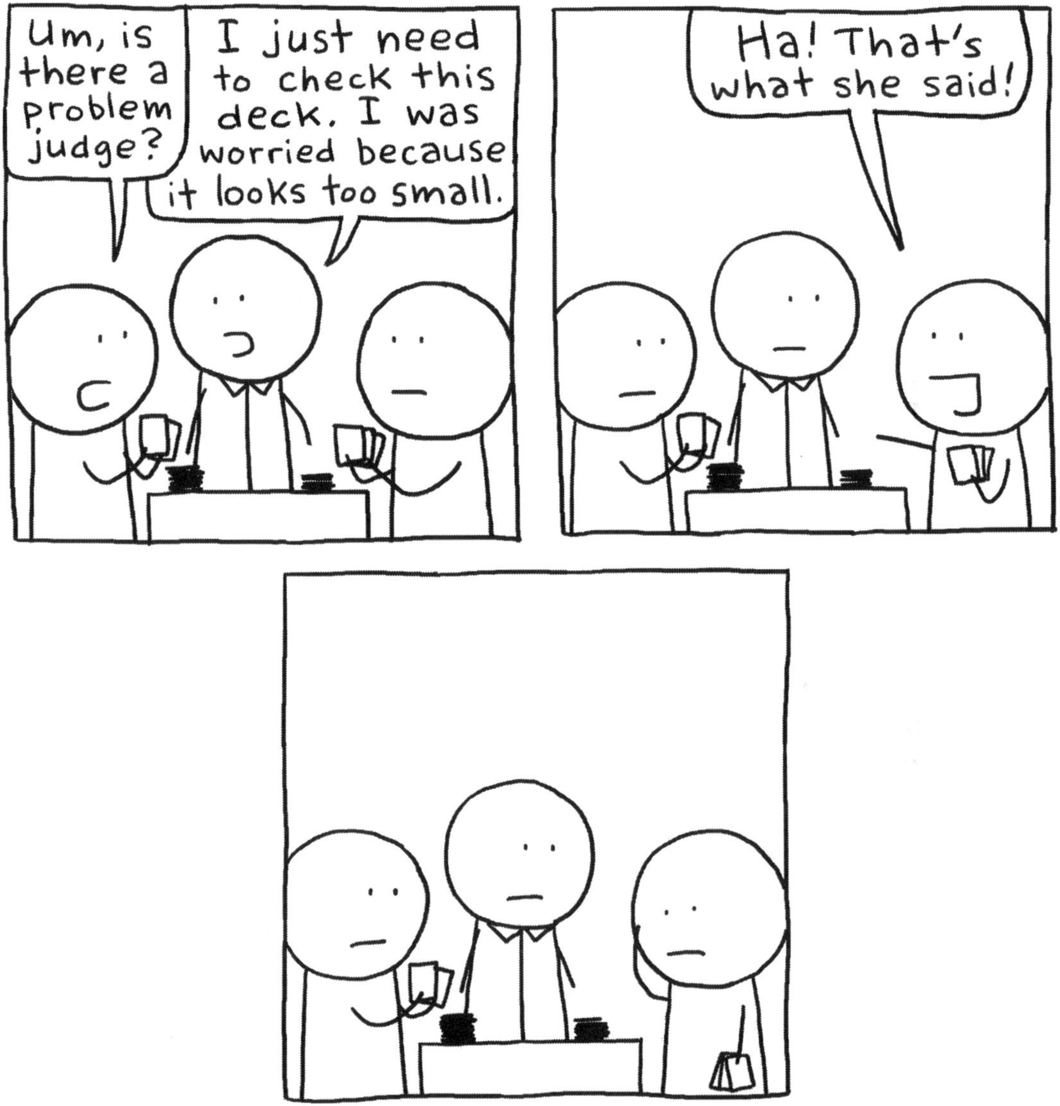
Um, is there a problem judge?
I just need to check this deck. I was worried because it looks too small.
Ha! That's what she said!

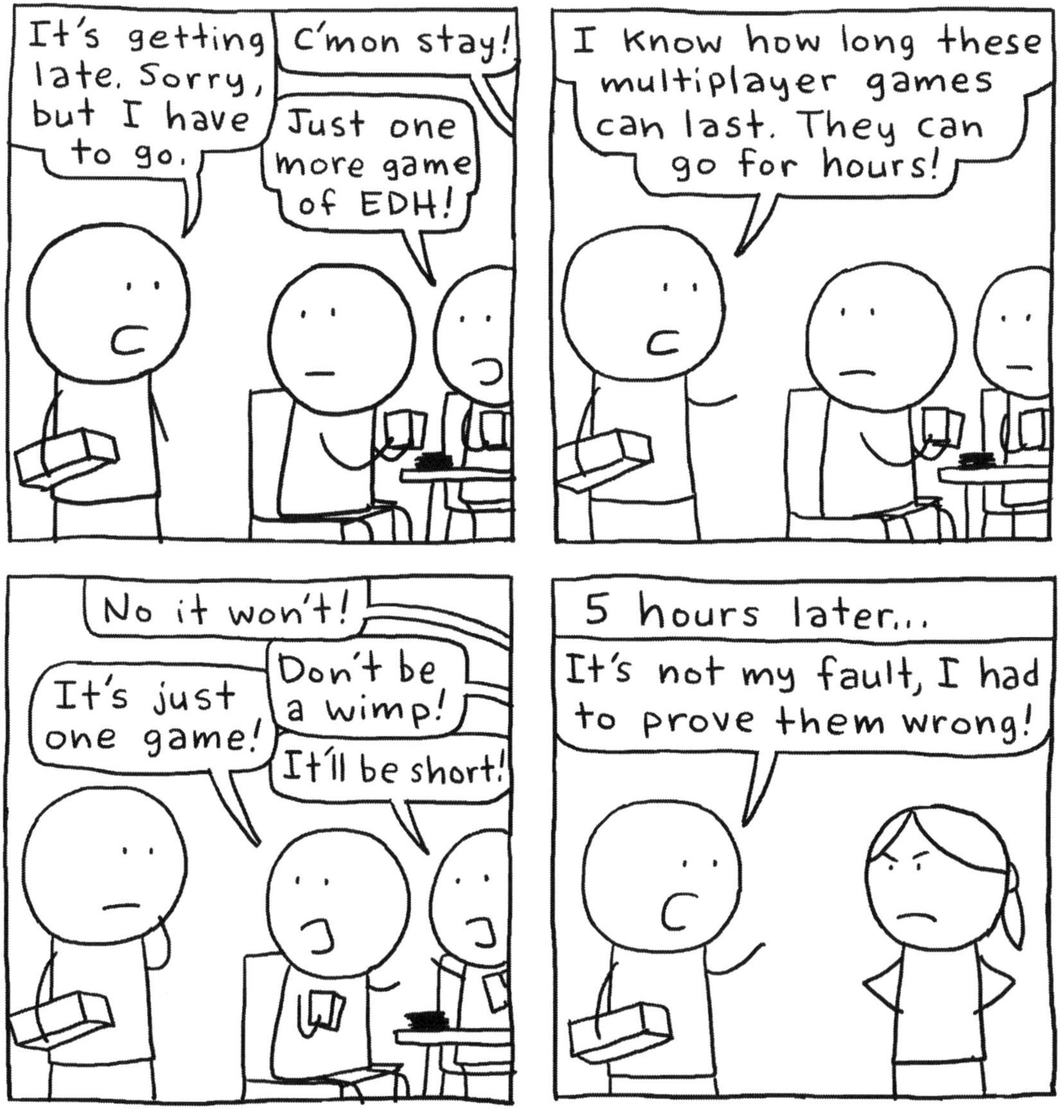
It's getting late. Sorry, but I have to go.
C'mon stay!
Just one more game of EDH!
I know how long these multiplayer games can last. They can go for hours!
No it won't!
It's just one game!
Don't be a wimp!
It'll be short!
5 hours later...
It's not my fault, I had to prove them wrong!

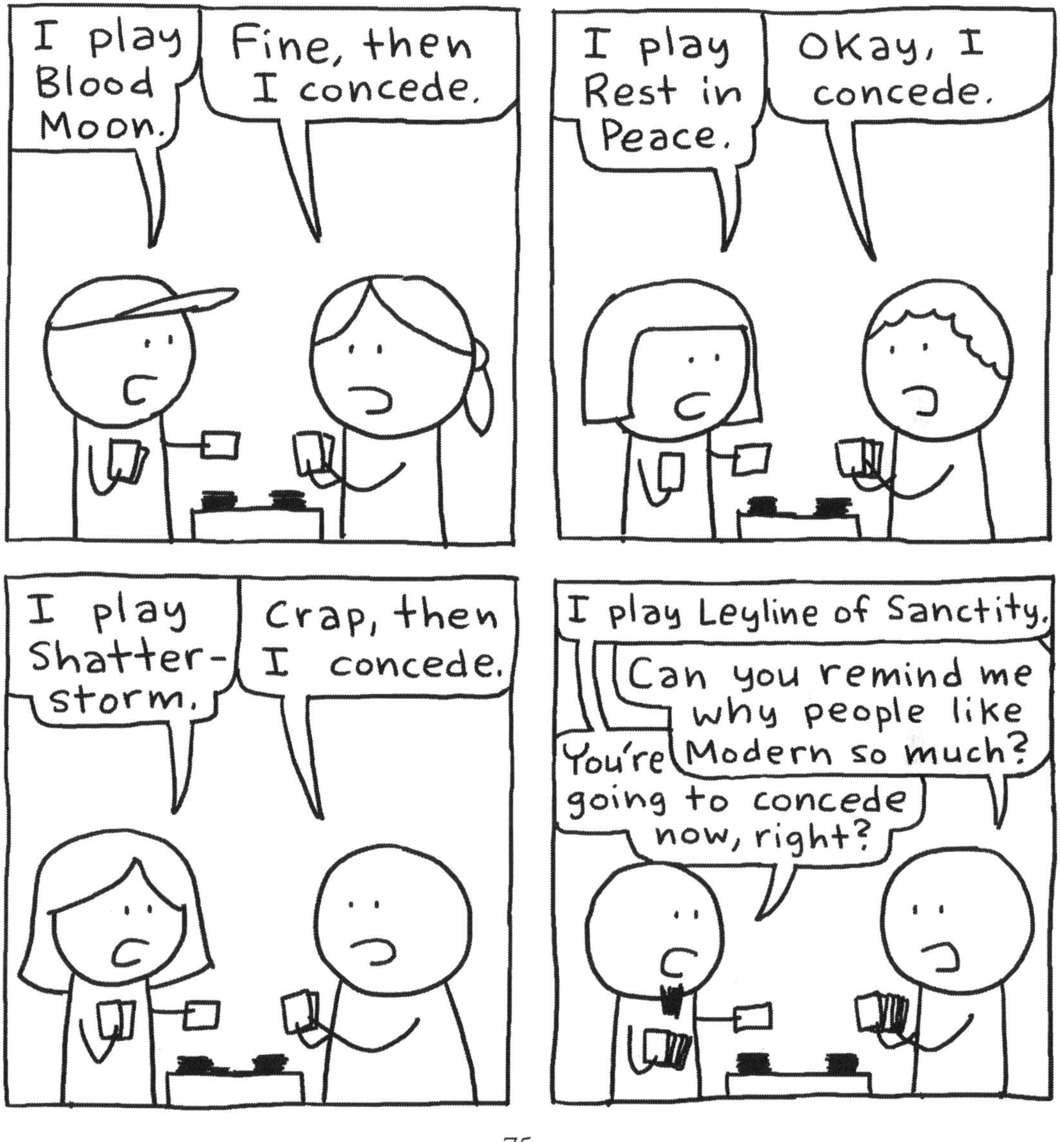
I play Blood Moon.
Fine, then I concede.
I play Rest in Peace.
Okay, I concede.
I play Shatter-storm.
Crap, then I concede.
I play Leyline of Sanctity.
Can you remind me why people like Modern so much?
You're going to concede now, right?

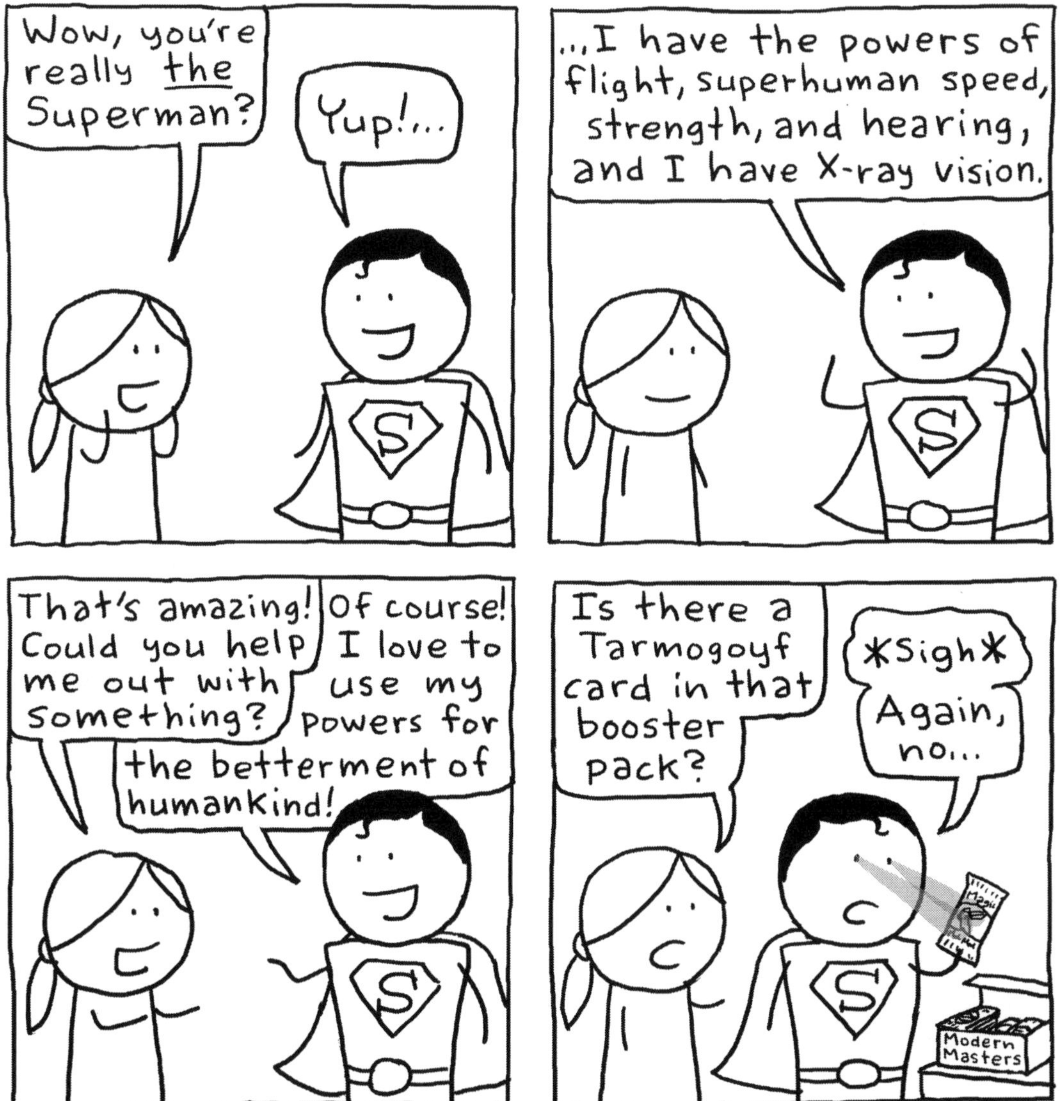
Wow, you're really the Superman?
Yup!...
...I have the powers of flight, superhuman speed, strength, and hearing, and I have X-ray vision.
That's amazing! Could you help me out with something?
Of course! I love to use my powers for the betterment of humankind!
Is there a Tarmogoyf card in that booster pack?
Sigh Again, no...
Modern Masters

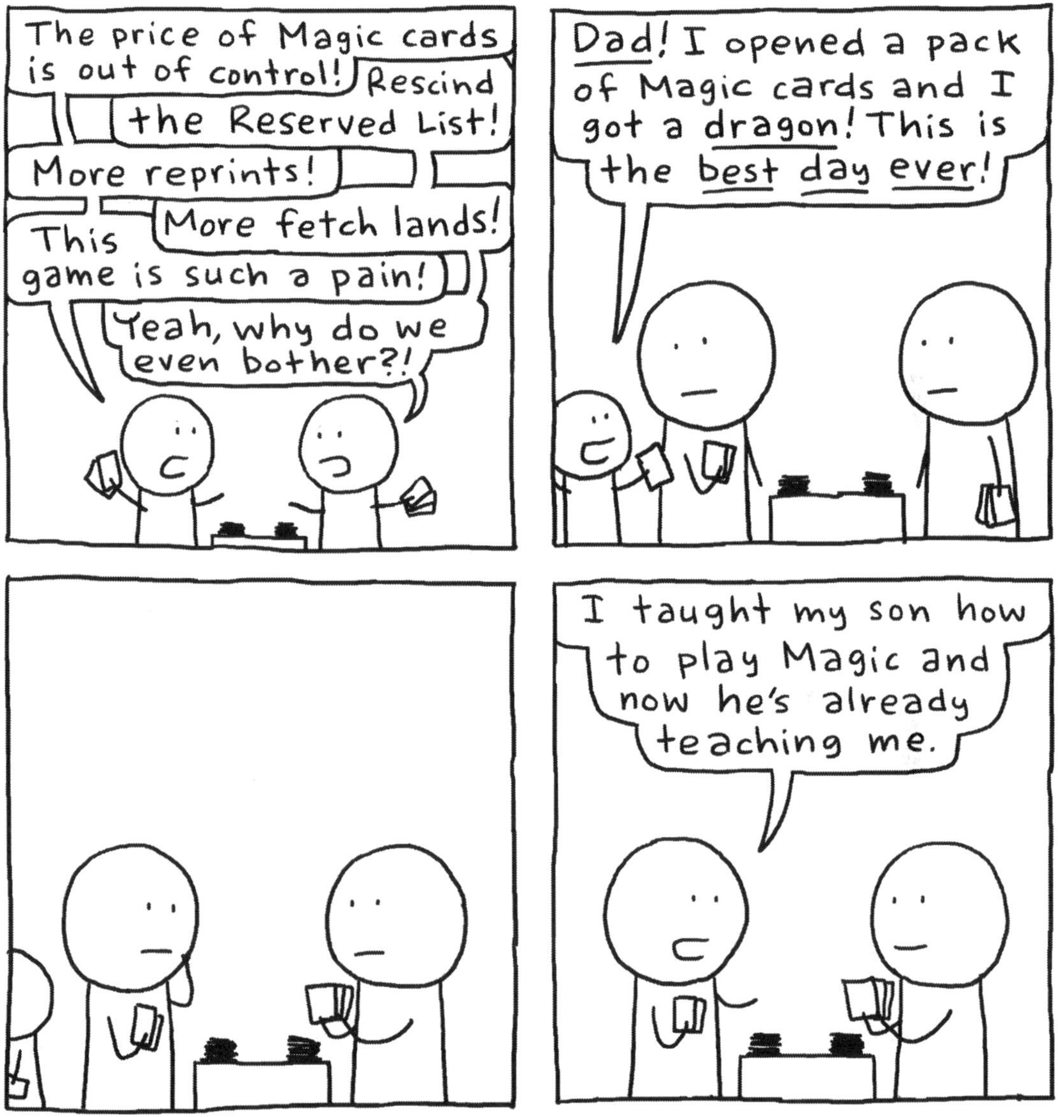
The price of Magic cards is out of control!
Rescind the Reserved List!
More reprints!
More fetch lands!
This game is such a pain!
Yeah, why do we even bother?!
Dad! I opened a pack of Magic cards and I got a dragon! This is the best day ever!
I taught my son how to play Magic and now he's already teaching me.

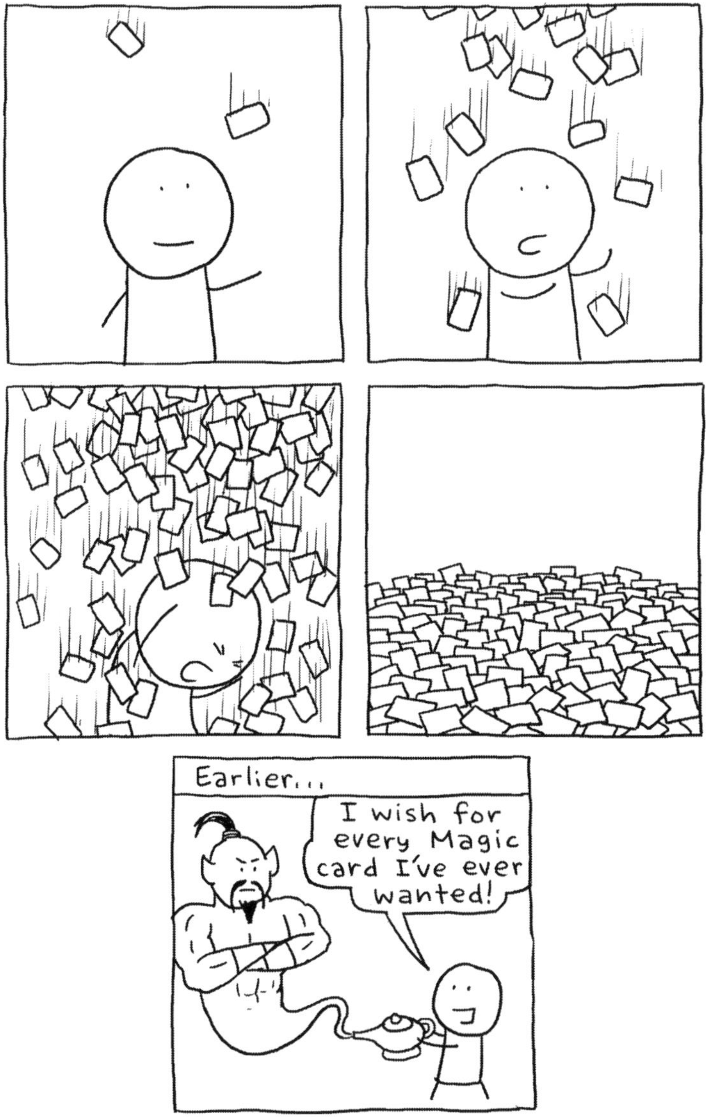
Earlier...
I wish for every Magic card I've ever wanted!

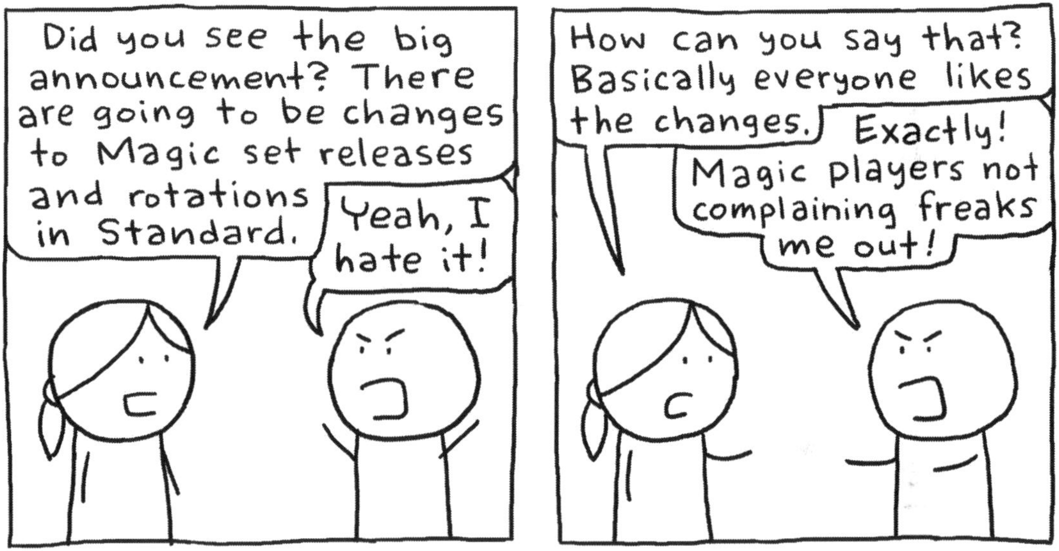
Did you see the big announcement? There are going to be changes to Magic set releases and rotations in Standard.
Yeah, I hate it!
How can you say that? Basically everyone likes the changes.
Exactly! Magic players not complaining freaks me out!

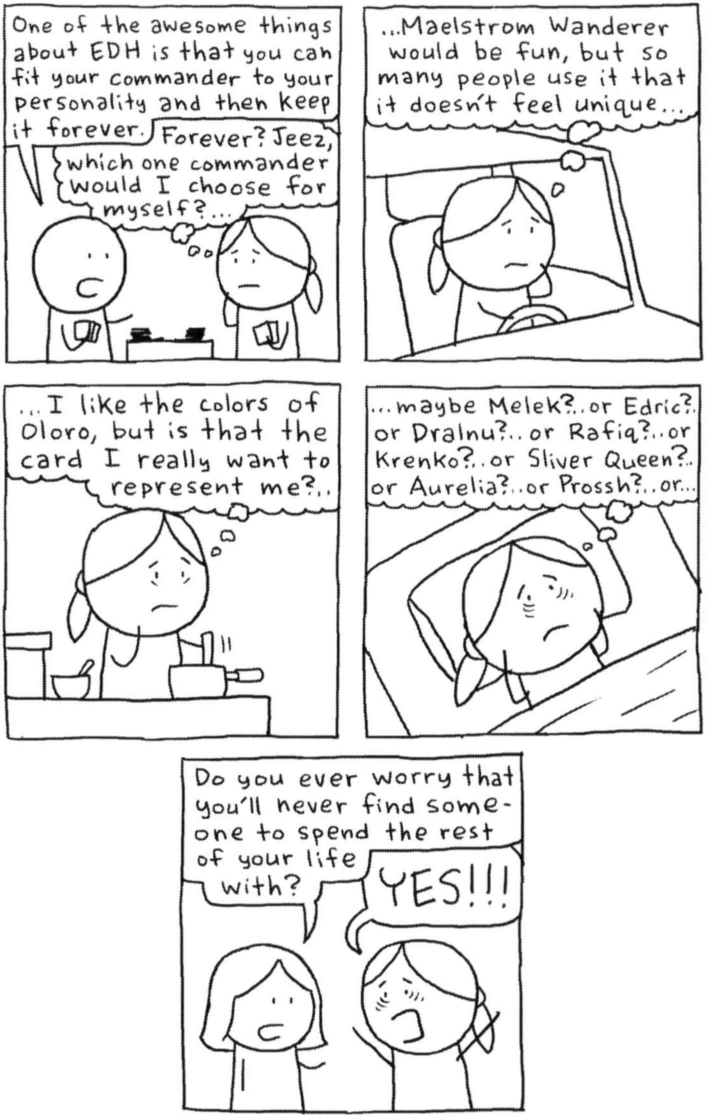
One of the awesome things about EDH is that you can fit your commander to your personality and then keep it forever.
Forever? Jeez, which one commander would I choose for myself?...
...Maelstrom Wanderer would be fun, but so many people use it that it doesn't feel unique...
...I like the colors of Oloro, but is that the card I really want to represent me?..
...maybe Melek?..or Edric?..or Dralnu?..or Rafiq?..or Krenko?..or Sliver Queen?..or Aurelia?..or Prossh?..or...
Do you ever worry that you'll never find some-one to spend the rest of your life with?
YES!!!

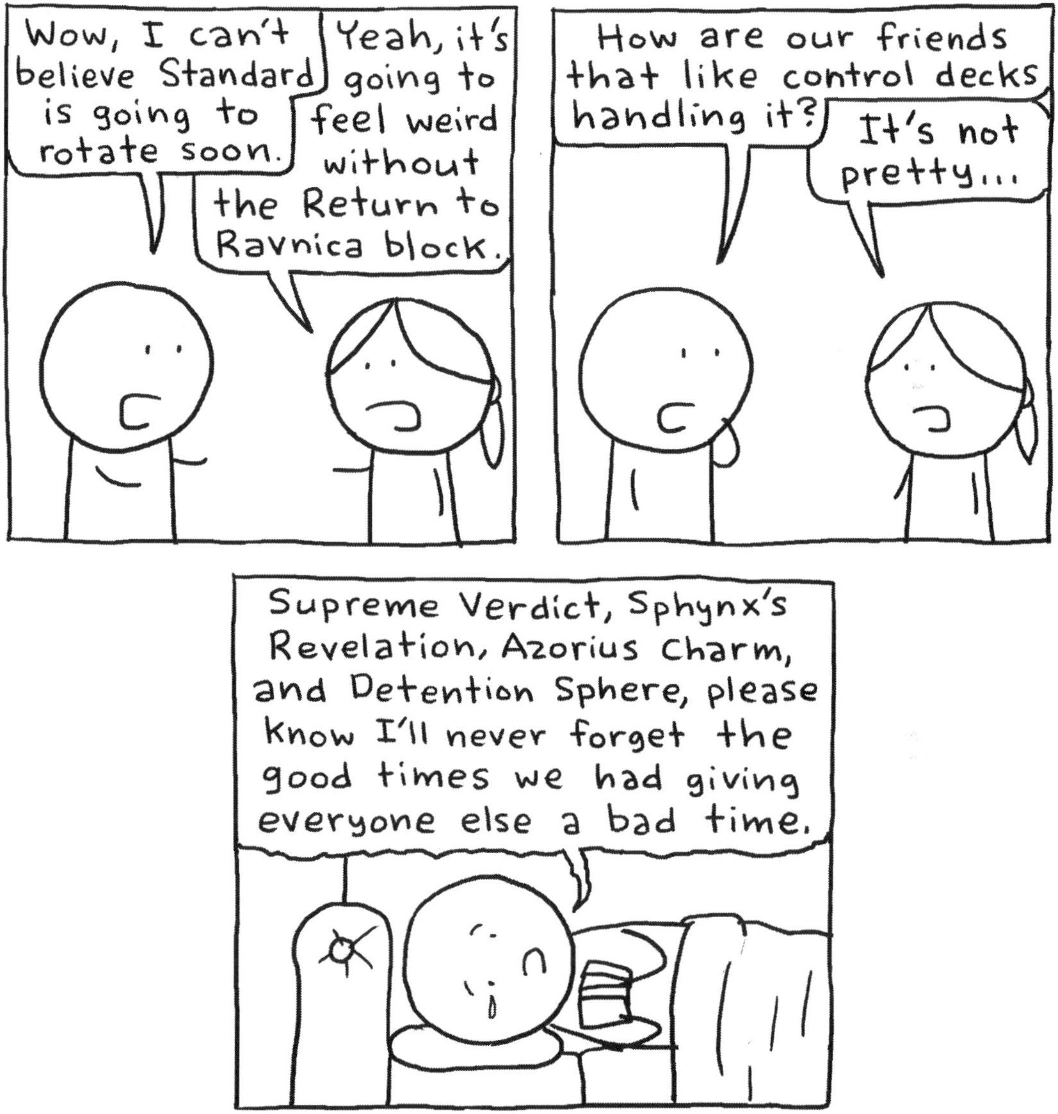
Wow, I can't believe Standard is going to rotate soon.
Yeah, it's going to feel weird without the Return to Ravnica block.
How are our friends that like control decks handling it?
It's not pretty...
Supreme Verdict, Sphynx's Revelation, Azorius Charm, and Detention Sphere, please know I'll never forget the good times we had giving everyone else a bad time.

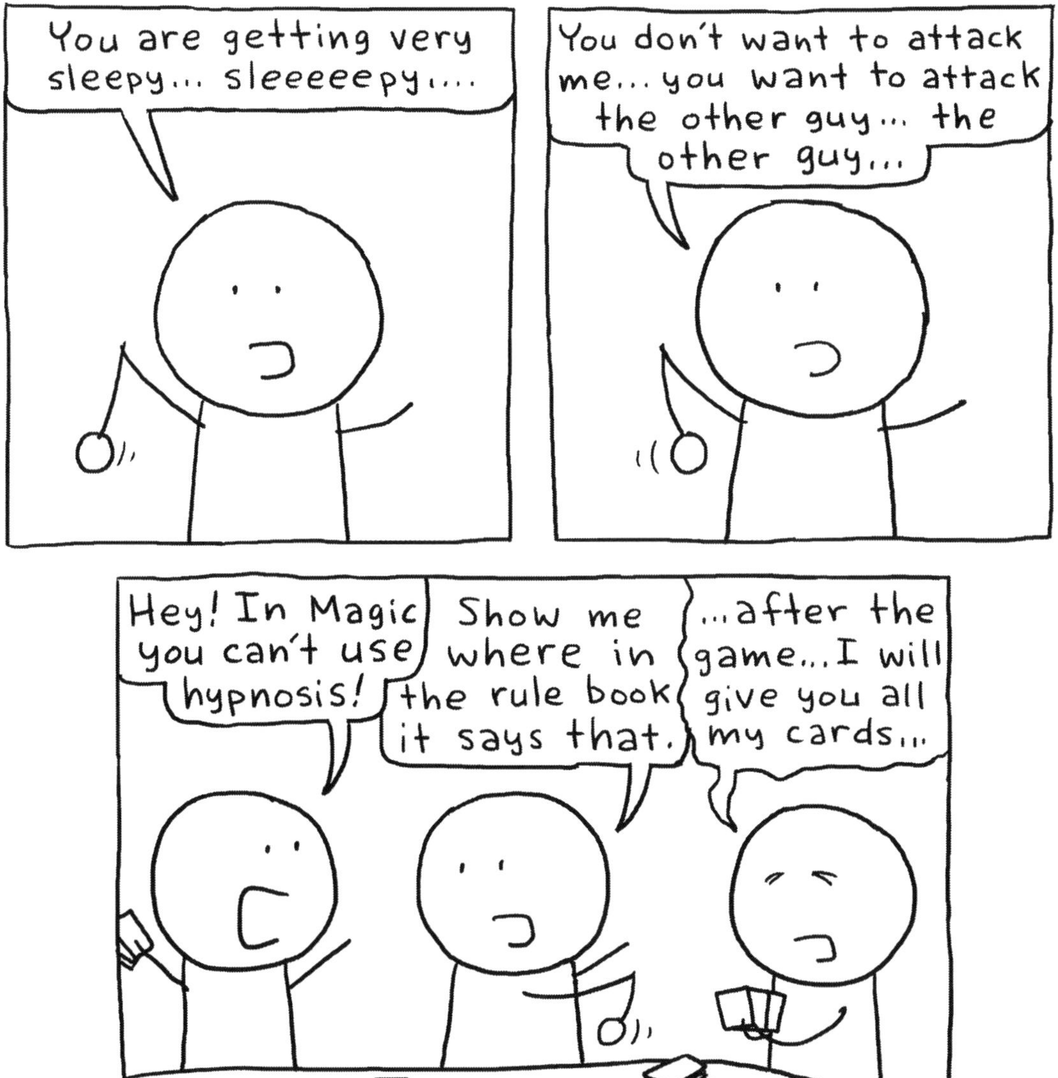
You are getting very sleepy... sleeeeeepy....
You don't want to attack me... you want to attack the other guy... the other guy...
Hey! In Magic you can't use hypnosis!
Show me where in the rule book it says that.
...after the game...I will give you all my cards...

The Pros and Cons of Magic Online

Cons	Pros
- Clunky interface - Expensive - Slows down computer - Misclicks - Card bugs - Trading system overrun with bots - Client crashes	- I can scream obscenities at the top of my lungs in the comfort of my own home

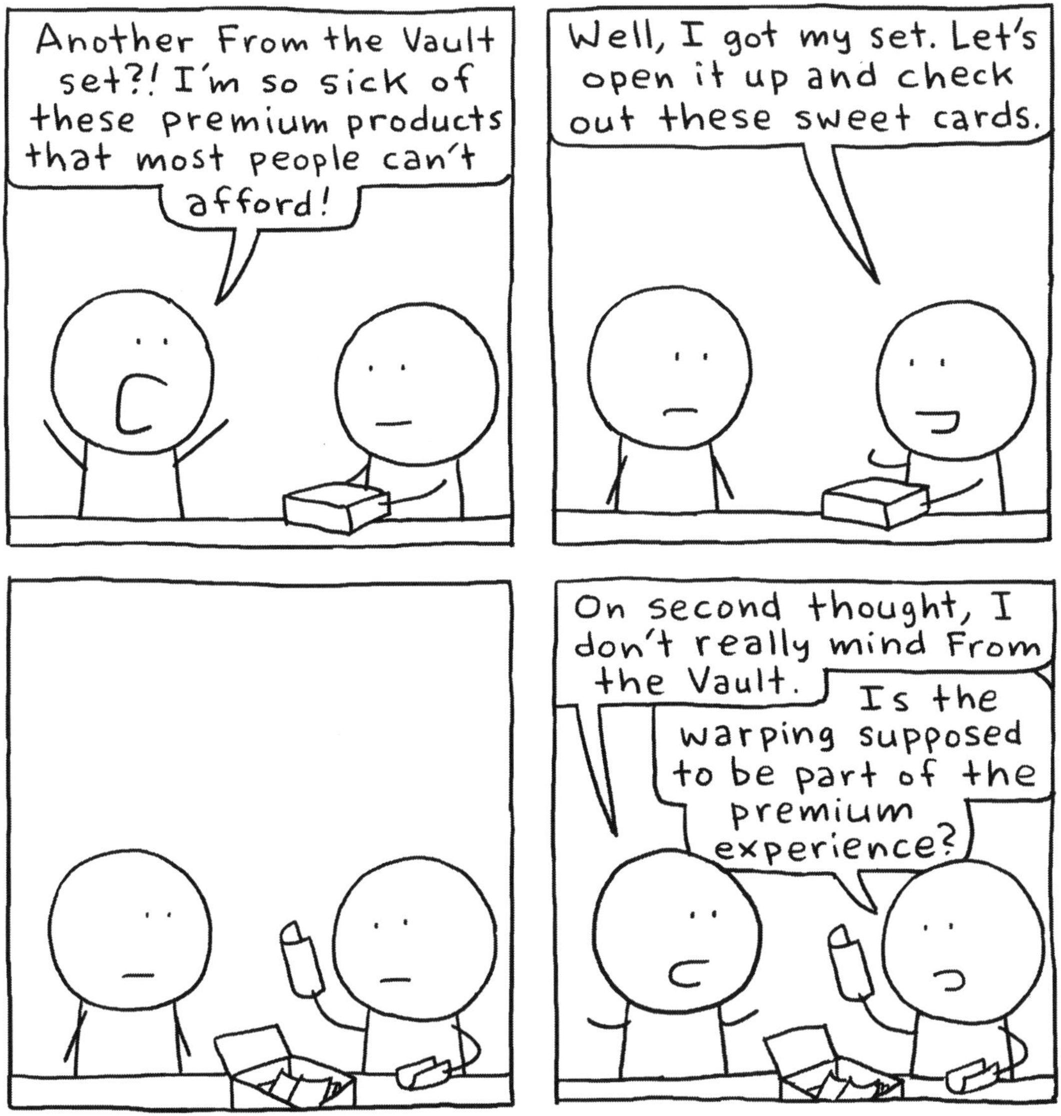
Another From the Vault set?! I'm so sick of these premium products that most people can't afford!
Well, I got my set. Let's open it up and check out these sweet cards.
On second thought, I don't really mind From the Vault.
Is the warping supposed to be part of the premium experience?

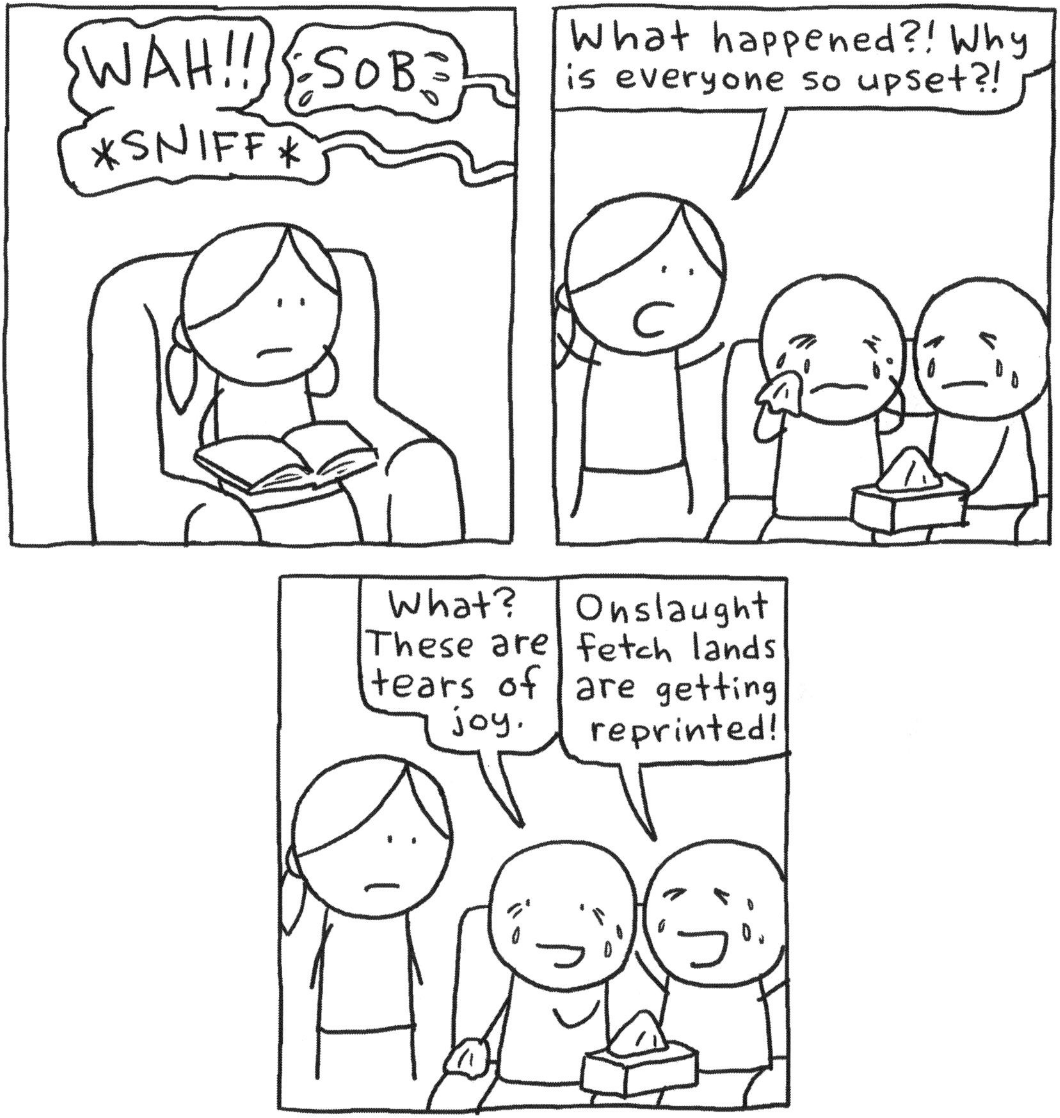
WAH!!
SOB
SNIFF
What happened?! Why is everyone so upset?!
What? These are tears of joy.
Onslaught fetch lands are getting reprinted!

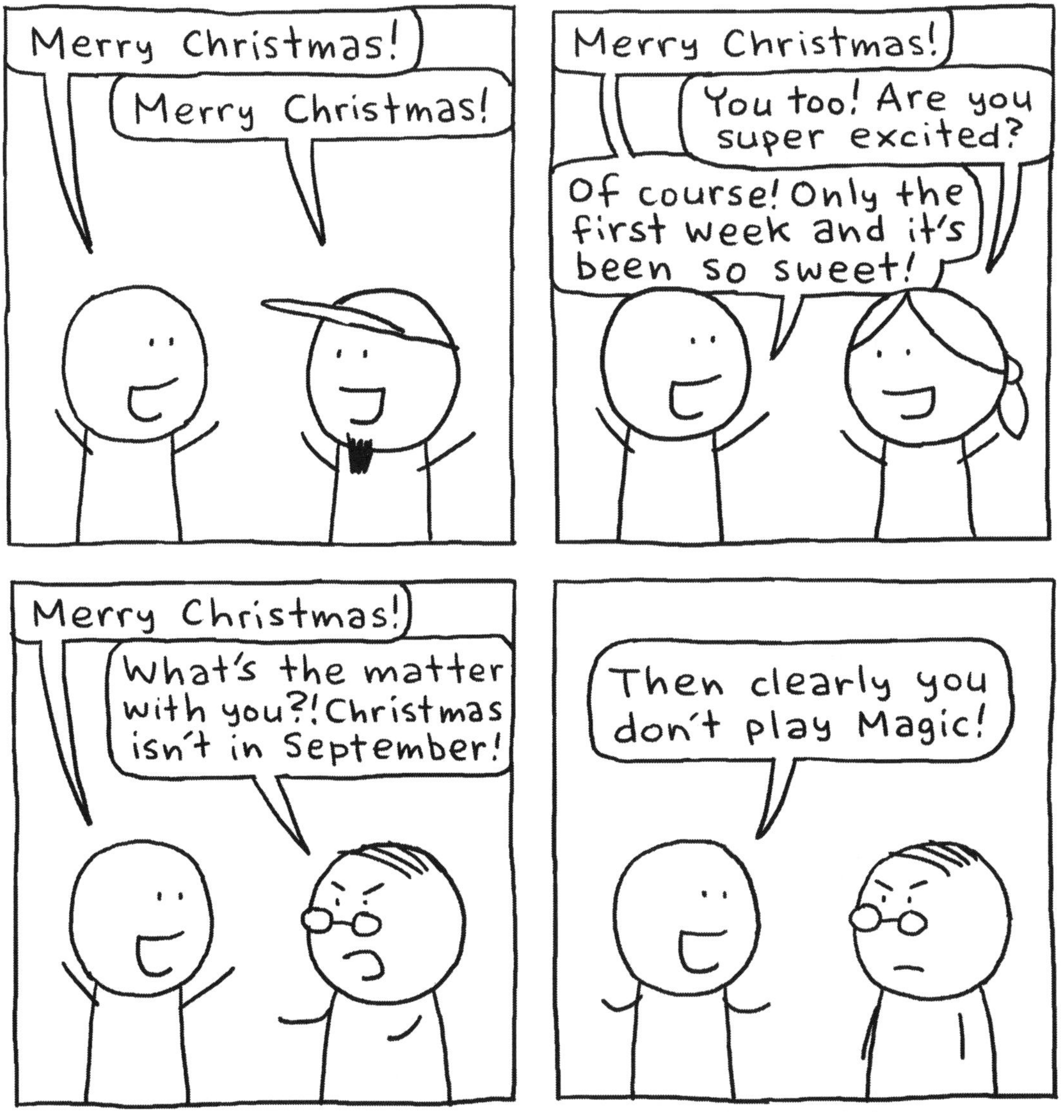
Merry Christmas!
Merry Christmas!
Merry Christmas!
You too! Are you super excited?
Of course! Only the first week and it's been so sweet!
Merry Christmas!
What's the matter with you?! Christmas isn't in September!
Then clearly you don't play Magic!

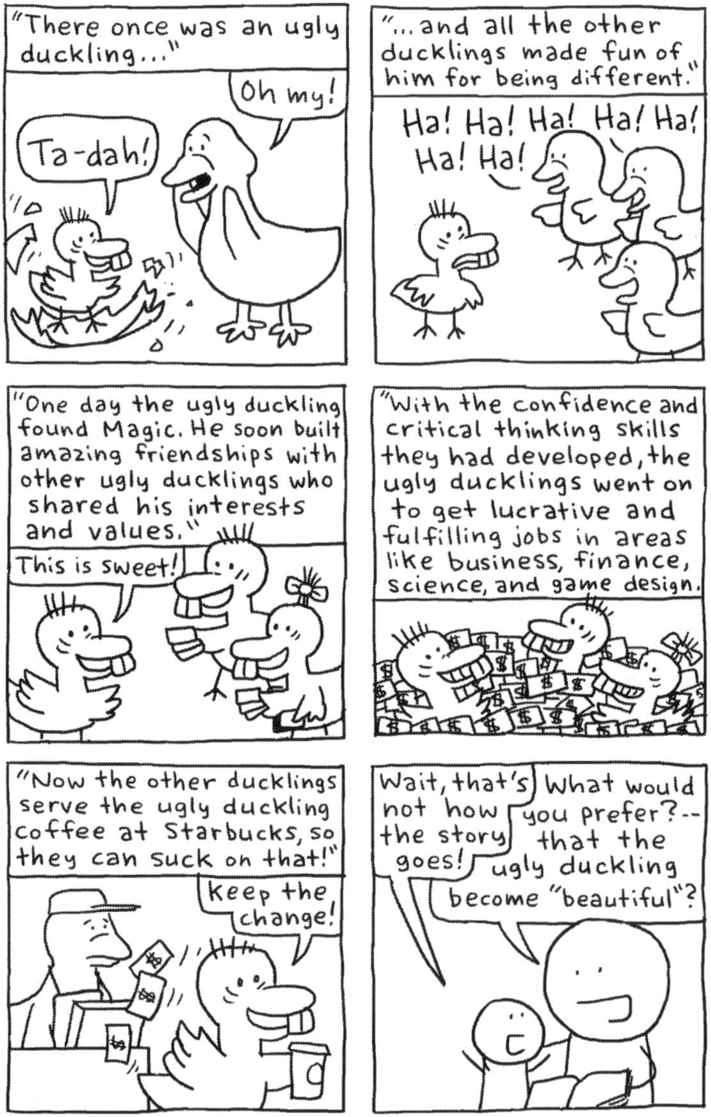
"There once was an ugly duckling..."
Oh my!
Ta-dah!
"...and all the other ducklings made fun of him for being different."
Ha! Ha! Ha! Ha! Ha! Ha! Ha!
"One day the ugly duckling found Magic. He soon built amazing friendships with other ugly ducklings who shared his interests and values."
This is sweet!
"With the confidence and critical thinking skills they had developed, the ugly ducklings went on to get lucrative and fulfilling jobs in areas like business, finance, science, and game design.
"Now the other ducklings serve the ugly duckling coffee at Starbucks, so they can suck on that!"
Keep the change!
Wait, that's not how the story goes!
What would you prefer?-- that the ugly duckling become "beautiful"?

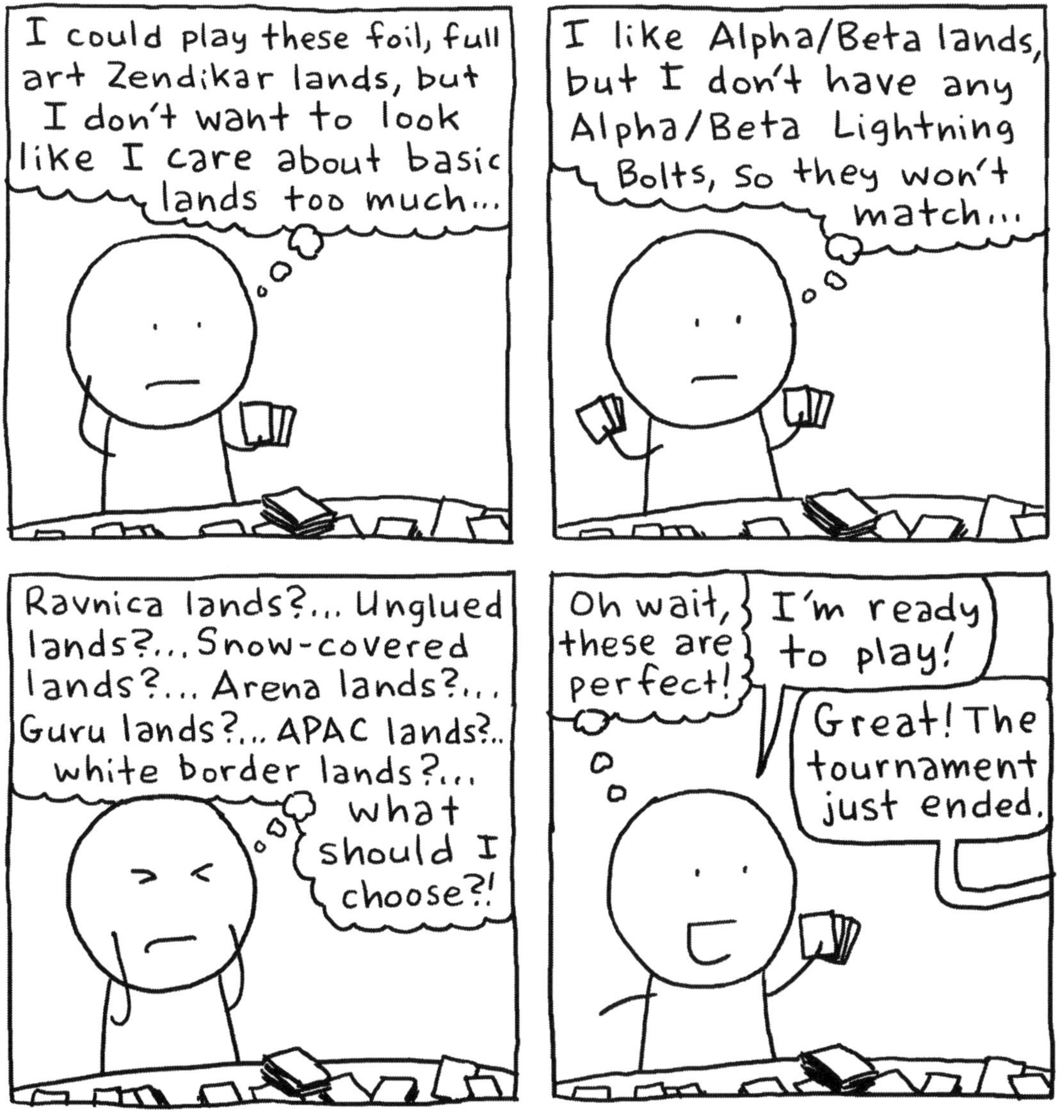
I could play these foil, full art Zendikar lands, but I don't want to look like I care about basic lands too much...
I like Alpha/Beta lands, but I don't have any Alpha/Beta Lightning Bolts, so they won't match...
Ravnica lands?... Unglued lands?... Snow-covered lands?... Arena lands?... Guru lands?... APAC lands?.. white border lands?...
what should I choose?!
Oh wait, these are perfect!
I'm ready to play!
Great! The tournament just ended.

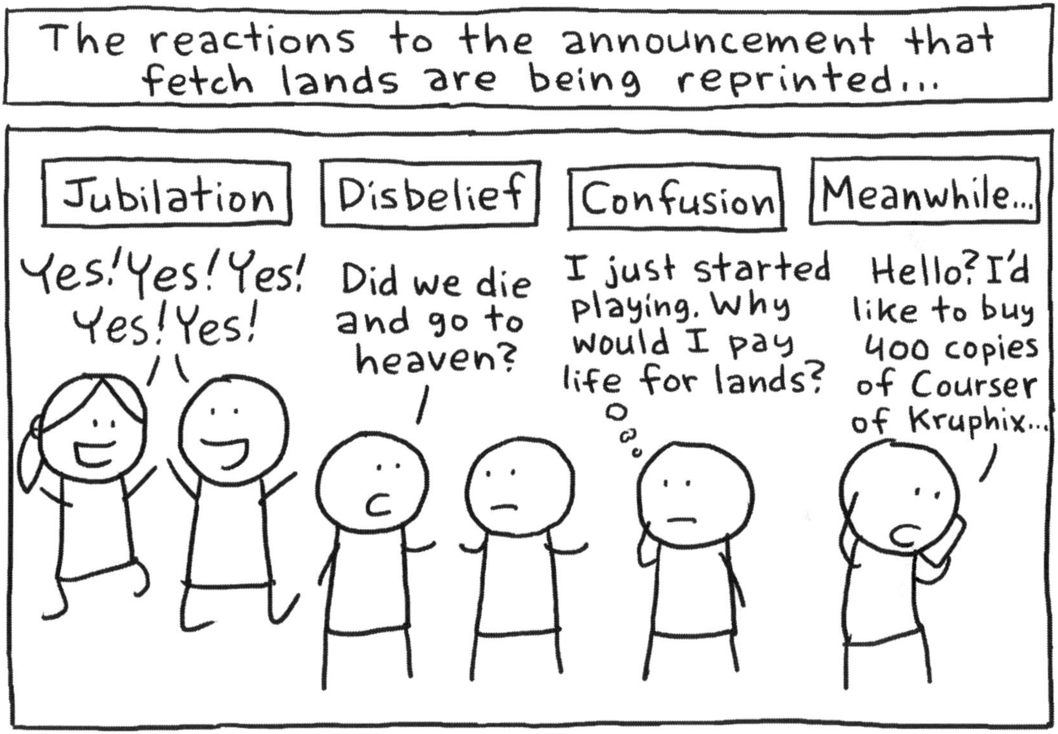
The reactions to the announcement that fetch lands are being reprinted...
Jubilation
Disbelief
Confusion
Meanwhile...
Yes! Yes! Yes! Yes! Yes!
Did we die and go to heaven?
I just started playing. Why would I pay life for lands?
Hello? I'd like to buy 400 copies of Courser of Kruphix...

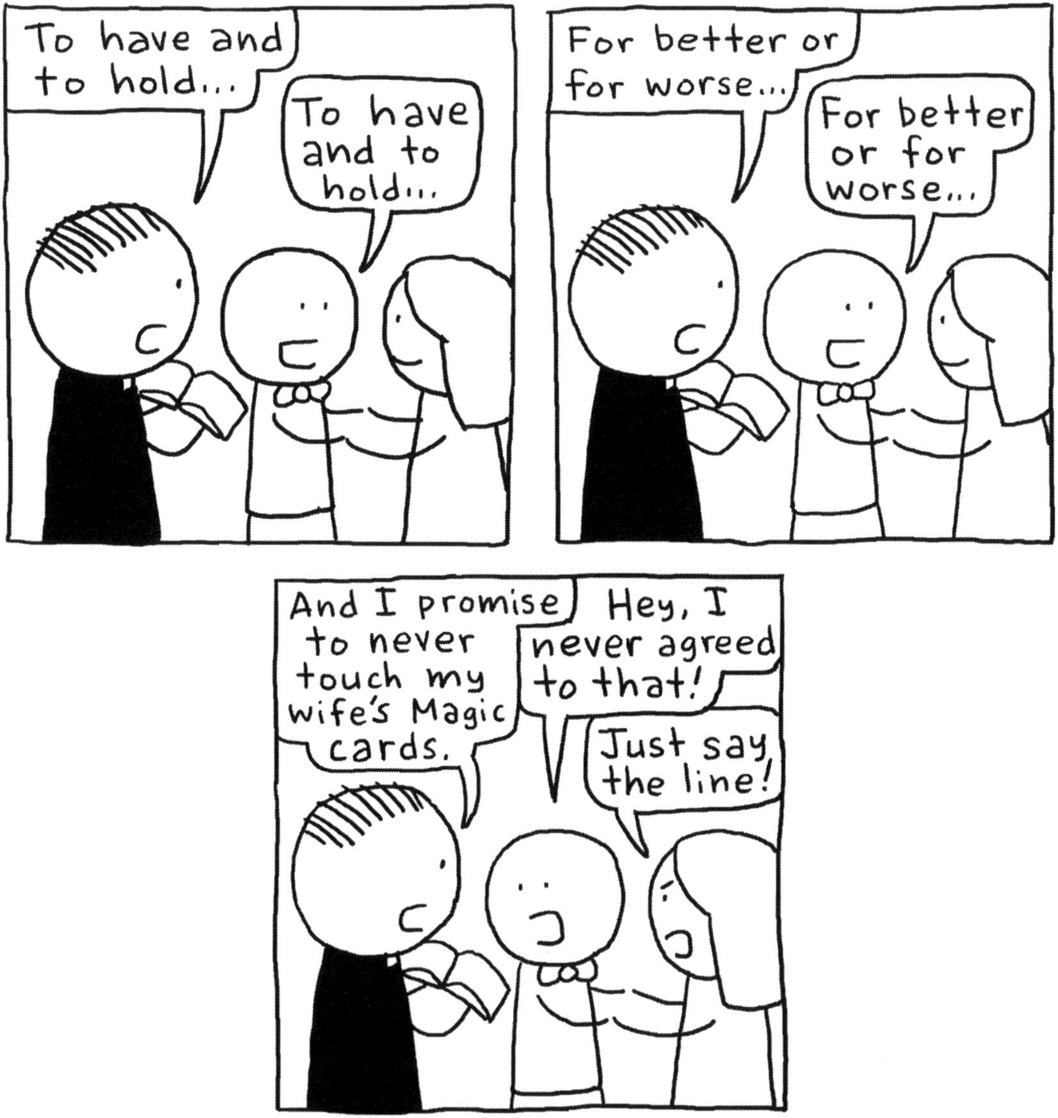
To have and to hold...
To have and to hold...
For better or for worse...
For better or for worse...
And I promise to never touch my wife's Magic cards.
Hey, I never agreed to that!
Just say the line!

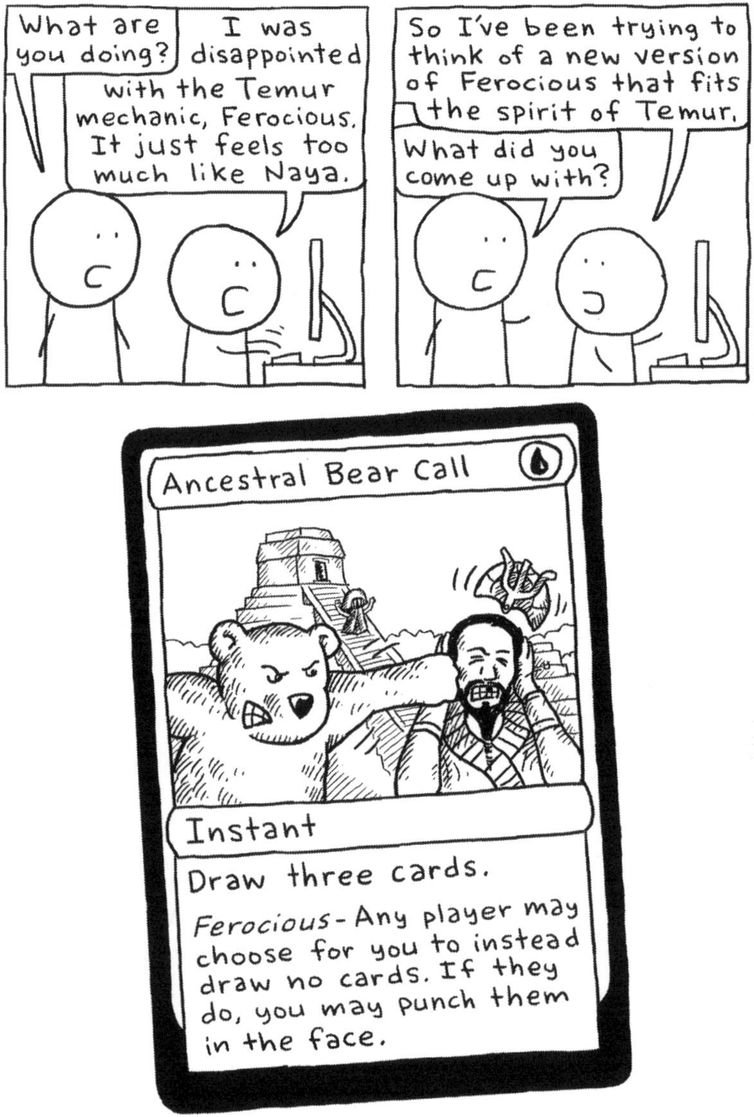
What are you doing?
I was disappointed with the Temur mechanic, Ferocious. It just feels too much like Naya.
So I've been trying to think of a new version of Ferocious that fits the spirit of Temur.
What did you come up with?
Ancestral Bear Call
Instant
Draw three cards.
Ferocious - Any player may choose for you to instead draw no cards. If they do, you may punch them in the face.

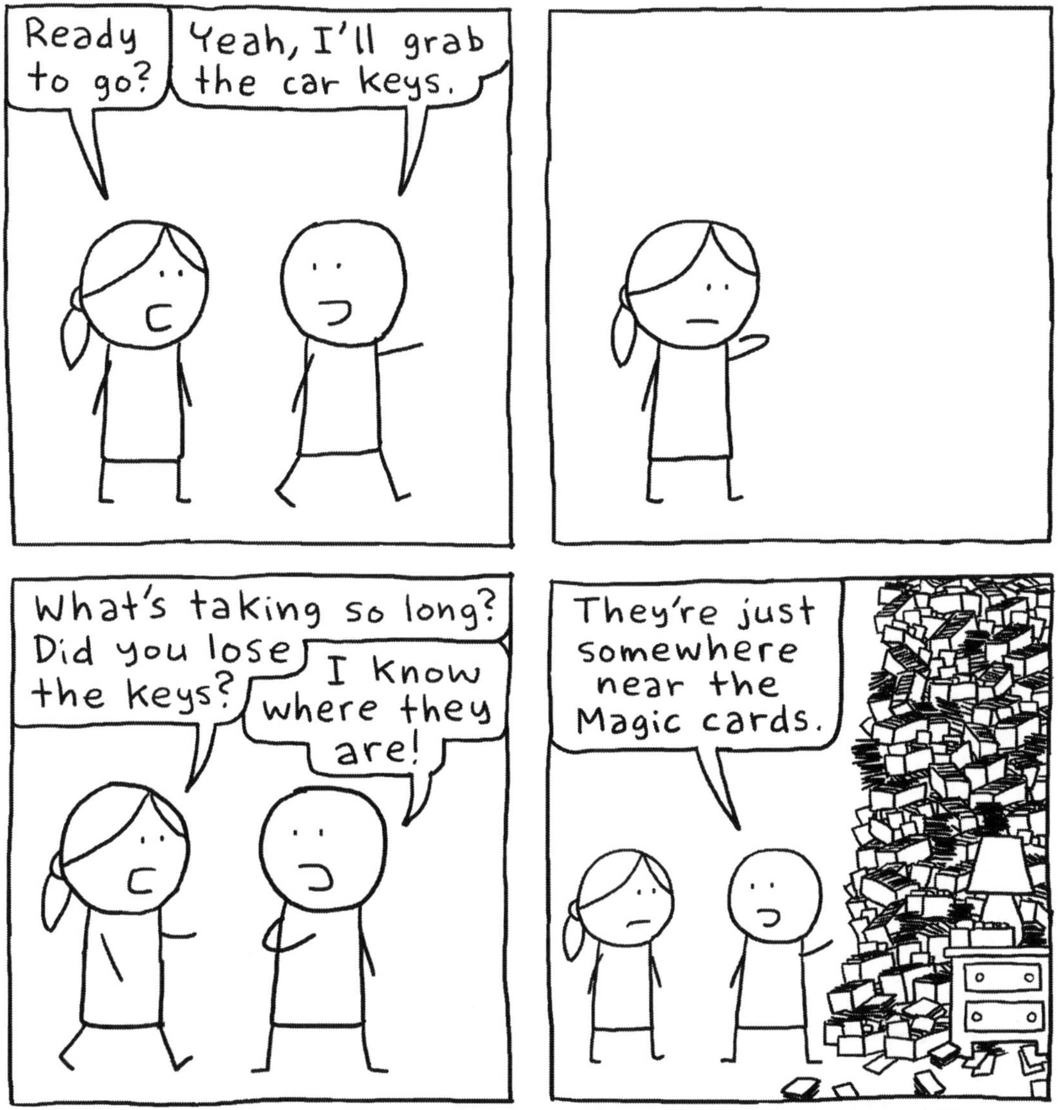
Ready to go?
Yeah, I'll grab the car keys.
What's taking so long? Did you lose the keys?
I know where they are!
They're just somewhere near the Magic cards.

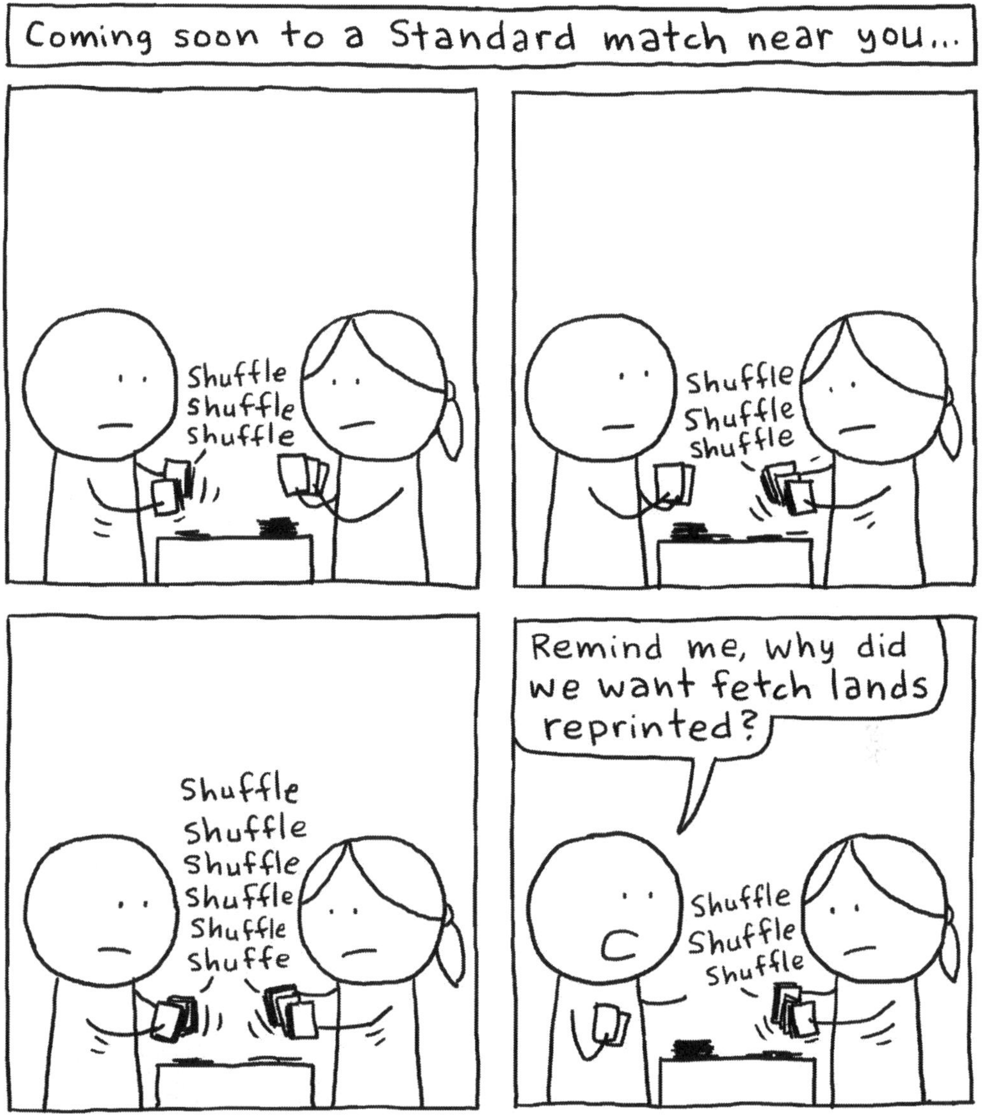
Coming soon to a Standard match near you...
Shuffle
Shuffle
Shuffle
Shuffle
Shuffle
Shuffle
Shuffle
Shuffle
Shuffle
Shuffle
Shuffle
Shuffe
Remind me, why did we want fetch lands reprinted?
Shuffle
Shuffle
Shuffle

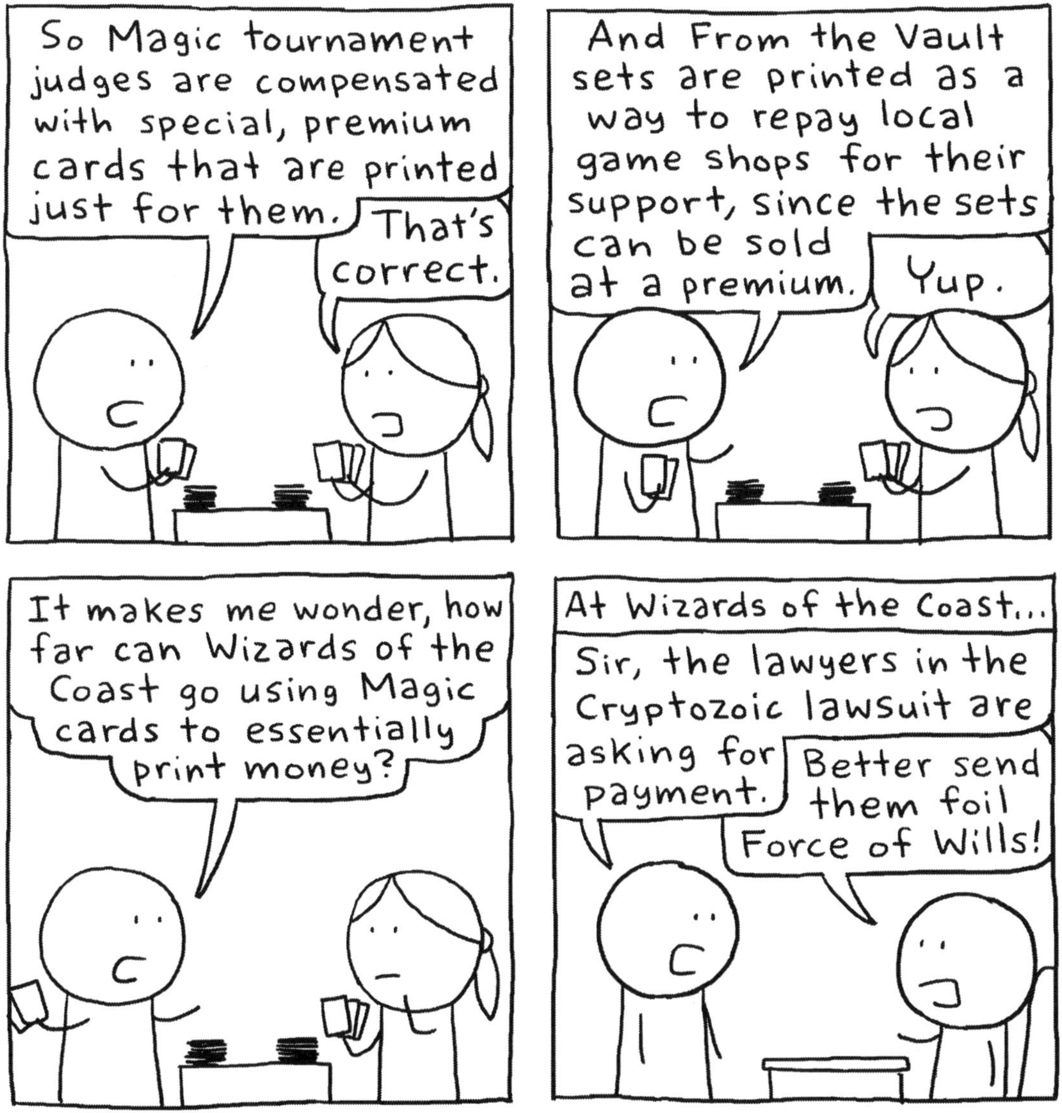
So Magic tournament judges are compensated with special, premium cards that are printed just for them.
That's correct.
And From the Vault sets are printed as a way to repay local game shops for their support, since the sets can be sold at a premium.
Yup.
It makes me wonder, how far can Wizards of the Coast go using Magic cards to essentially print money?
At Wizards of the Coast...
Sir, the lawyers in the Cryptozoic lawsuit are asking for payment.
Better send them foil Force of Wills!

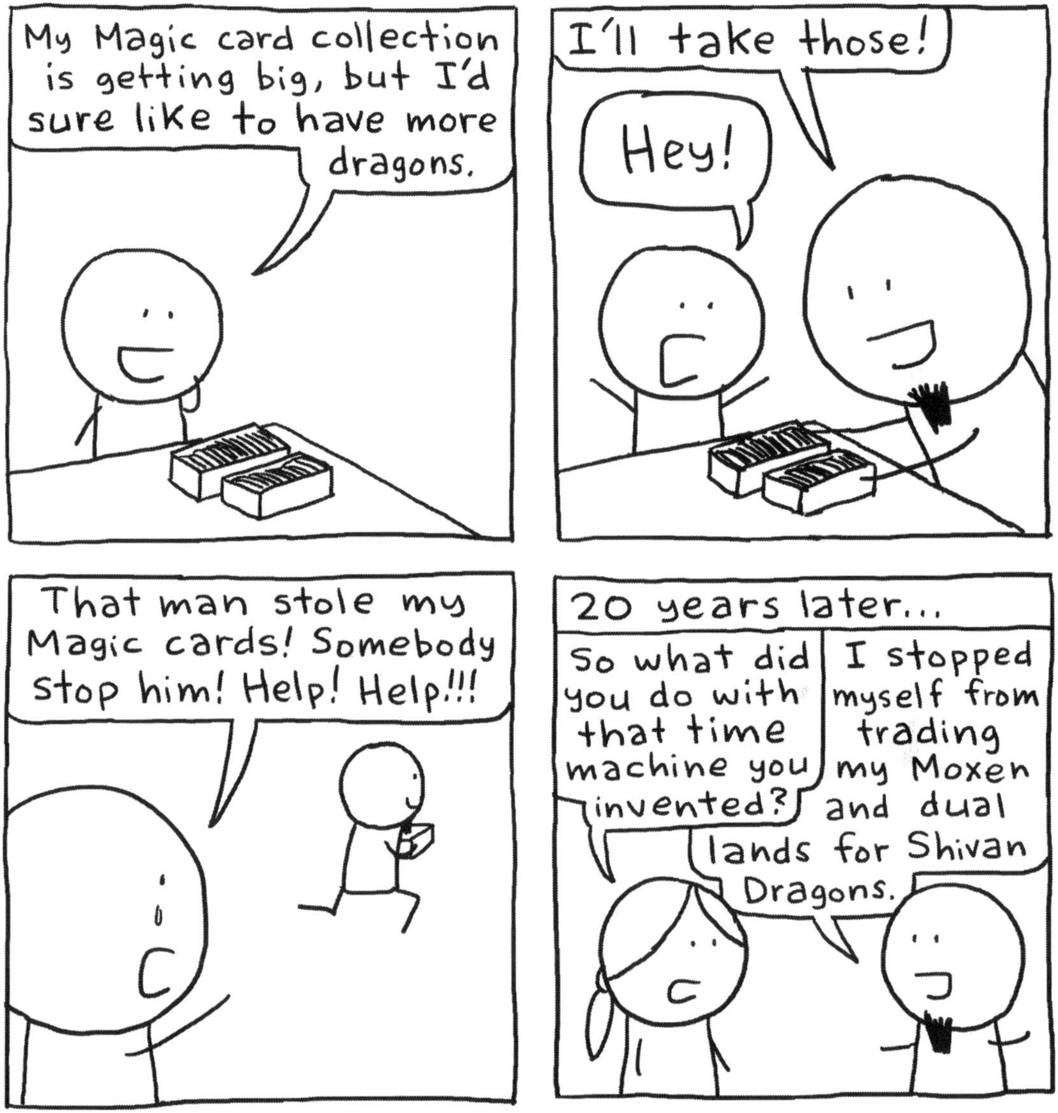
My Magic card collection is getting big, but I'd sure like to have more dragons.
I'll take those!
Hey!
That man stole my Magic cards! Somebody stop him! Help! Help!!!
20 years later...
So what did you do with that time machine you invented?
I stopped myself from trading my Moxen and dual lands for Shivan Dragons.

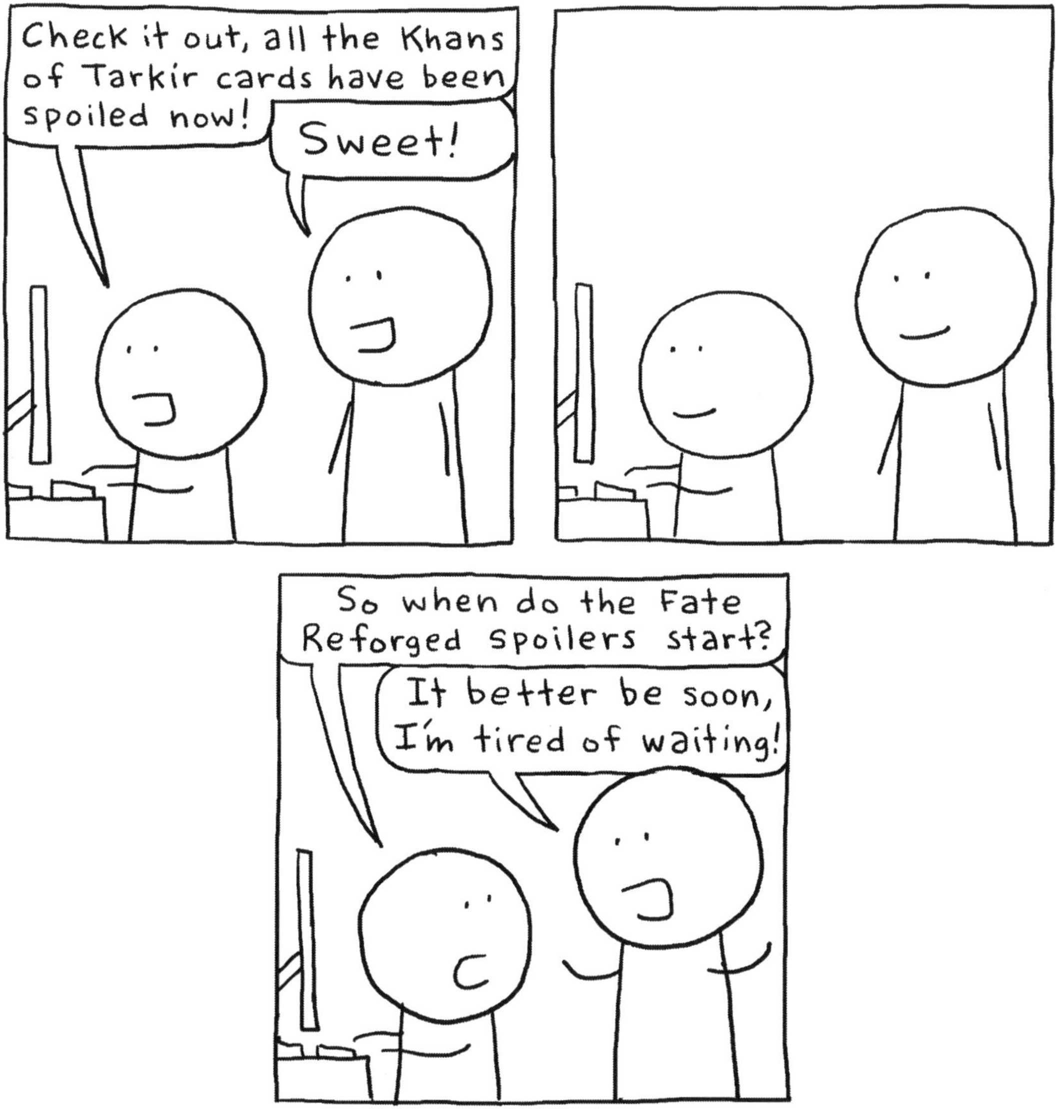
Check it out, all the Khans of Tarkir cards have been spoiled now!
Sweet!
So when do the Fate Reforged spoilers start?
It better be soon, I'm tired of waiting!

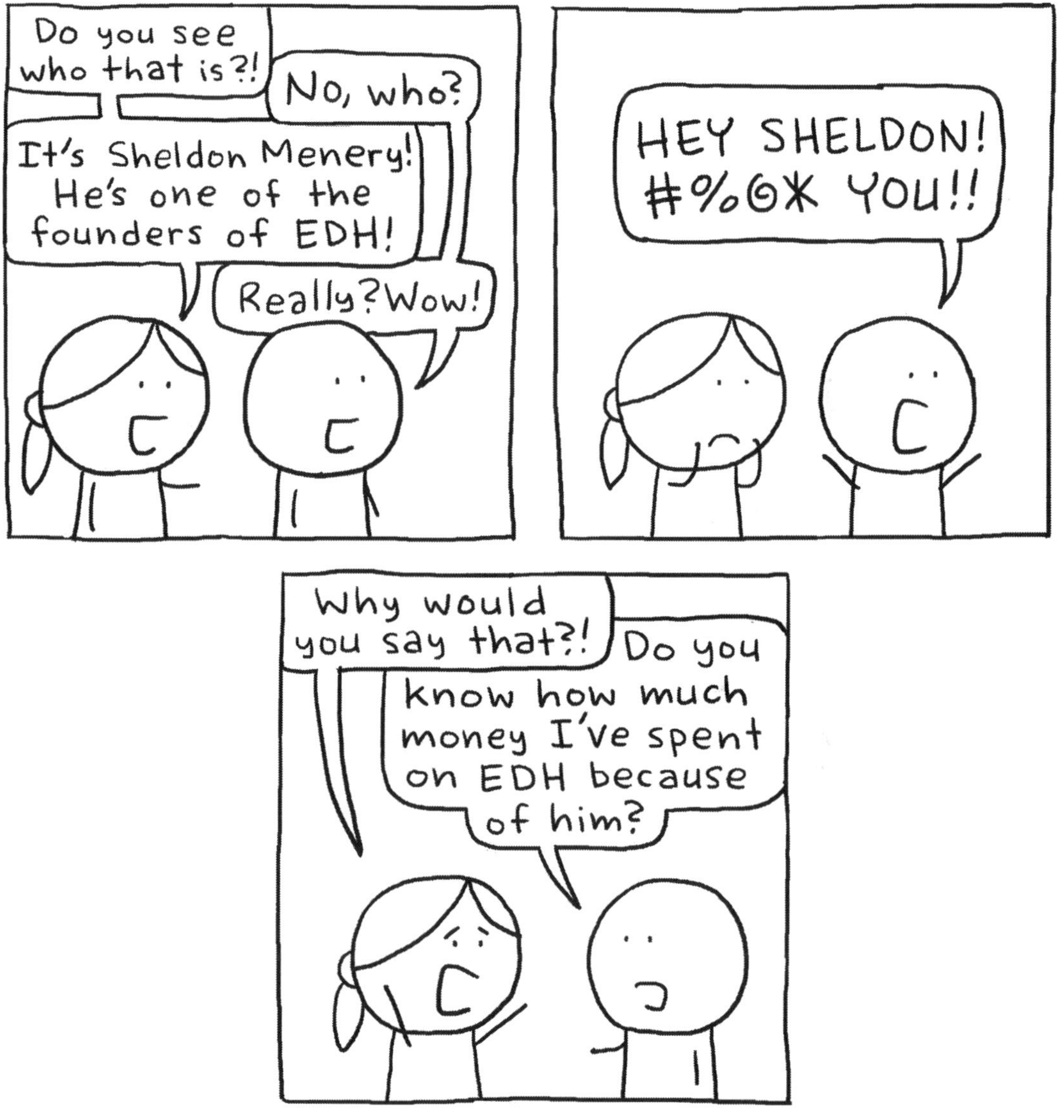
Do you see who that is?!
No, who?
It's Sheldon Menery! He's one of the founders of EDH!
Really? Wow!
HEY SHELDON! #%@* YOU!!
Why would you say that?!
Do you know how much money I've spent on EDH because of him?

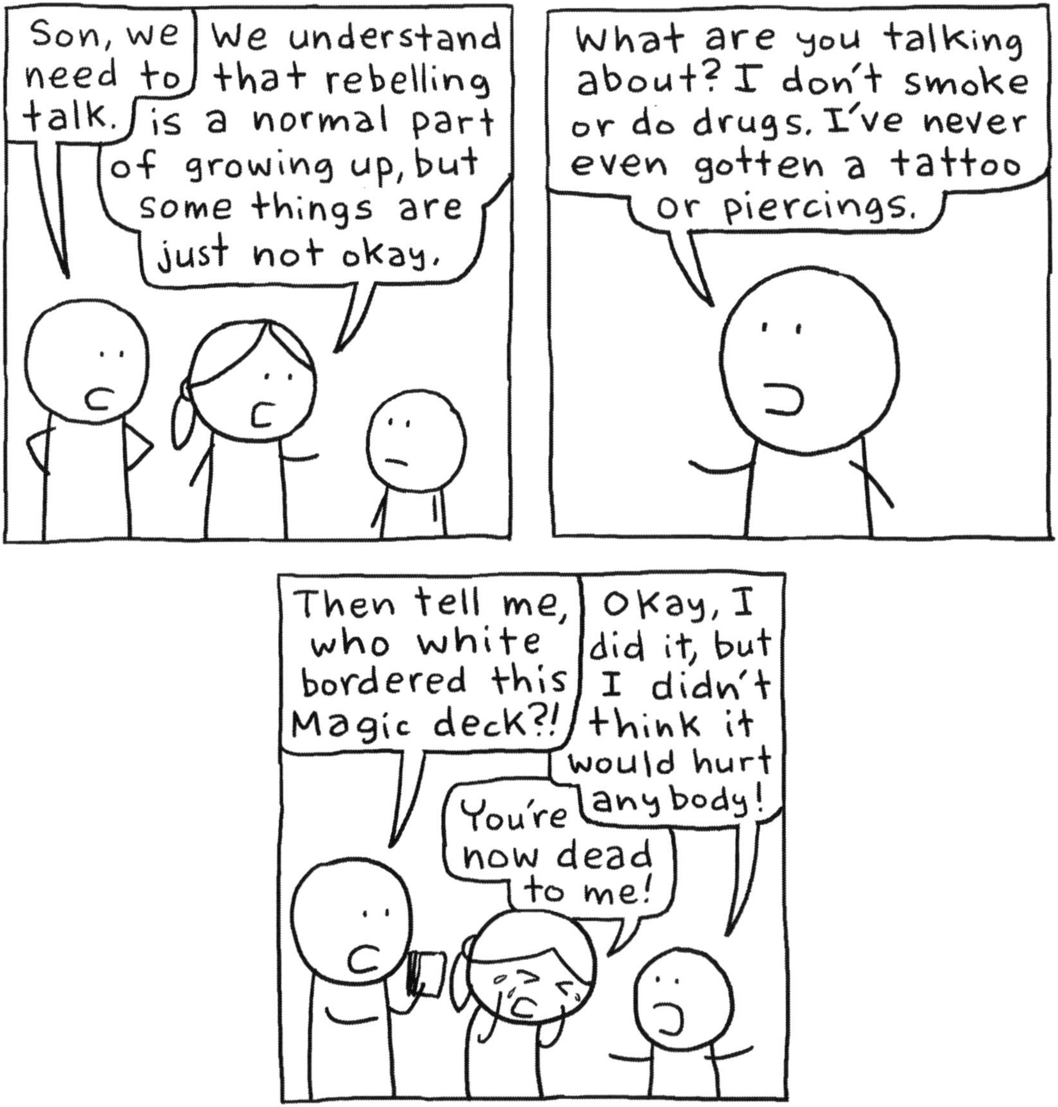
Son, we need to talk.
We understand that rebelling is a normal part of growing up, but some things are just not okay.
What are you talking about? I don't smoke or do drugs. I've never even gotten a tattoo or piercings.
Then tell me, who white bordered this Magic deck?!
Okay, I did it, but I didn't think it would hurt anybody!
You're now dead to me!

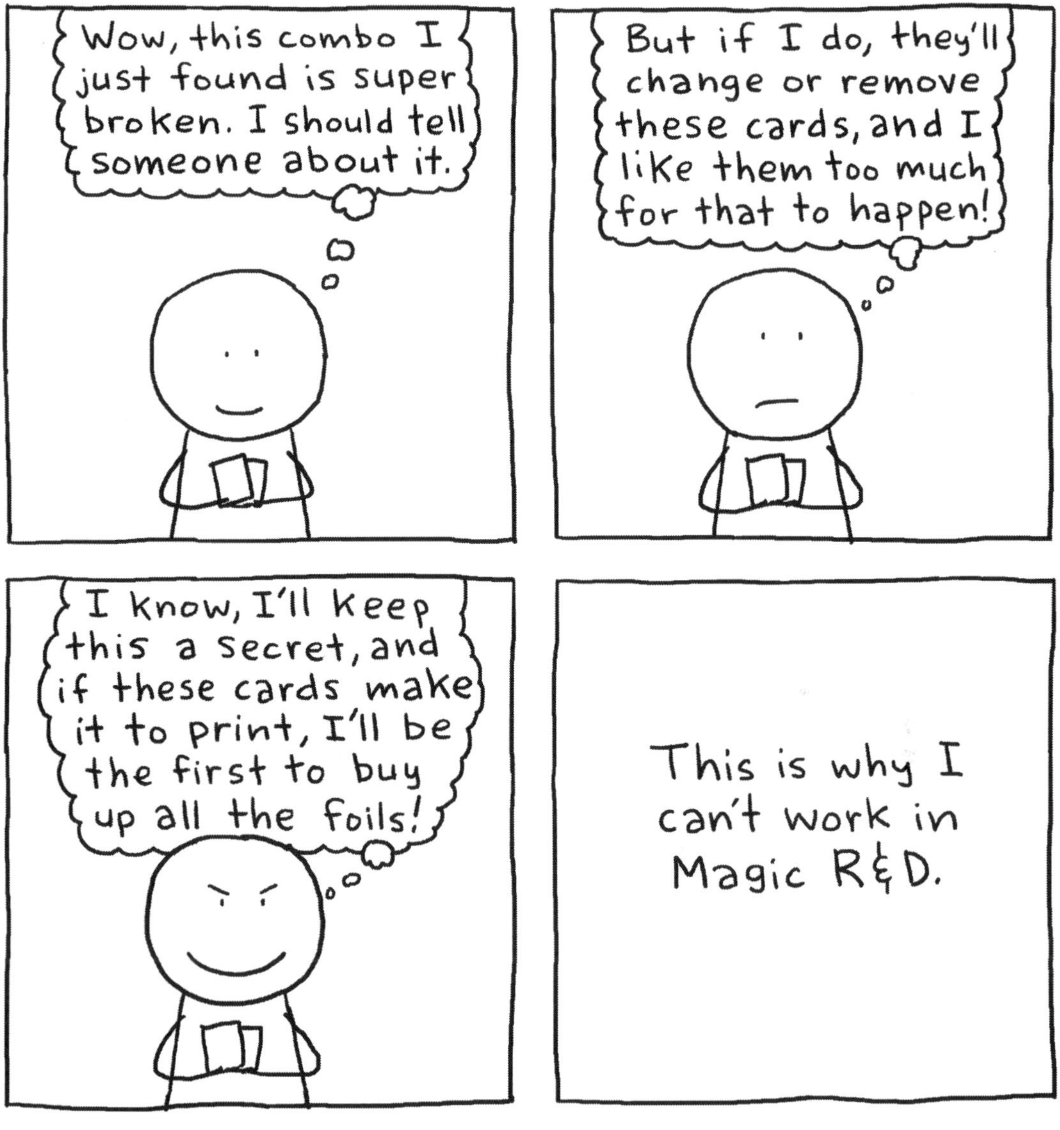
Wow, this combo I just found is super broken. I should tell someone about it.
But if I do, they'll change or remove these cards, and I like them too much for that to happen!
I know, I'll keep this a secret, and if these cards make it to print, I'll be the first to buy up all the foils!
This is why I can't work in Magic R&D.

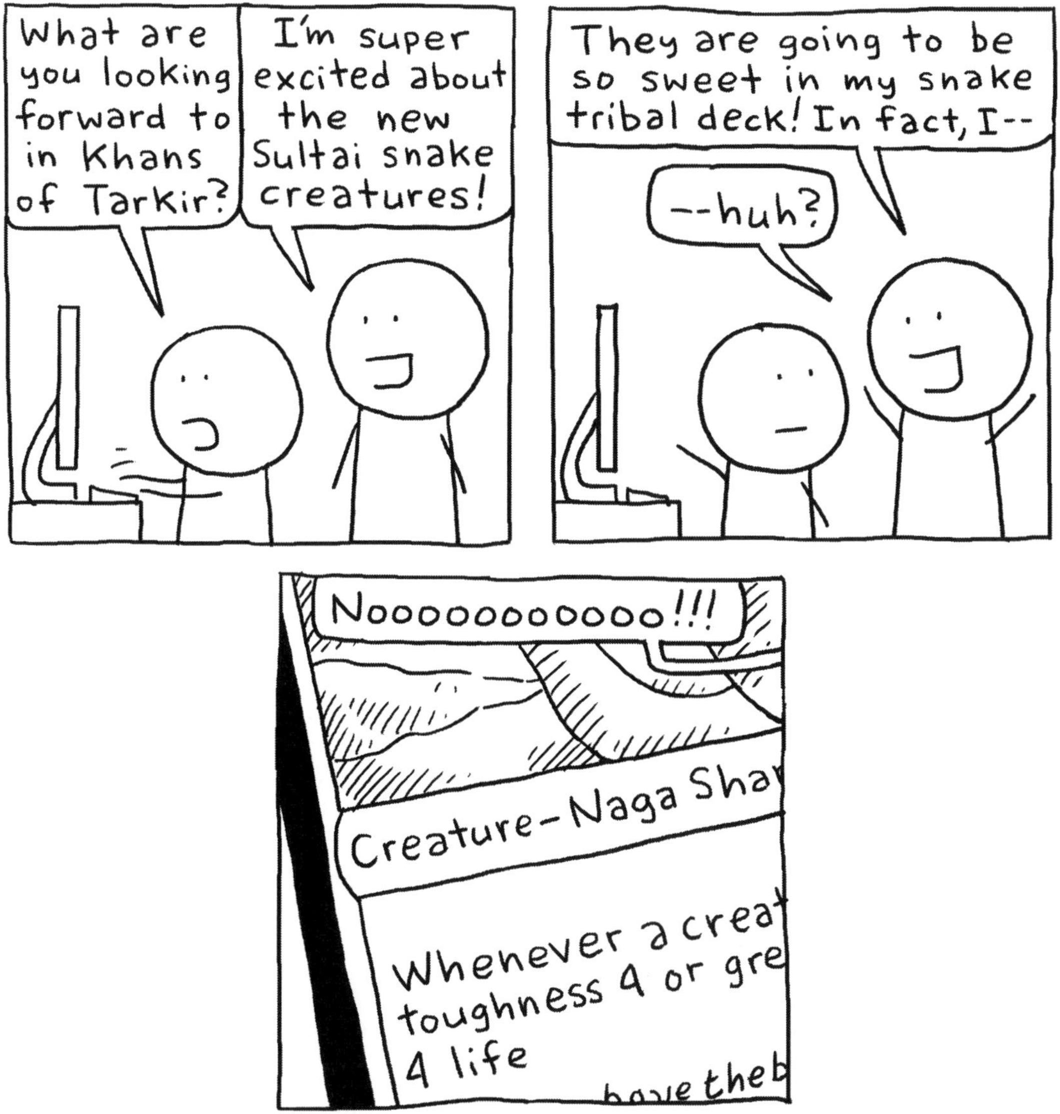
What are you looking forward to in Khans of Tarkir?
I'm super excited about the new Sultai snake creatures!
They are going to be so sweet in my snake tribal deck! In fact, I--
--huh?
Nooooooooooo!!!
Creature–Naga Sha
Whenever a creat
toughness 4 or gre
4 life

Hey, nice face tattoo! I like to play counter-spell decks too!
What did I say wrong?

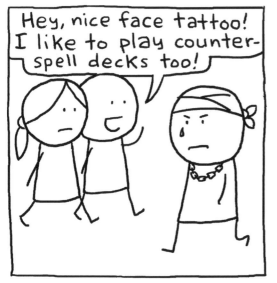

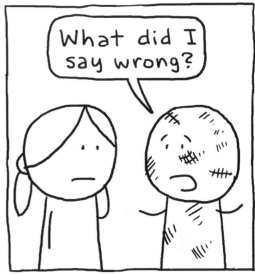

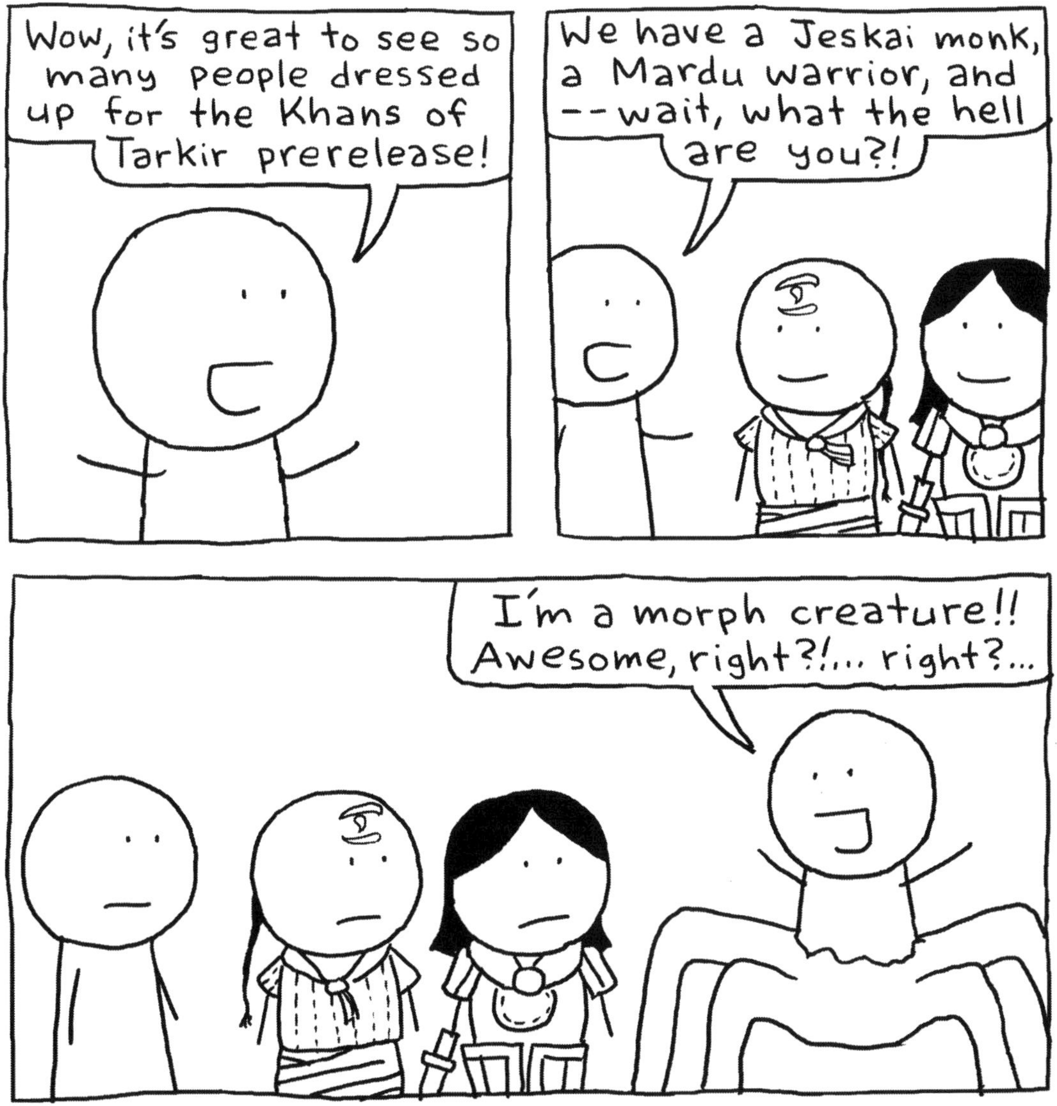
Wow, it's great to see so many people dressed up for the Khans of Tarkir prerelease!
We have a Jeskai monk, a Mardu warrior, and --wait, what the hell are you?!
I'm a morph creature!! Awesome, right?!... right?...

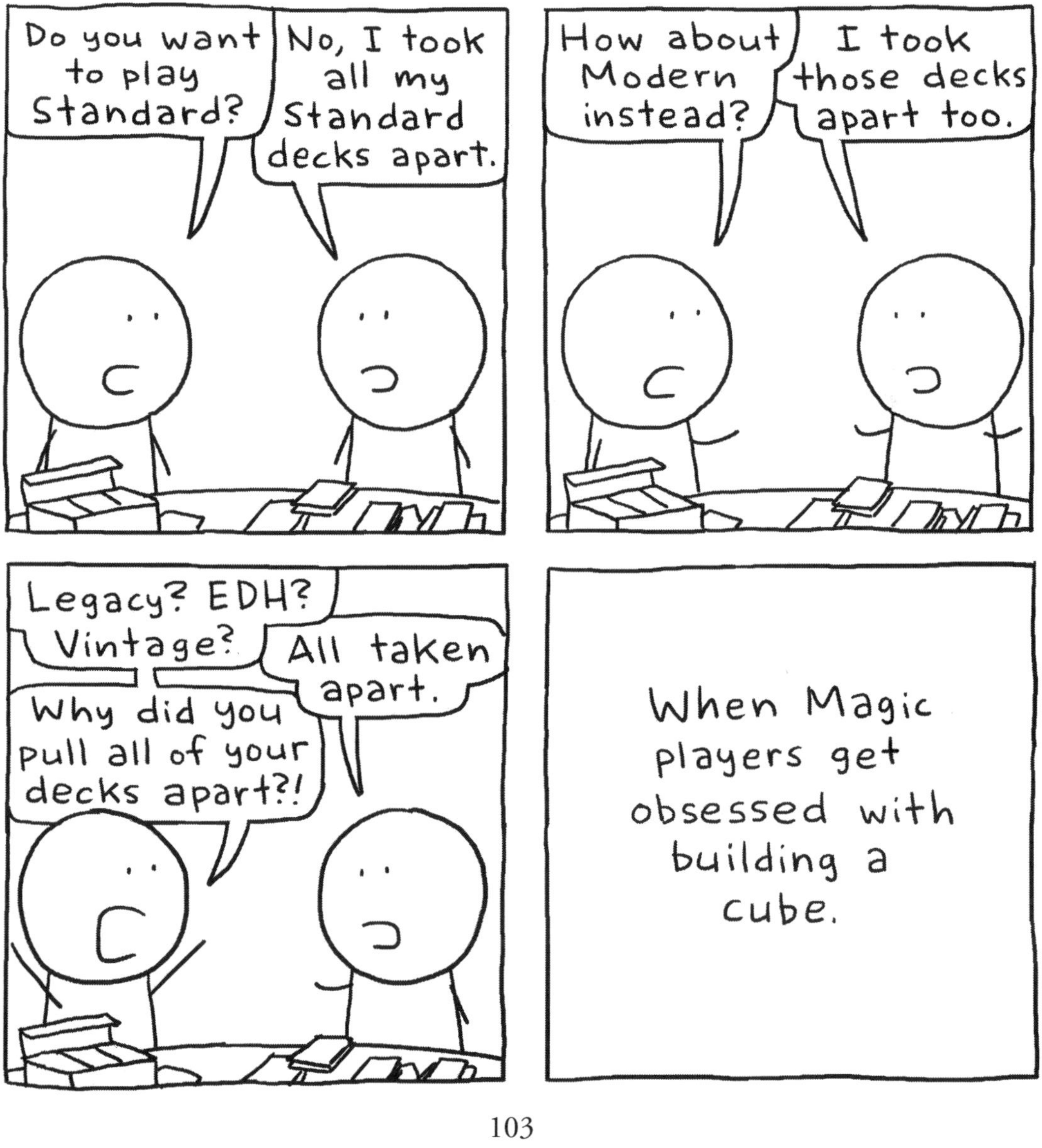
Do you want to play Standard?
No, I took all my Standard decks apart.
How about Modern instead?
I took those decks apart too.
Legacy? EDH? Vintage?
All taken apart.
Why did you pull all of your decks apart?!
When Magic players get obsessed with building a cube.

One of the things I really like about playing Magic is that it teaches you how to think critically and rationally.
You topdecked that?! Why are you always so lucky?! This game hates me!!

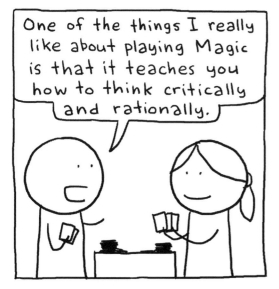

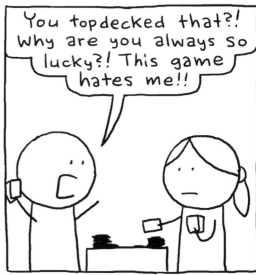

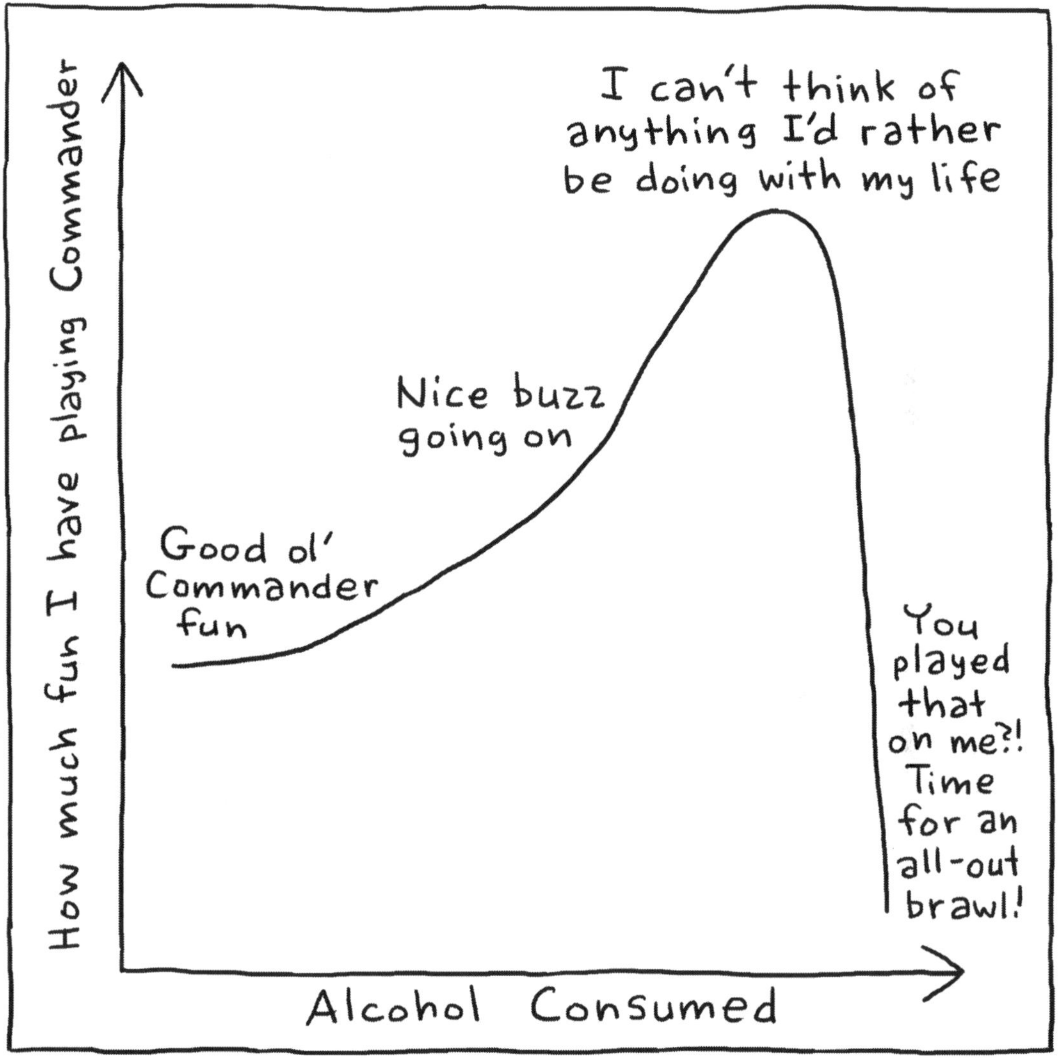
How much fun I have playing Commander
I can't think of anything I'd rather be doing with my life
Nice buzz going on
Good ol' Commander fun
You played that on me?! Time for an all-out brawl!
Alcohol Consumed

How I spend my time in the shower...

30 minutes thinking about Magic deck ideas and cards I want.

1 minute frantically washing because I'm late for something.

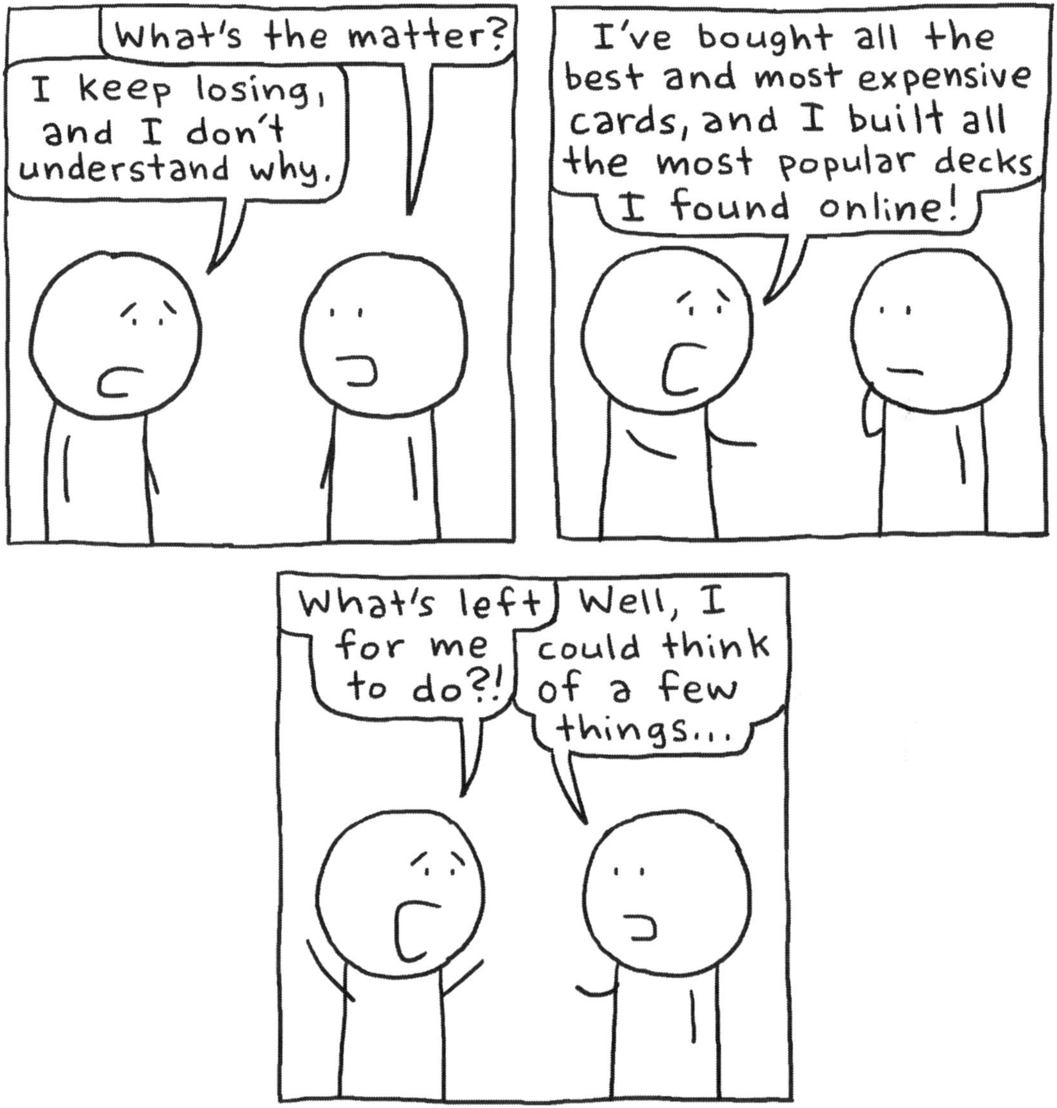
What's the matter?
I keep losing, and I don't understand why.
I've bought all the best and most expensive cards, and I built all the most popular decks I found online!
What's left for me to do?!
Well, I could think of a few things...

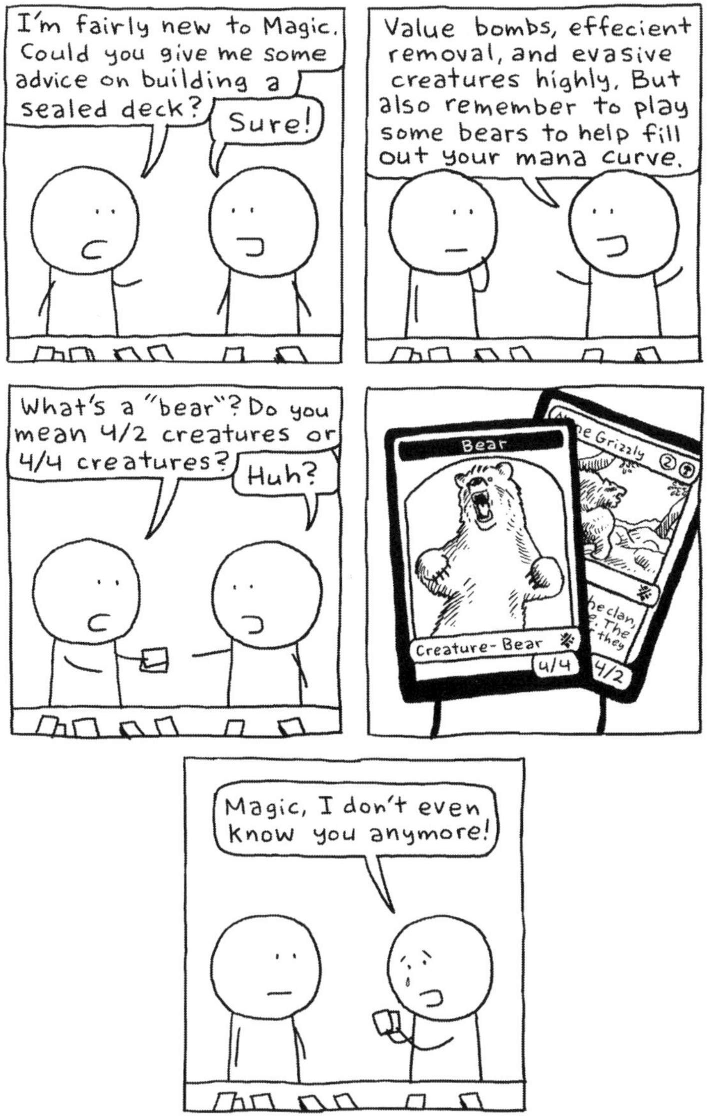
I'm fairly new to Magic. Could you give me some advice on building a sealed deck?
Sure!
Value bombs, effecient removal, and evasive creatures highly. But also remember to play some bears to help fill out your mana curve.
What's a "bear"? Do you mean 4/2 creatures or 4/4 creatures?
Huh?
Bear
Creature- Bear
4/4
4/2
Magic, I don't even know you anymore!

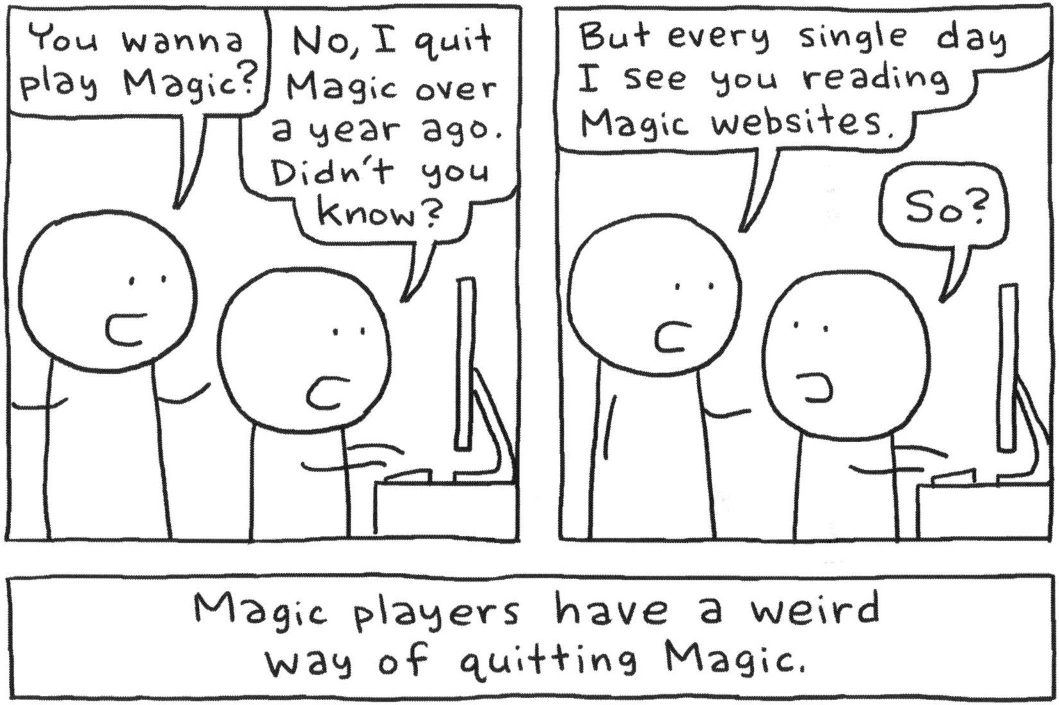
You wanna play Magic?
No, I quit Magic over a year ago. Didn't you know?
But every single day I see you reading Magic websites.
So?
Magic players have a weird way of quitting Magic.

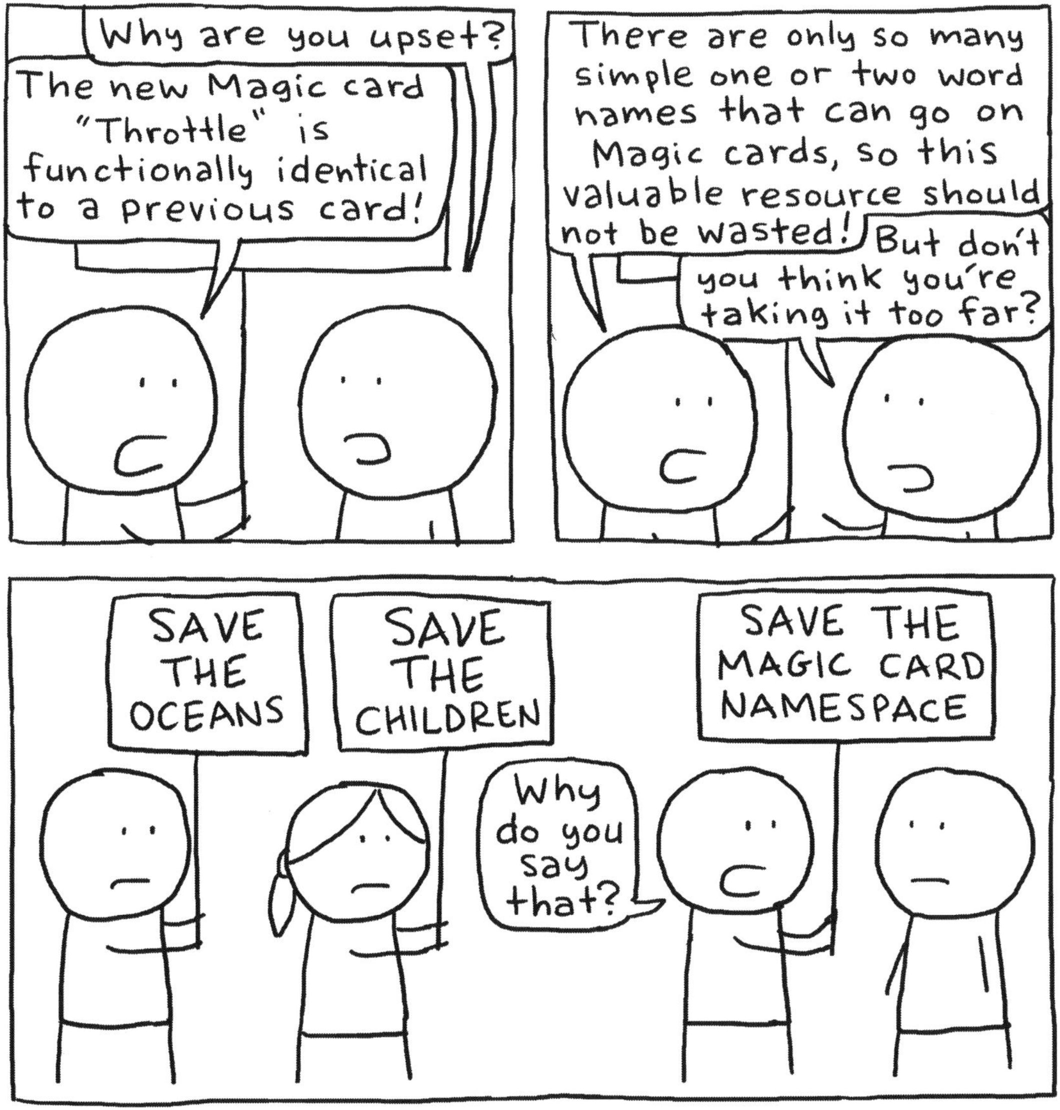
Why are you upset?
The new Magic card "Throttle" is functionally identical to a previous card!
There are only so many simple one or two word names that can go on Magic cards, so this valuable resource should not be wasted!
But don't you think you're taking it too far?
SAVE THE OCEANS
SAVE THE CHILDREN
Why do you say that?
SAVE THE MAGIC CARD NAMESPACE

Guess what? I finally got a BLACK LOTUS!
Sweet! I want to see!
This is so disappointing...

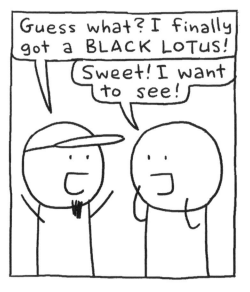

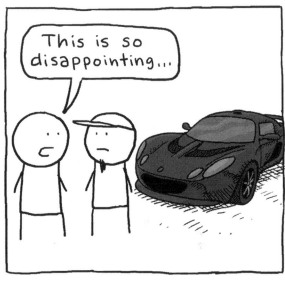

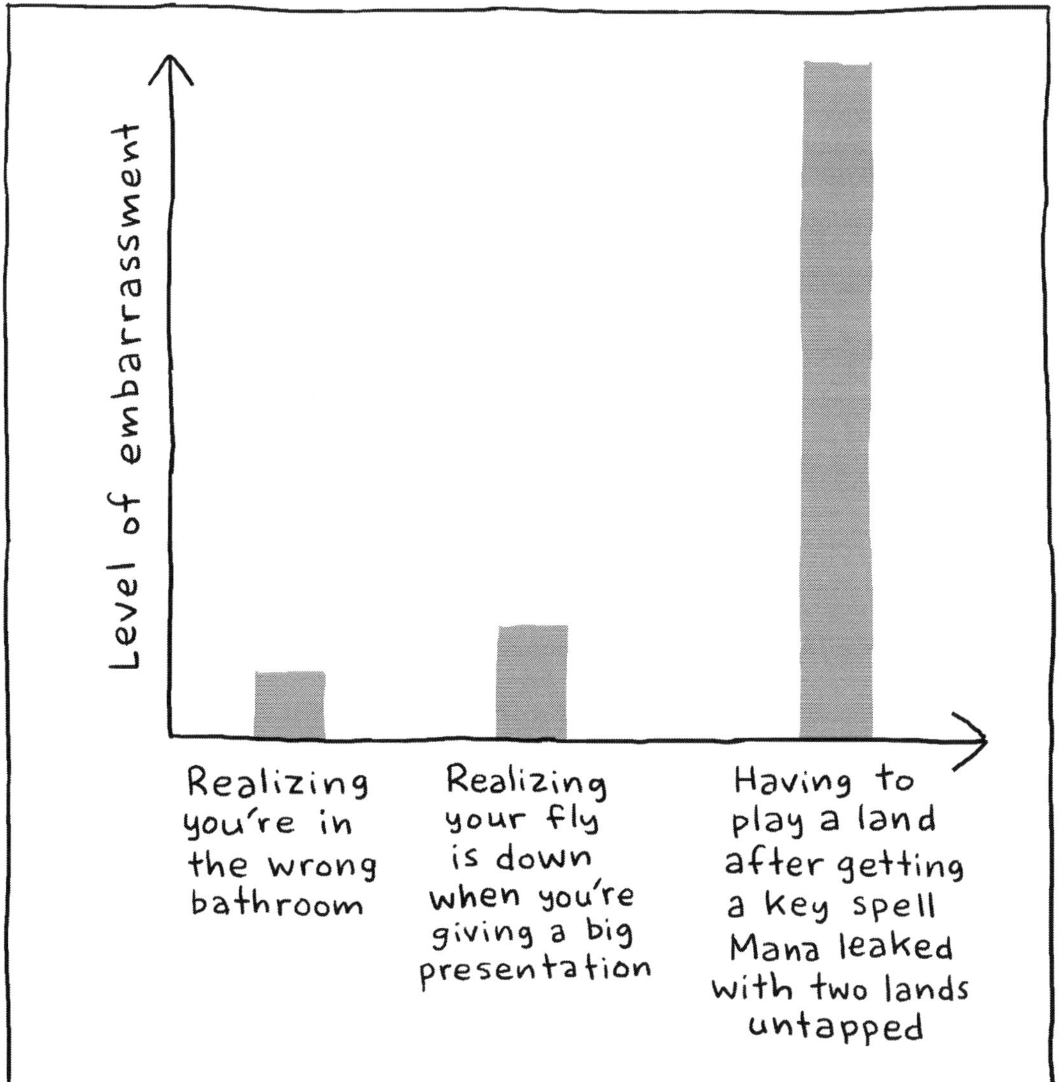
Level of embarrassment
Realizing you're in the wrong bathroom
Realizing your fly is down when you're giving a big presentation
Having to play a land after getting a key spell Mana leaked with two lands untapped

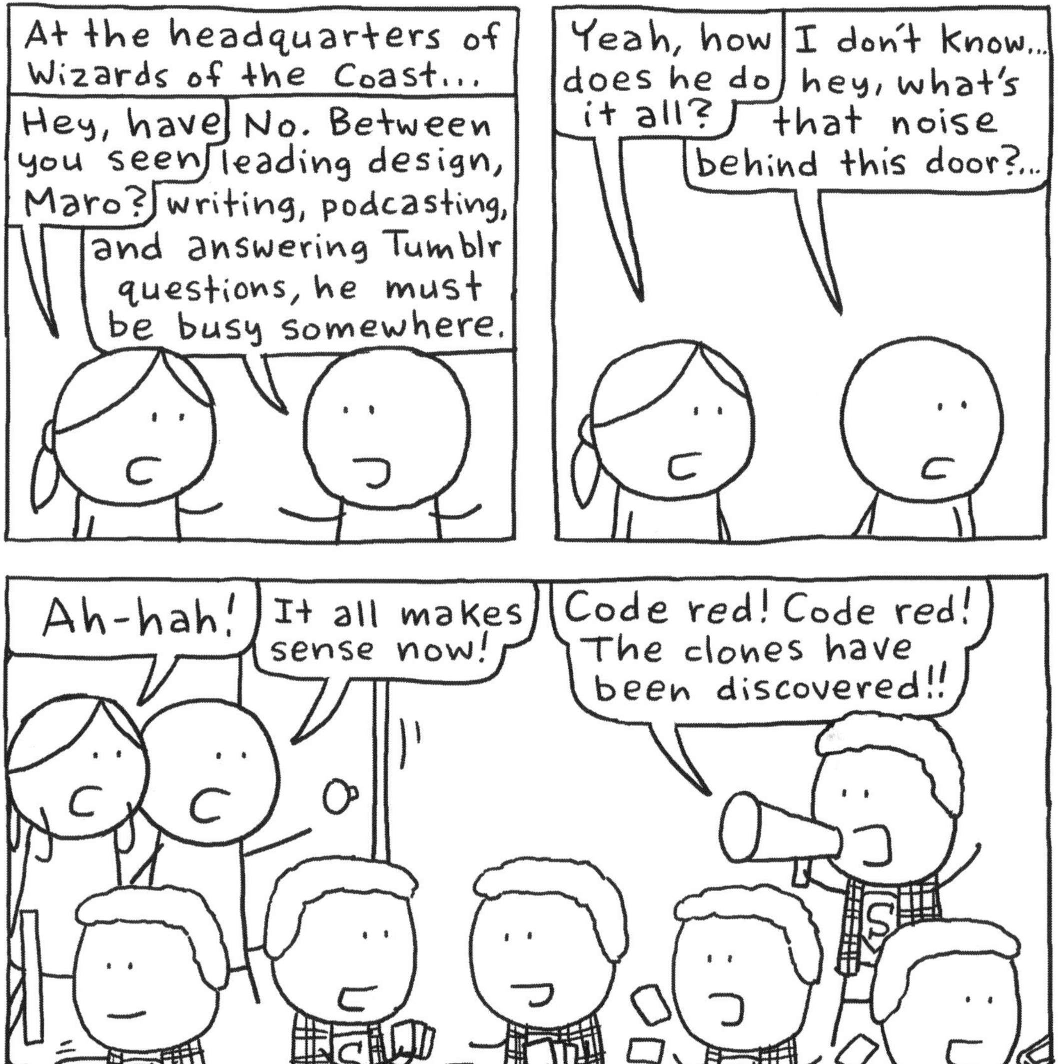
At the headquarters of Wizards of the Coast...
Hey, have you seen Maro?
No. Between leading design, writing, podcasting, and answering Tumblr questions, he must be busy somewhere.
Yeah, how does he do it all?
I don't know... hey, what's that noise behind this door?...
Ah-hah!
It all makes sense now!
Code red! Code red! The clones have been discovered!!

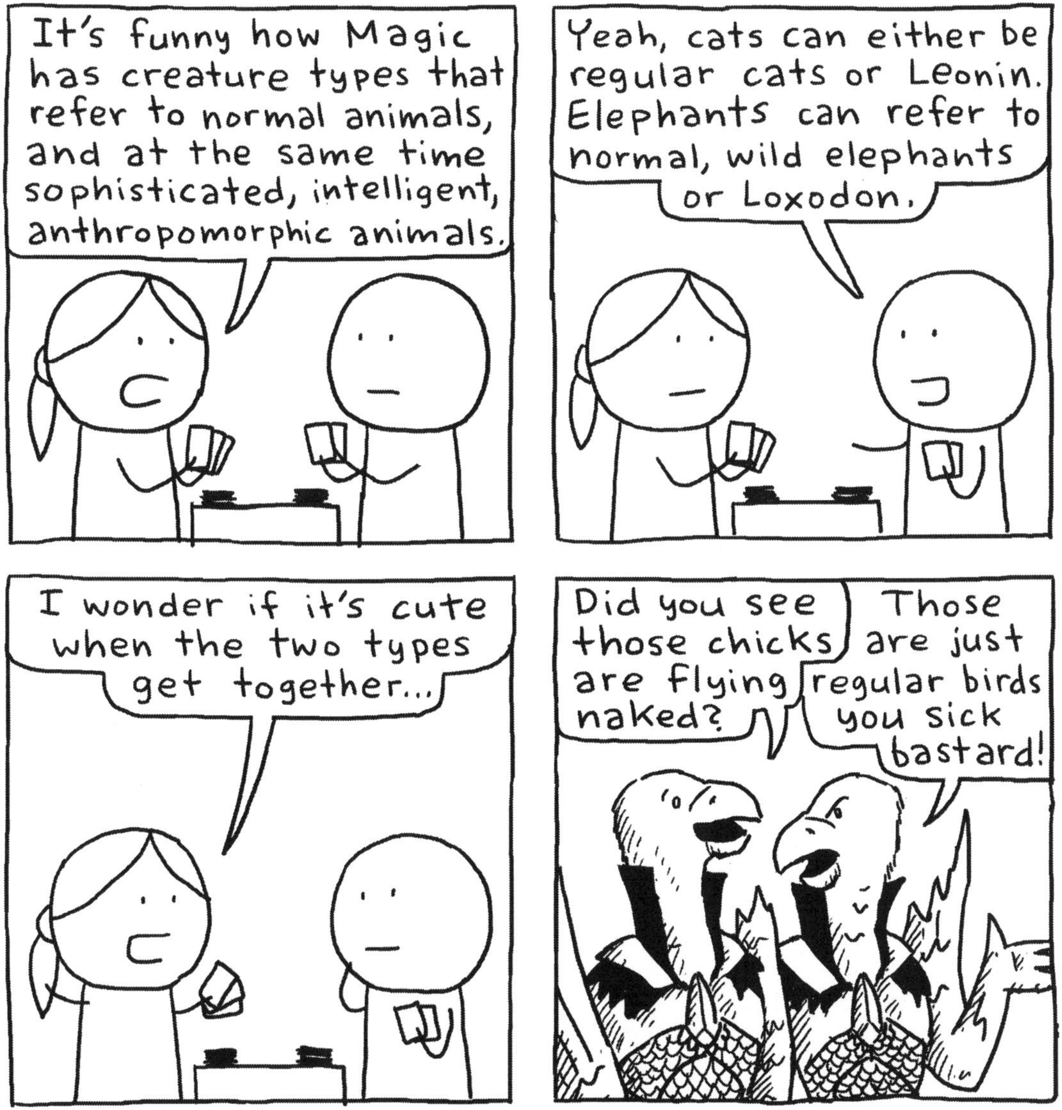
It's funny how Magic has creature types that refer to normal animals, and at the same time sophisticated, intelligent, anthropomorphic animals.
Yeah, cats can either be regular cats or Leonin. Elephants can refer to normal, wild elephants or Loxodon.
I wonder if it's cute when the two types get together...
Did you see those chicks are flying naked?
Those are just regular birds you sick bastard!

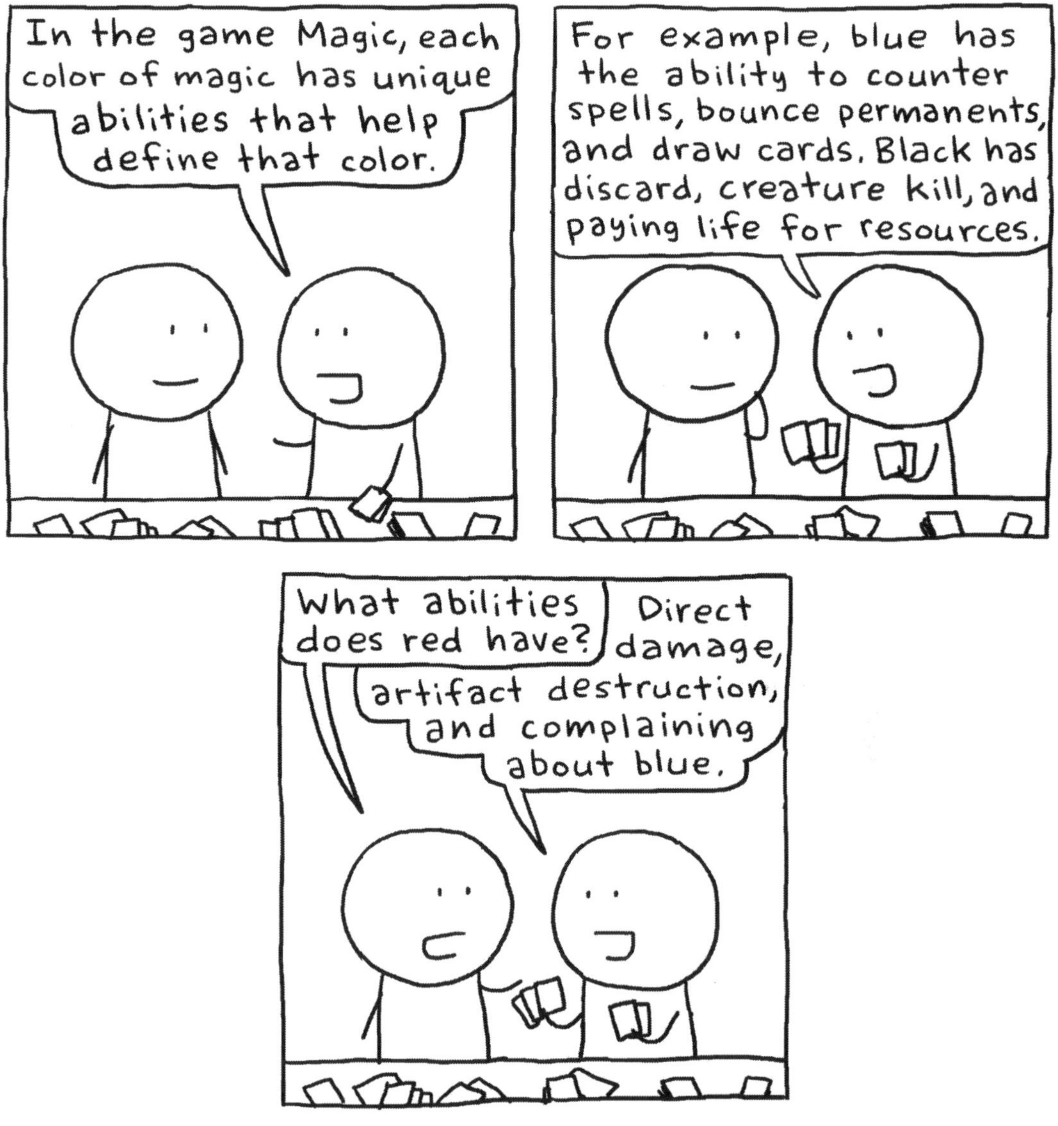
In the game Magic, each color of magic has unique abilities that help define that color.
For example, blue has the ability to counter spells, bounce permanents, and draw cards. Black has discard, creature kill, and paying life for resources.
What abilities does red have?
Direct damage, artifact destruction, and complaining about blue.

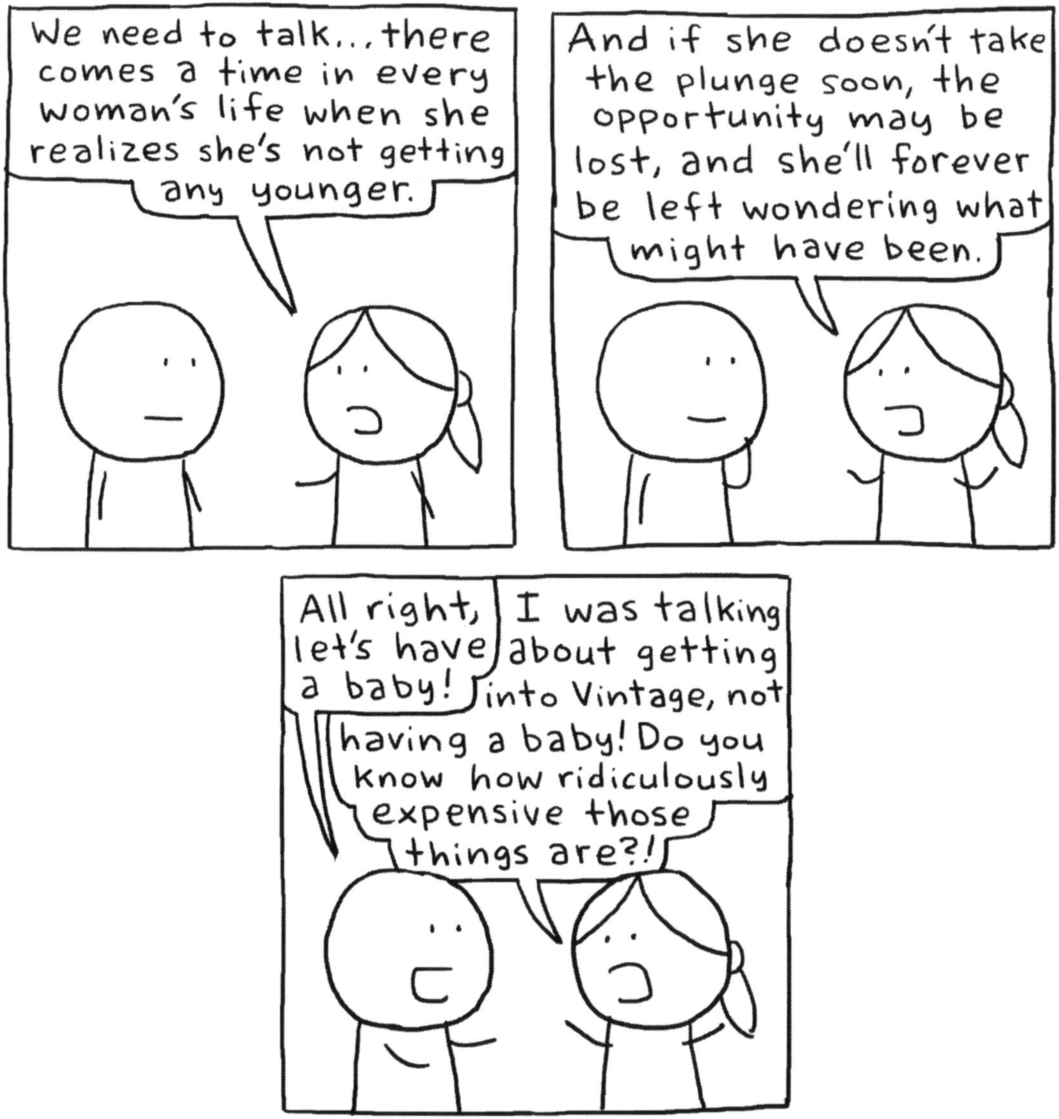
We need to talk... there comes a time in every woman's life when she realizes she's not getting any younger.
And if she doesn't take the plunge soon, the opportunity may be lost, and she'll forever be left wondering what might have been.
All right, let's have a baby!
I was talking about getting into Vintage, not having a baby! Do you know how ridiculously expensive those things are?!

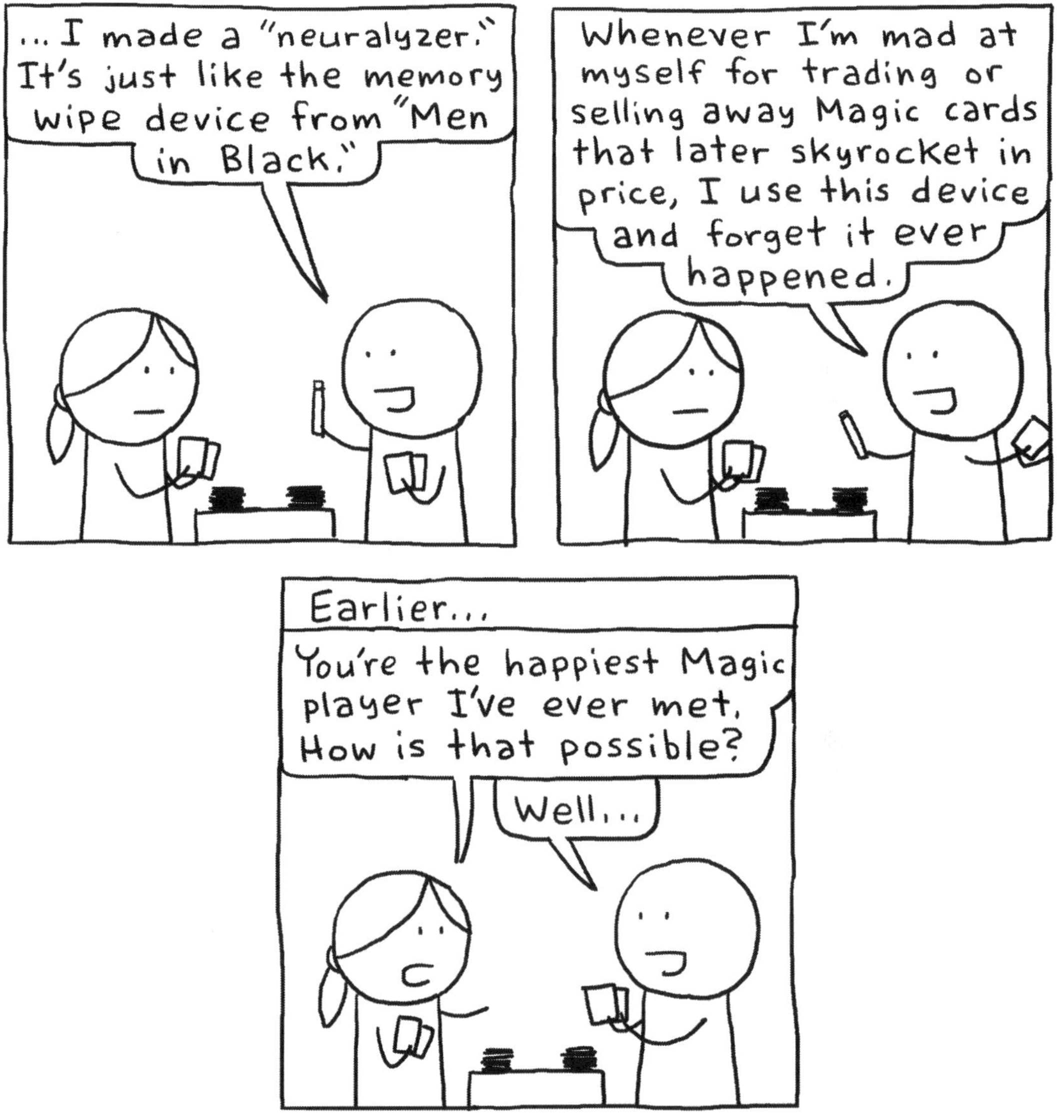
... I made a "neuralyzer." It's just like the memory wipe device from "Men in Black."
Whenever I'm mad at myself for trading or selling away Magic cards that later skyrocket in price, I use this device and forget it ever happened.
Earlier...
You're the happiest Magic player I've ever met. How is that possible?
Well...

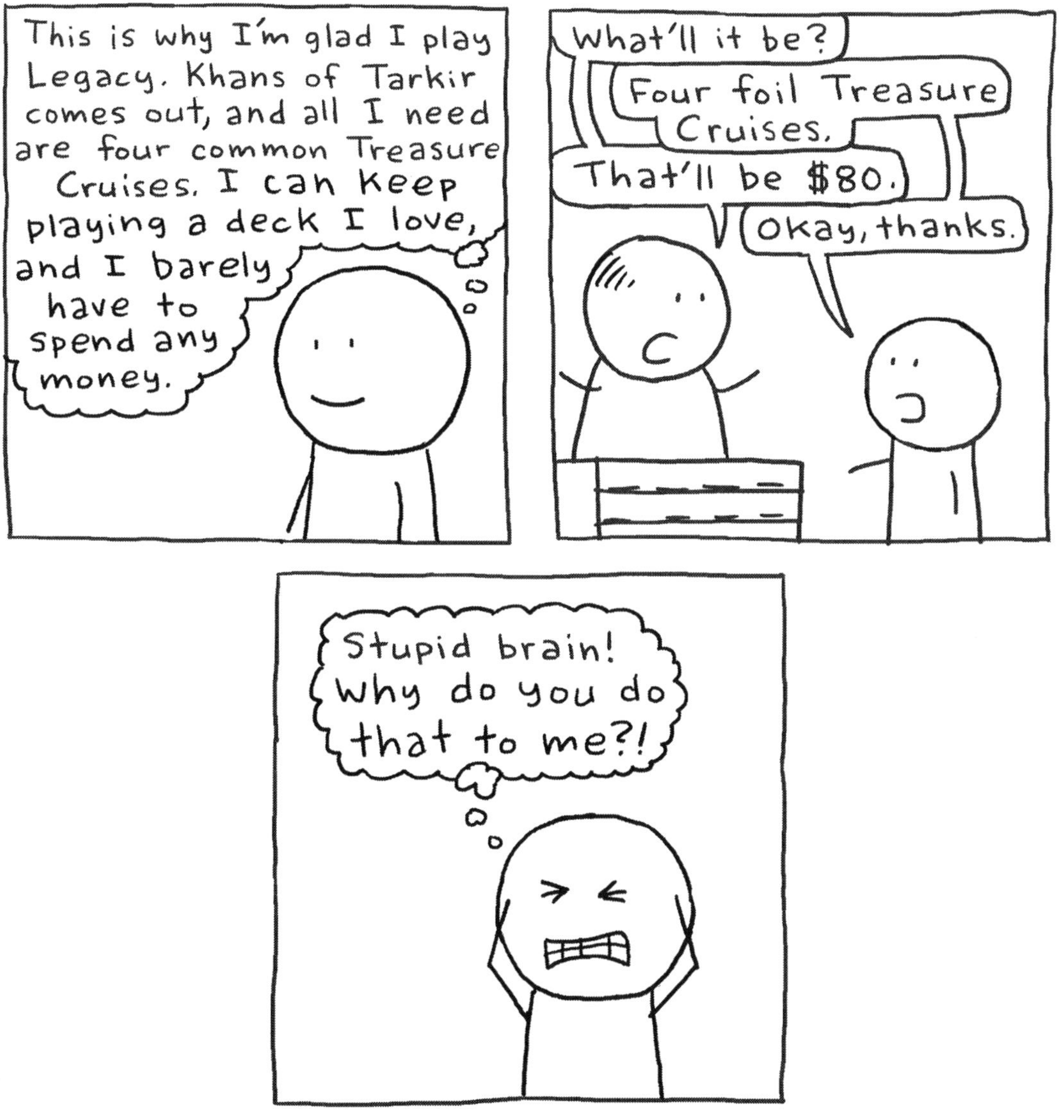
This is why I'm glad I play Legacy. Khans of Tarkir comes out, and all I need are four common Treasure Cruises. I can keep playing a deck I love, and I barely have to spend any money.
What'll it be?
Four foil Treasure Cruises.
That'll be $80.
Okay, thanks.
Stupid brain! Why do you do that to me?!

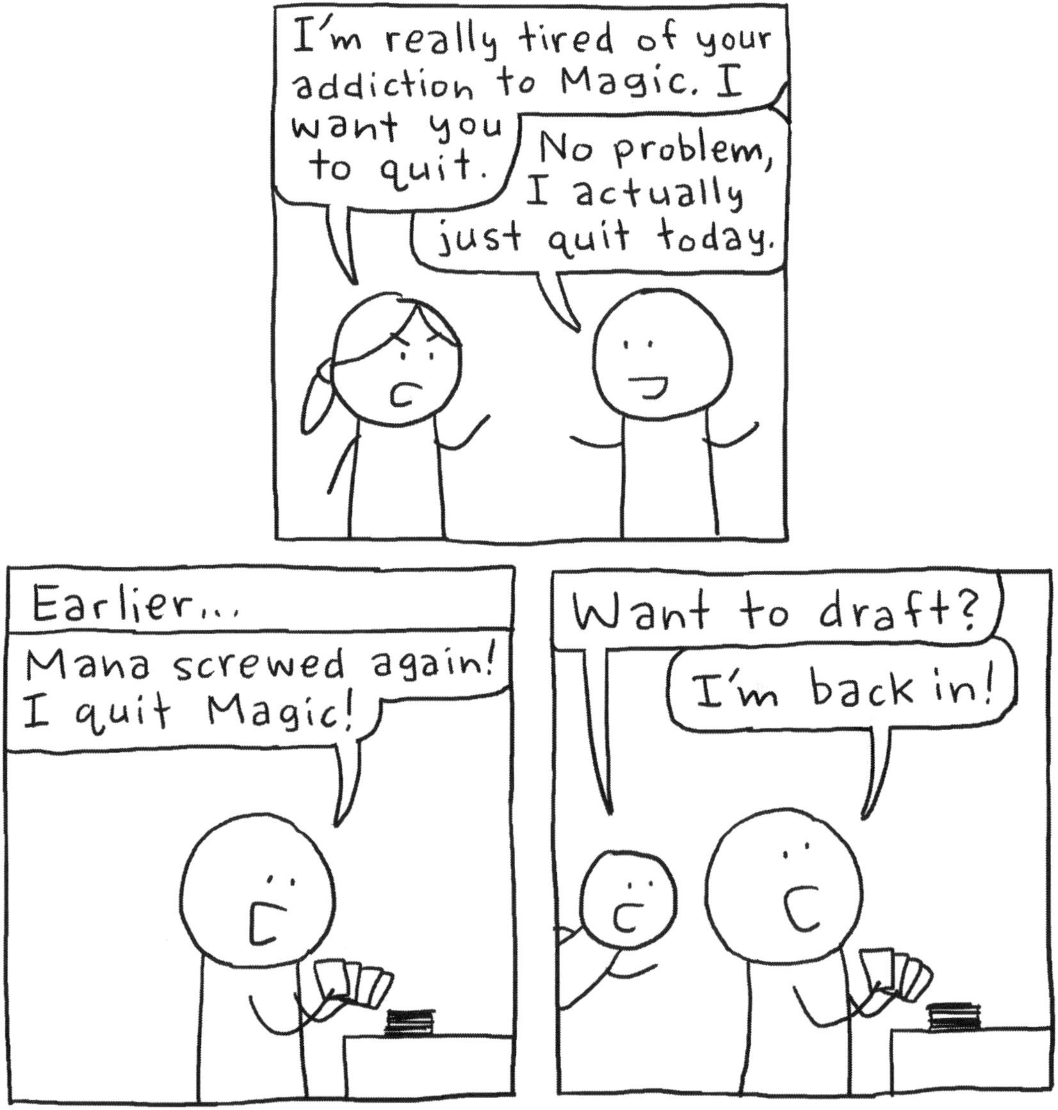
I'm really tired of your addiction to Magic. I want you to quit.
No problem, I actually just quit today.
Earlier...
Mana screwed again! I quit Magic!
Want to draft?
I'm back in!

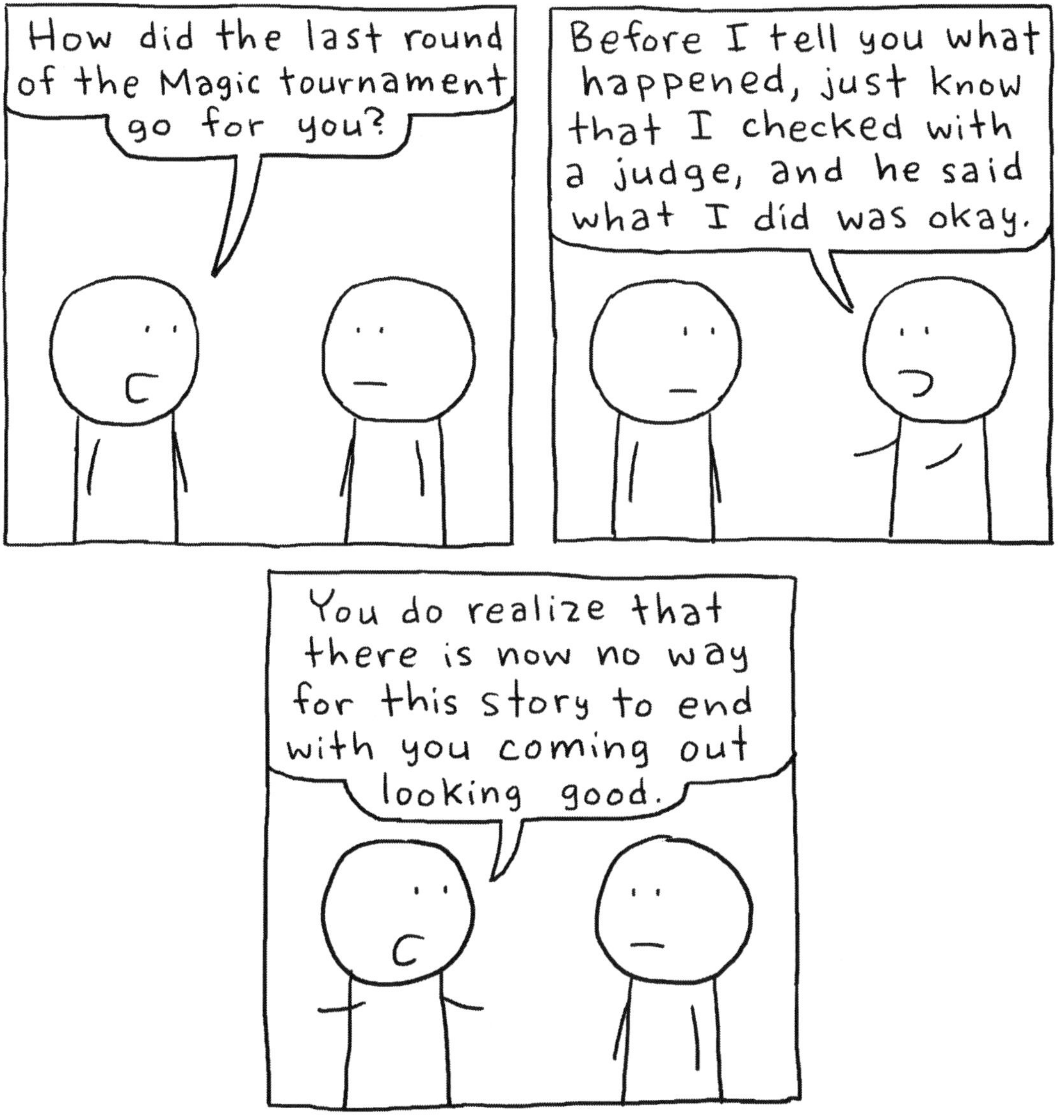
How did the last round of the Magic tournament go for you?
Before I tell you what happened, just know that I checked with a judge, and he said what I did was okay.
You do realize that there is now no way for this story to end with you coming out looking good.

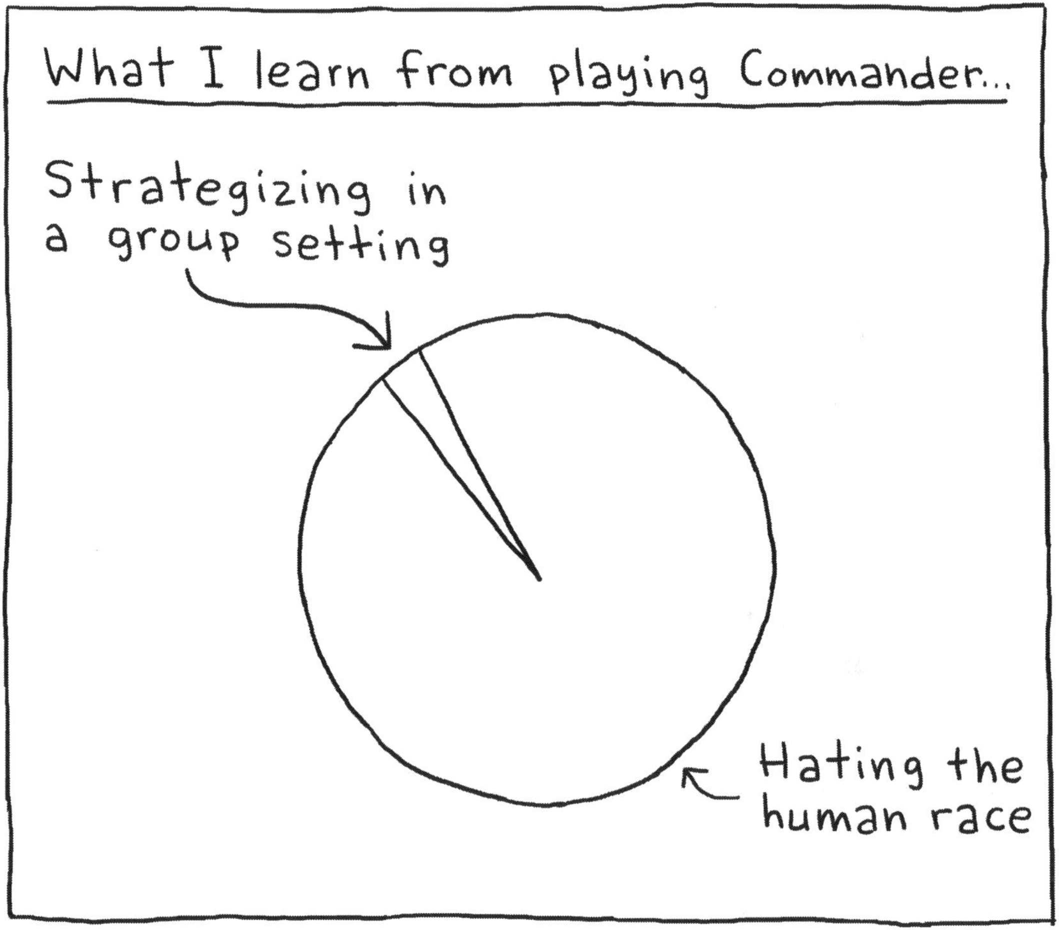
What I learn from playing Commander...
Strategizing in a group setting
Hating the human race

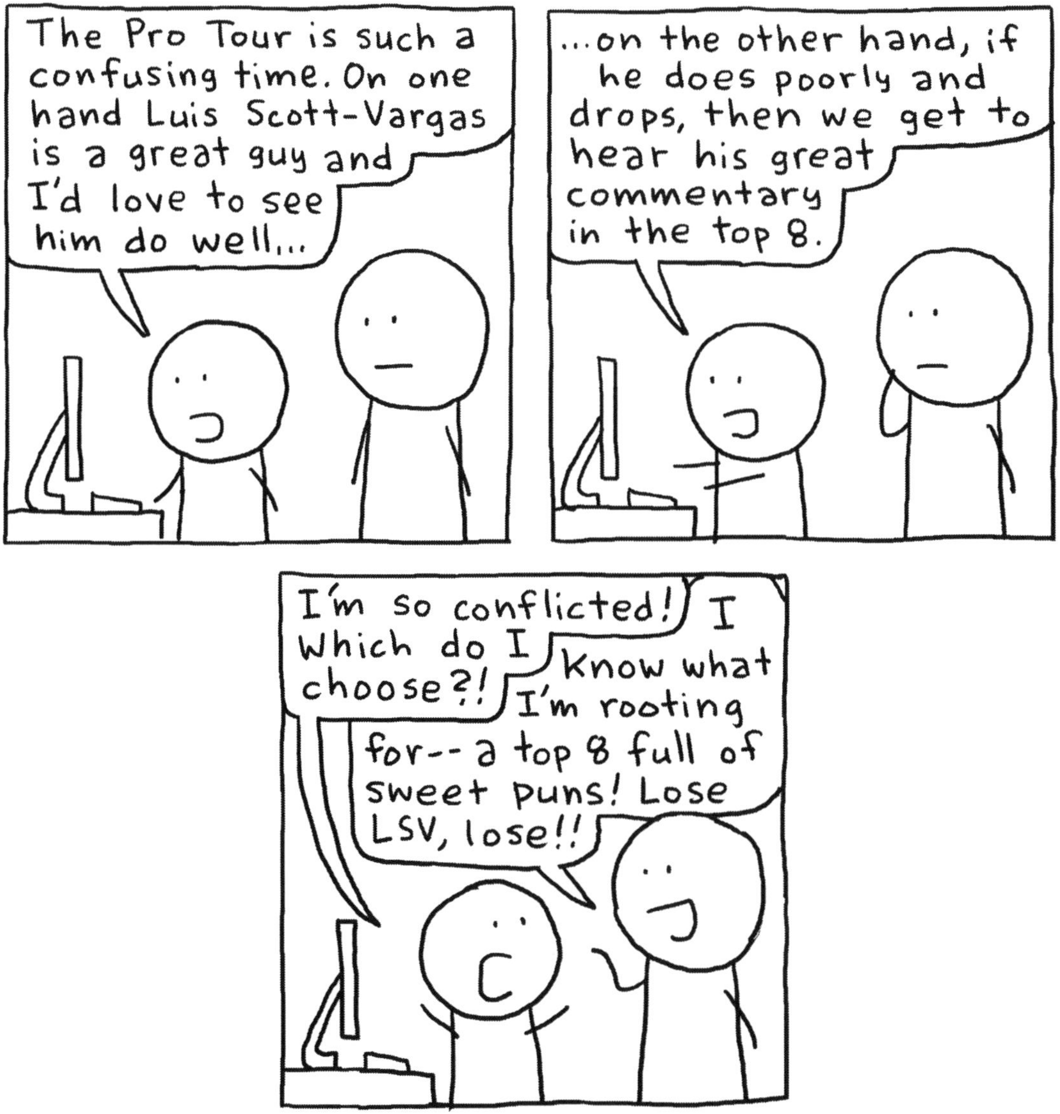
The Pro Tour is such a confusing time. On one hand Luis Scott-Vargas is a great guy and I'd love to see him do well...
...on the other hand, if he does poorly and drops, then we get to hear his great commentary in the top 8.
I'm so conflicted! Which do I choose?!
I know what I'm rooting for-- a top 8 full of sweet puns! Lose LSV, lose!!

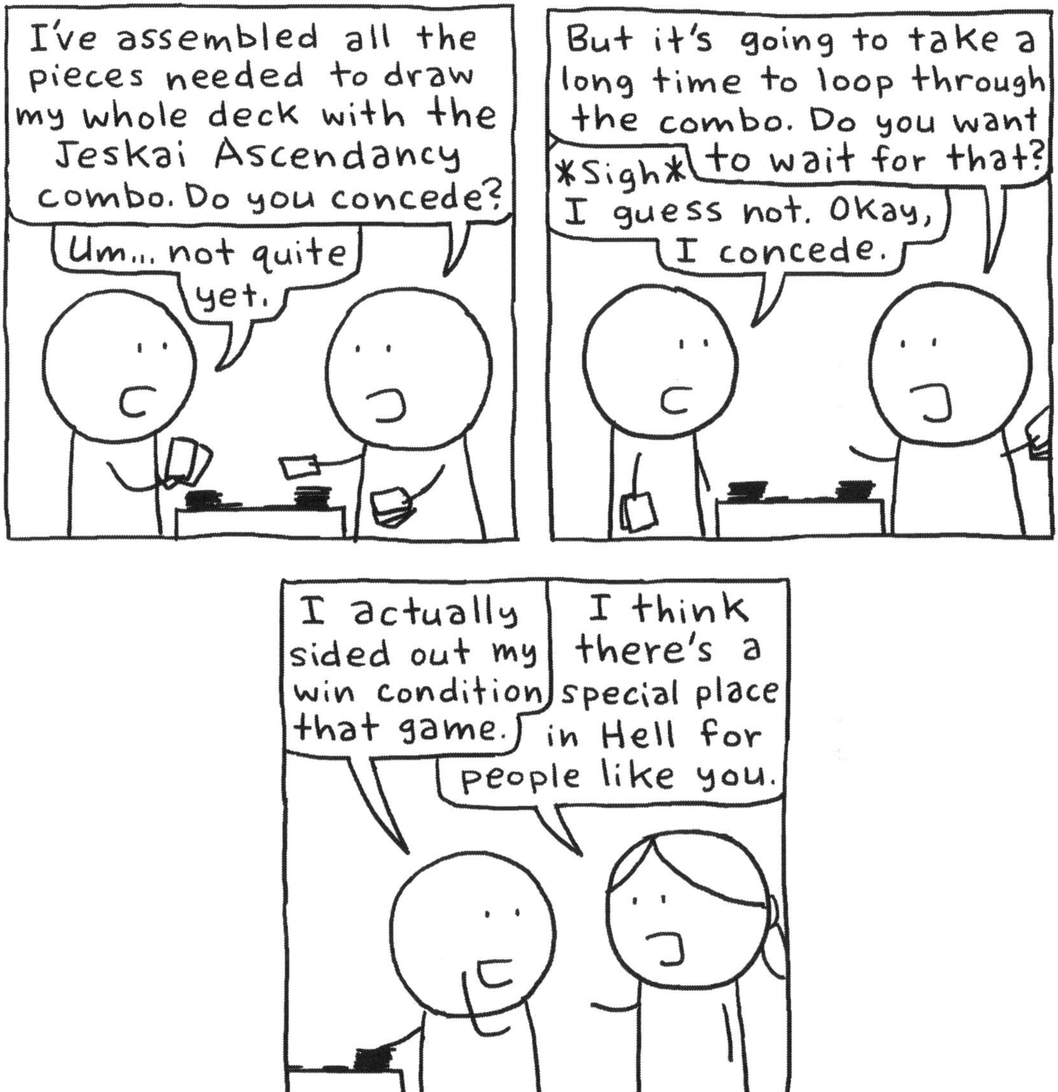
I've assembled all the pieces needed to draw my whole deck with the Jeskai Ascendancy combo. Do you concede?
Um... not quite yet.
But it's going to take a long time to loop through the combo. Do you want to wait for that?
Sigh I guess not. Okay, I concede.
I actually sided out my win condition that game.
I think there's a special place in Hell for people like you.

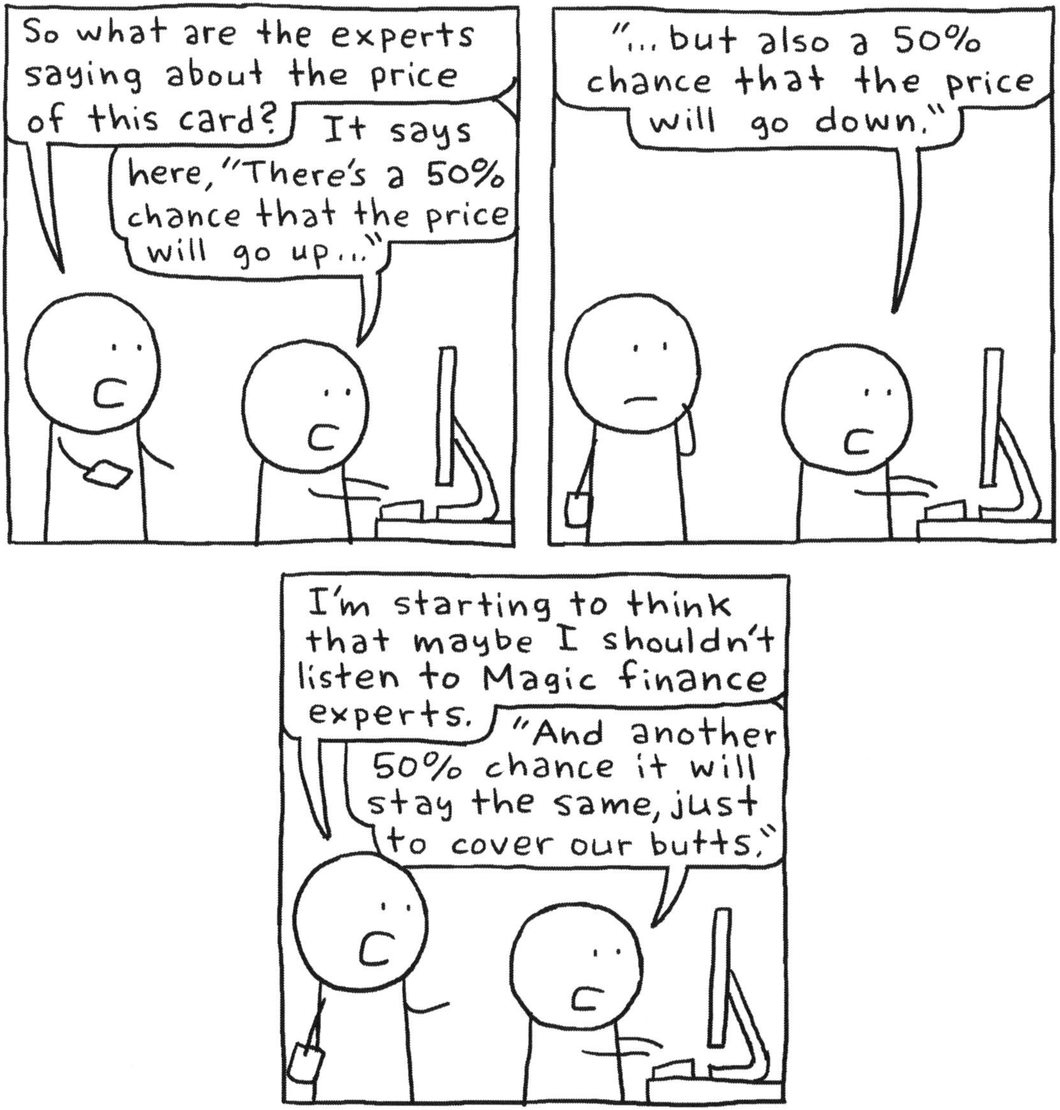
So what are the experts saying about the price of this card?
It says here, "There's a 50% chance that the price will go up..."
"...but also a 50% chance that the price will go down."
I'm starting to think that maybe I shouldn't listen to Magic finance experts.
"And another 50% chance it will stay the same, just to cover our butts."

Throughout most of the history of Magic...
Do you think Wizards of the Coast will ever again print a card like Ancestral Recall?
No way! Maybe if Hell freezes over.
After Khans of Tarkir...
Dammit Wizards.

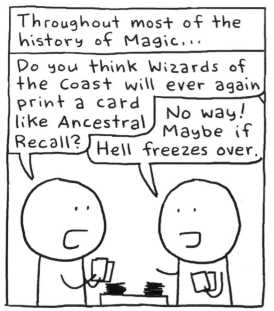

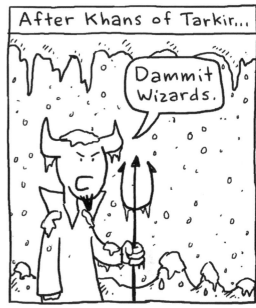

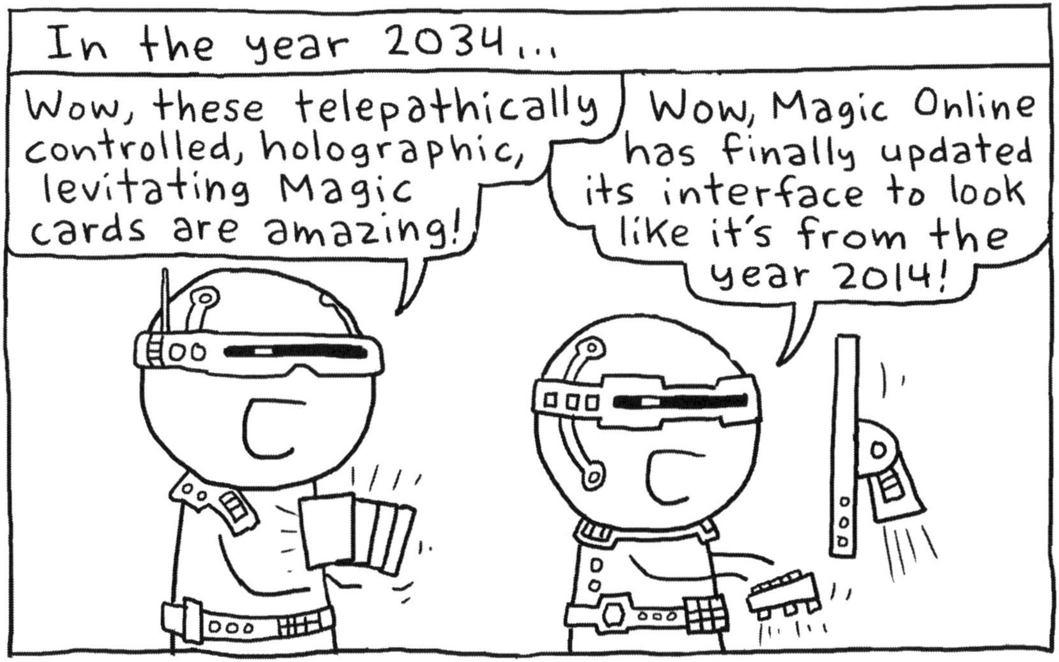
In the year 2034...
Wow, these telepathically controlled, holographic, levitating Magic cards are amazing!
Wow, Magic Online has finally updated its interface to look like it's from the year 2014!

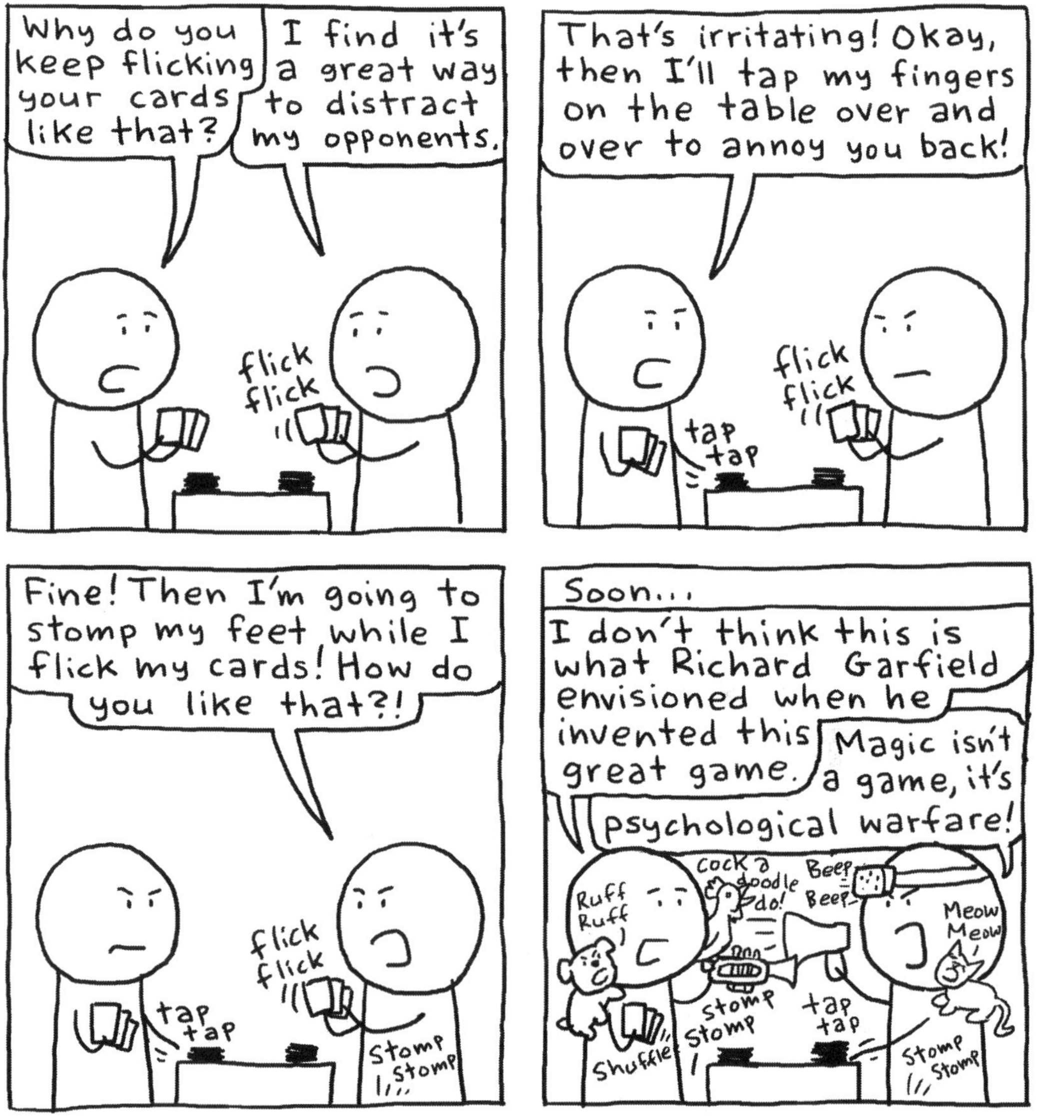
Why do you keep flicking your cards like that?
I find it's a great way to distract my opponents.
flick flick
That's irritating! Okay, then I'll tap my fingers on the table over and over to annoy you back!
flick flick
tap tap
Fine! Then I'm going to stomp my feet while I flick my cards! How do you like that?!
flick flick
tap tap
Stomp Stomp
Soon...
I don't think this is what Richard Garfield envisioned when he invented this great game.
Magic isn't a game, it's psychological warfare!
Ruff Ruff
Cock a doodle do!
Beep Beep
Meow Meow
Shuffle
Stomp Stomp
tap tap
Stomp Stomp

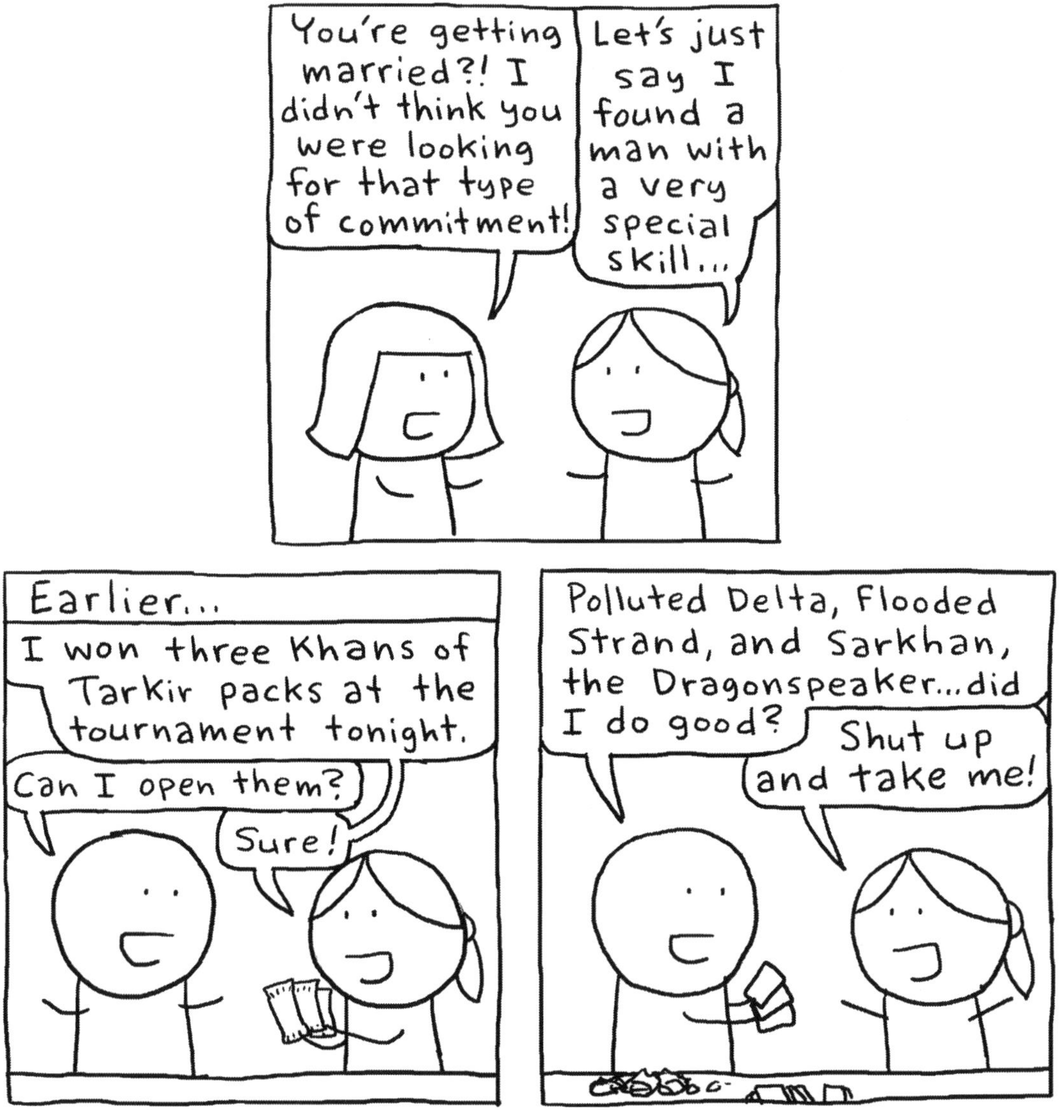
You're getting married?! I didn't think you were looking for that type of commitment!
Let's just say I found a man with a very special skill...
Earlier...
I won three Khans of Tarkir packs at the tournament tonight.
Can I open them?
Sure!
Polluted Delta, Flooded Strand, and Sarkhan, the Dragonspeaker...did I do good?
Shut up and take me!

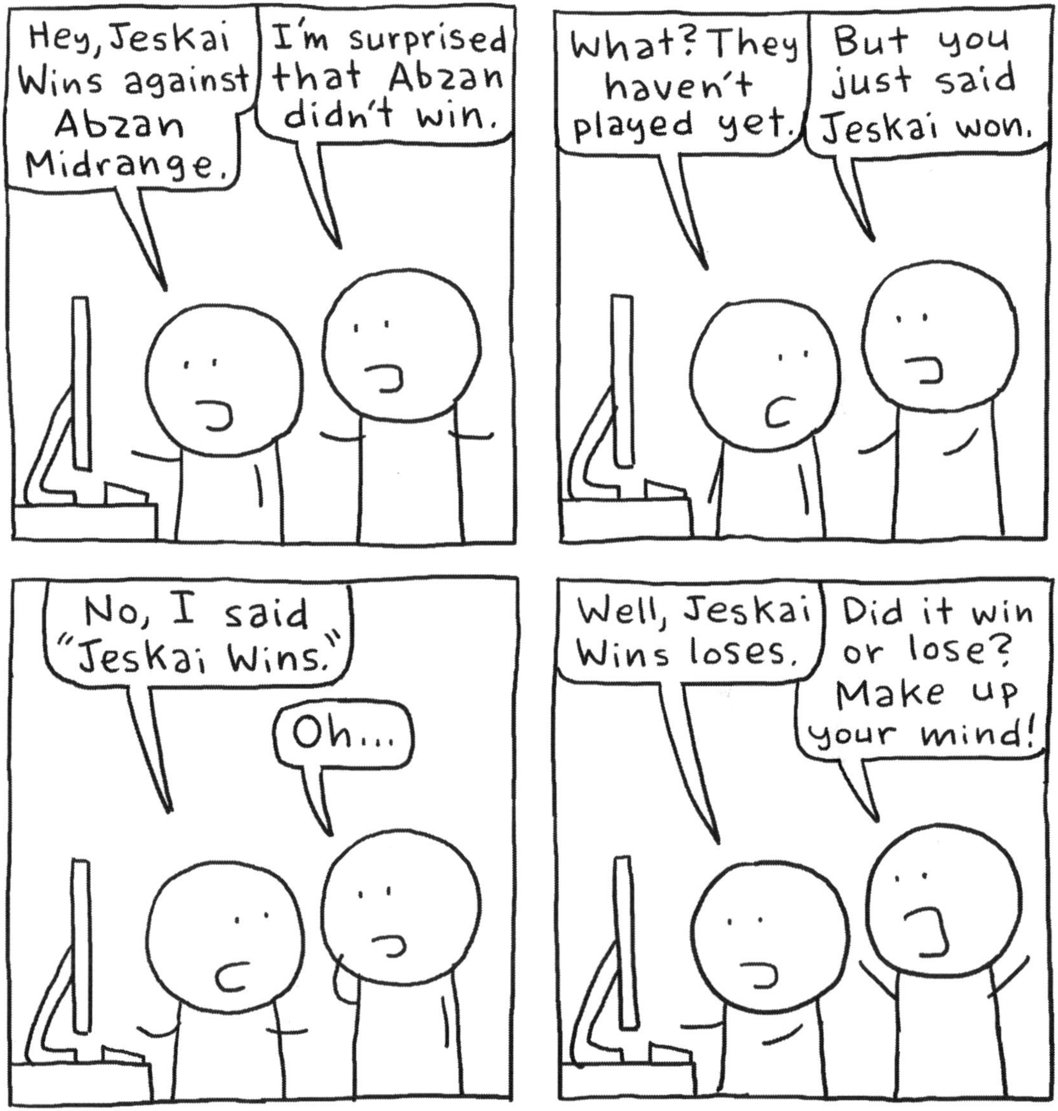
Hey, JesKai Wins against Abzan Midrange.
I'm surprised that Abzan didn't win.
What? They haven't played yet.
But you just said JesKai won.
No, I said "JesKai Wins."
Oh...
Well, JesKai Wins loses.
Did it win or lose? Make up your mind!

Bonus Comics

The following pages feature comics that have never appeared on the Cardboard Crack website. I hope you enjoy the chance to see them here for the first time!

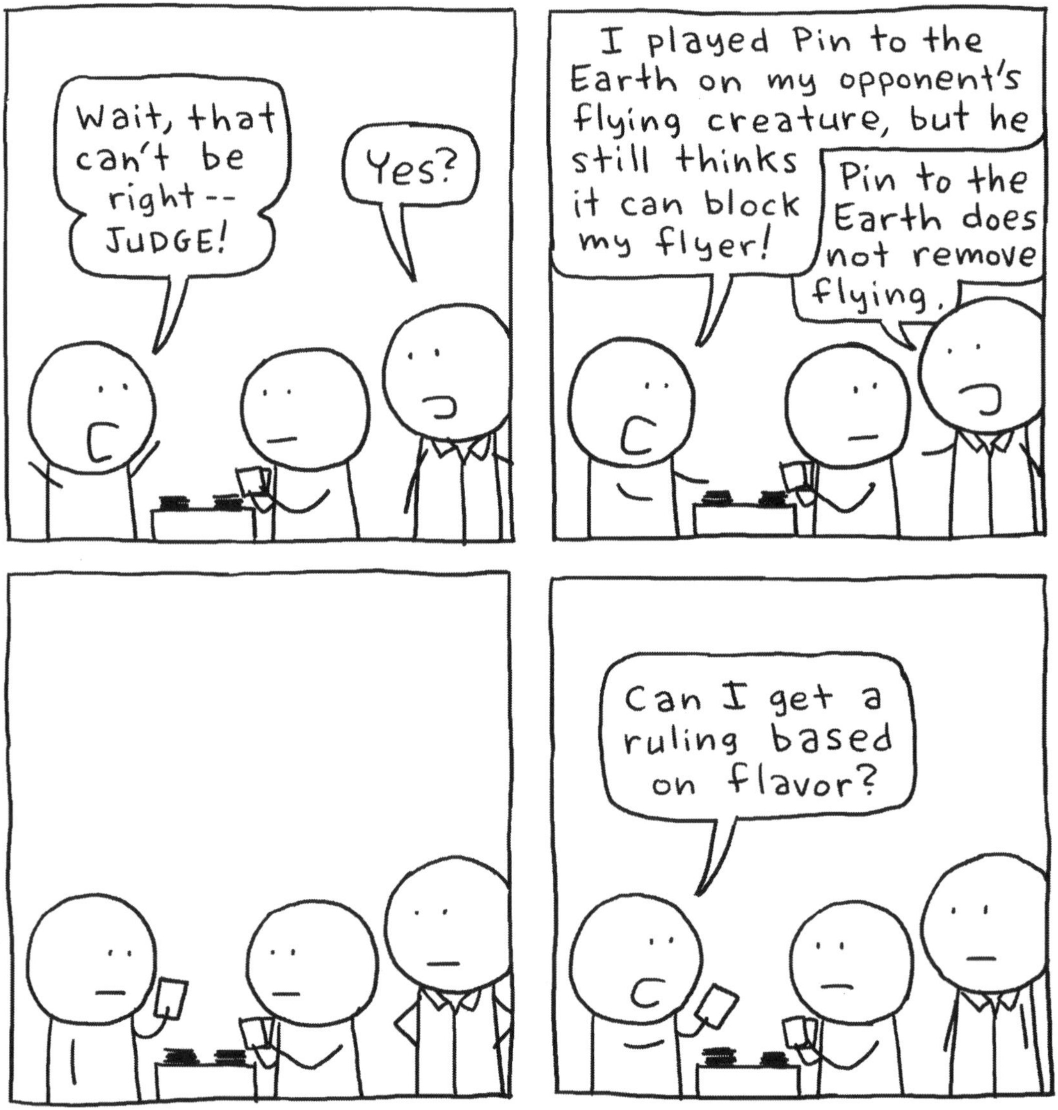
Wait, that can't be right -- JUDGE!
Yes?
I played Pin to the Earth on my opponent's flying creature, but he still thinks it can block my flyer!
Pin to the Earth does not remove flying.
Can I get a ruling based on flavor?

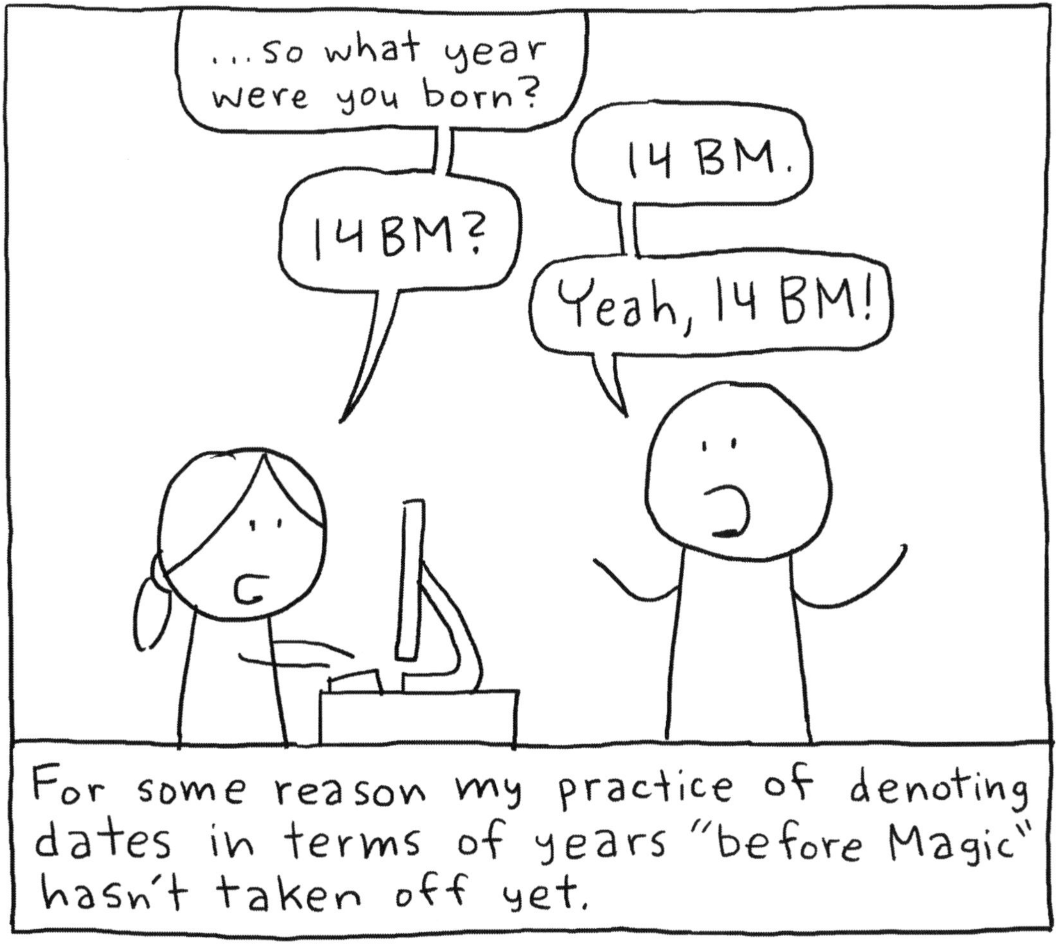
...so what year were you born?
14 BM?
14 BM.
Yeah, 14 BM!
For some reason my practice of denoting dates in terms of years "before Magic" hasn't taken off yet.

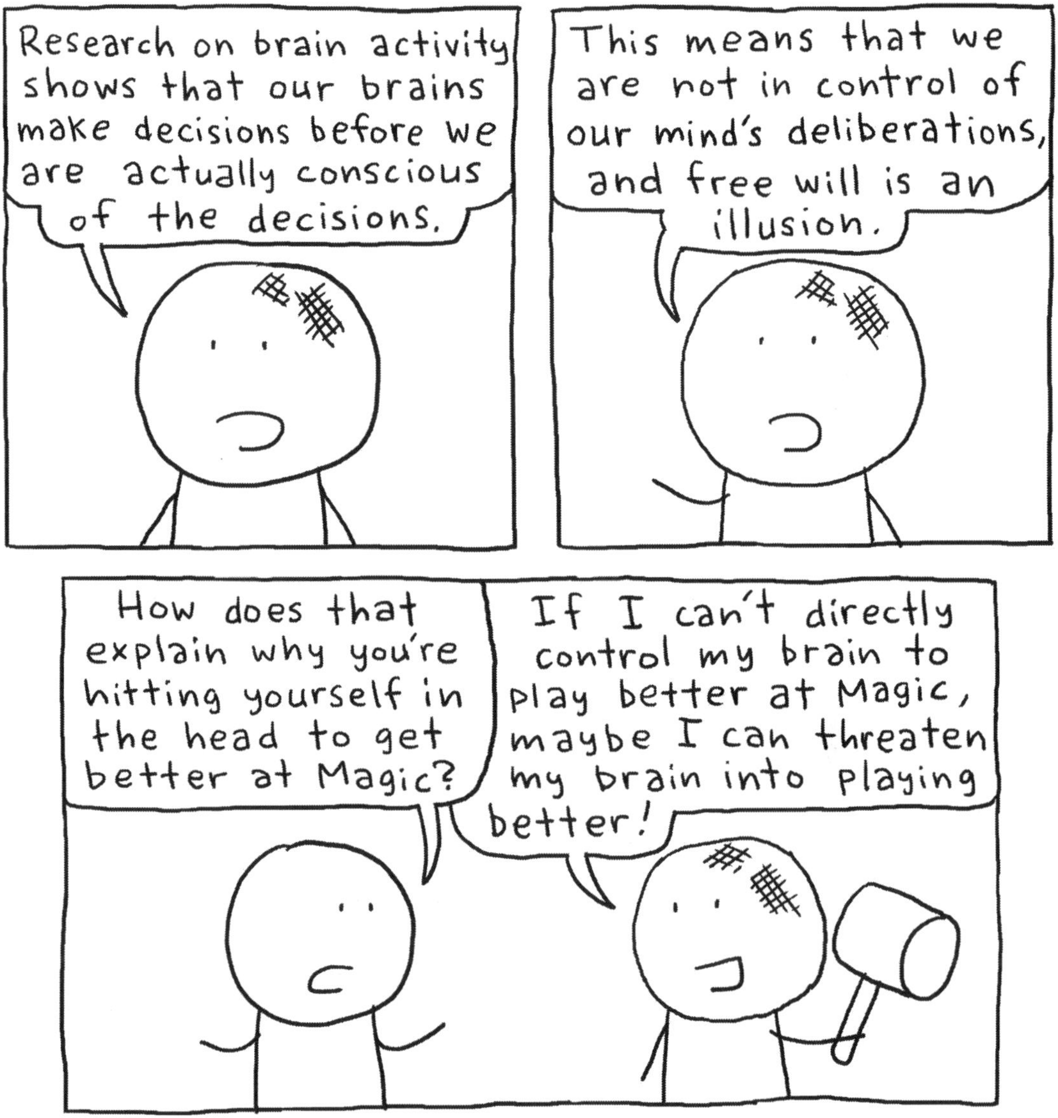

Research on brain activity shows that our brains make decisions before we are actually conscious of the decisions.
This means that we are not in control of our mind's deliberations, and free will is an illusion.
How does that explain why you're hitting yourself in the head to get better at Magic?
If I can't directly control my brain to play better at Magic, maybe I can threaten my brain into playing better!

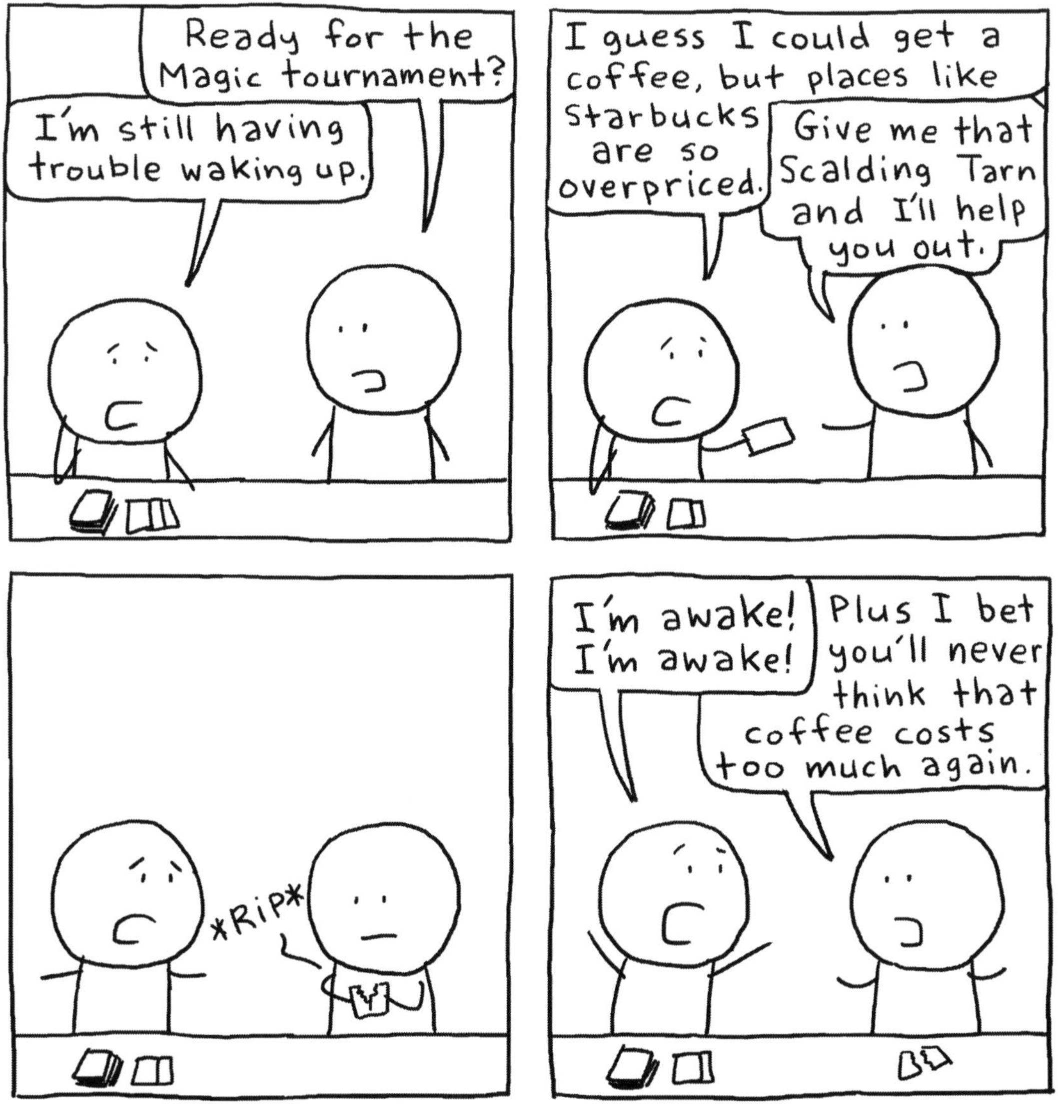
Ready for the Magic tournament?
I'm still having trouble waking up.
I guess I could get a coffee, but places like Starbucks are so overpriced.
Give me that Scalding Tarn and I'll help you out.
Rip
I'm awake! I'm awake!
Plus I bet you'll never think that coffee costs too much again.

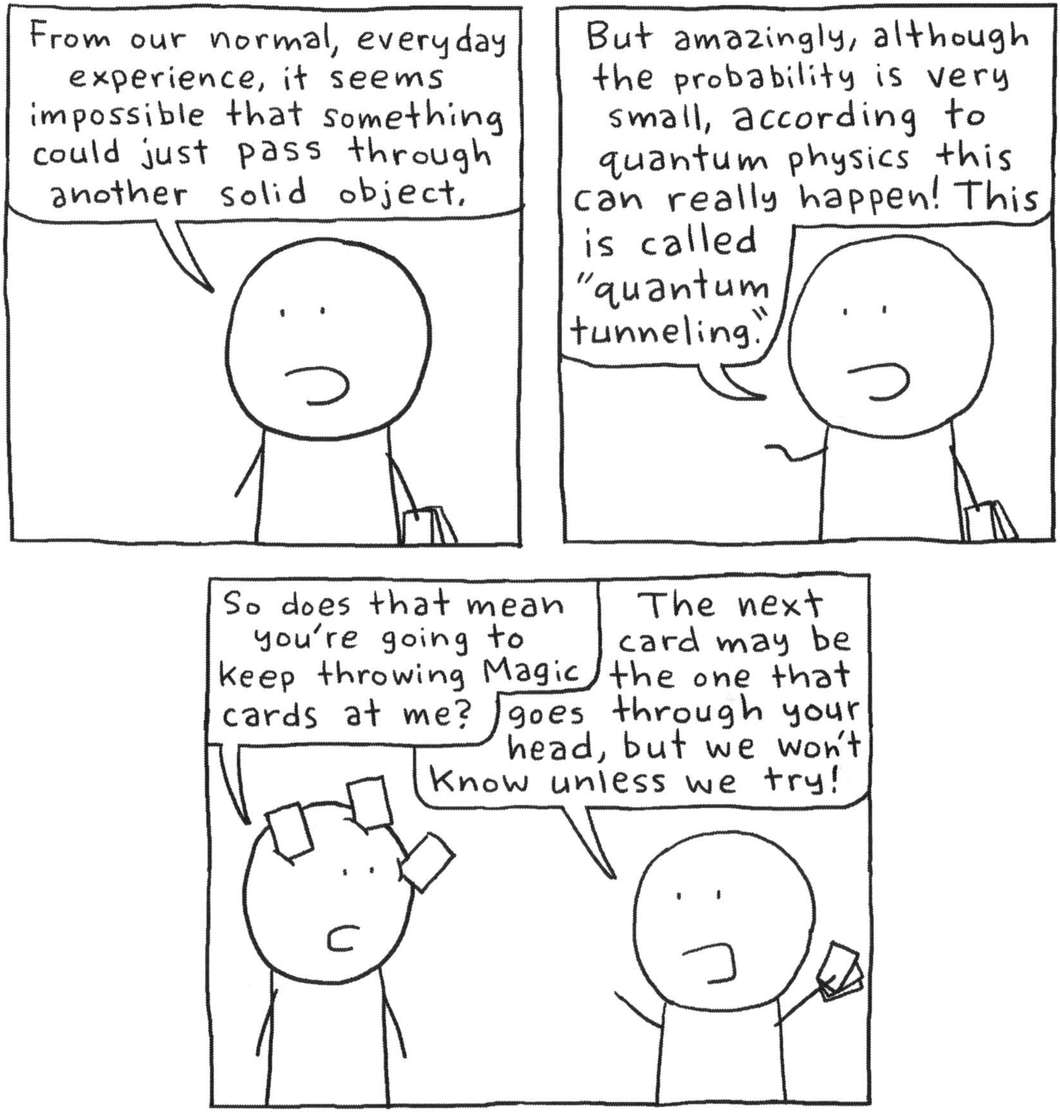
From our normal, everyday experience, it seems impossible that something could just pass through another solid object.
But amazingly, although the probability is very small, according to quantum physics this can really happen! This is called "quantum tunneling."
So does that mean you're going to keep throwing Magic cards at me?
The next card may be the one that goes through your head, but we won't know unless we try!

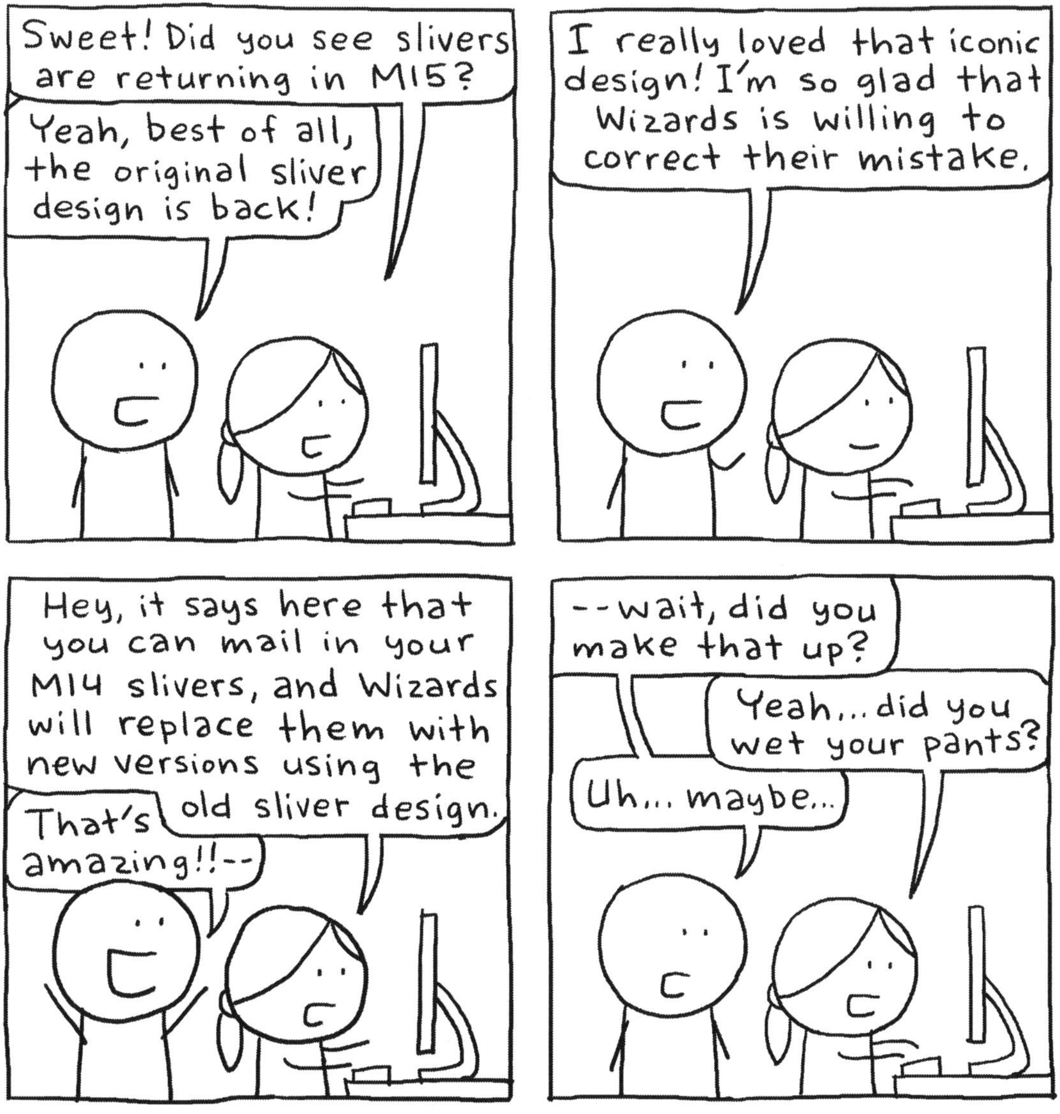
Sweet! Did you see slivers are returning in M15?
Yeah, best of all, the original sliver design is back!
I really loved that iconic design! I'm so glad that Wizards is willing to correct their mistake.
Hey, it says here that you can mail in your M14 slivers, and Wizards will replace them with new versions using the old sliver design.
That's amazing!!--
--wait, did you make that up?
Yeah... did you wet your pants?
Uh... maybe...

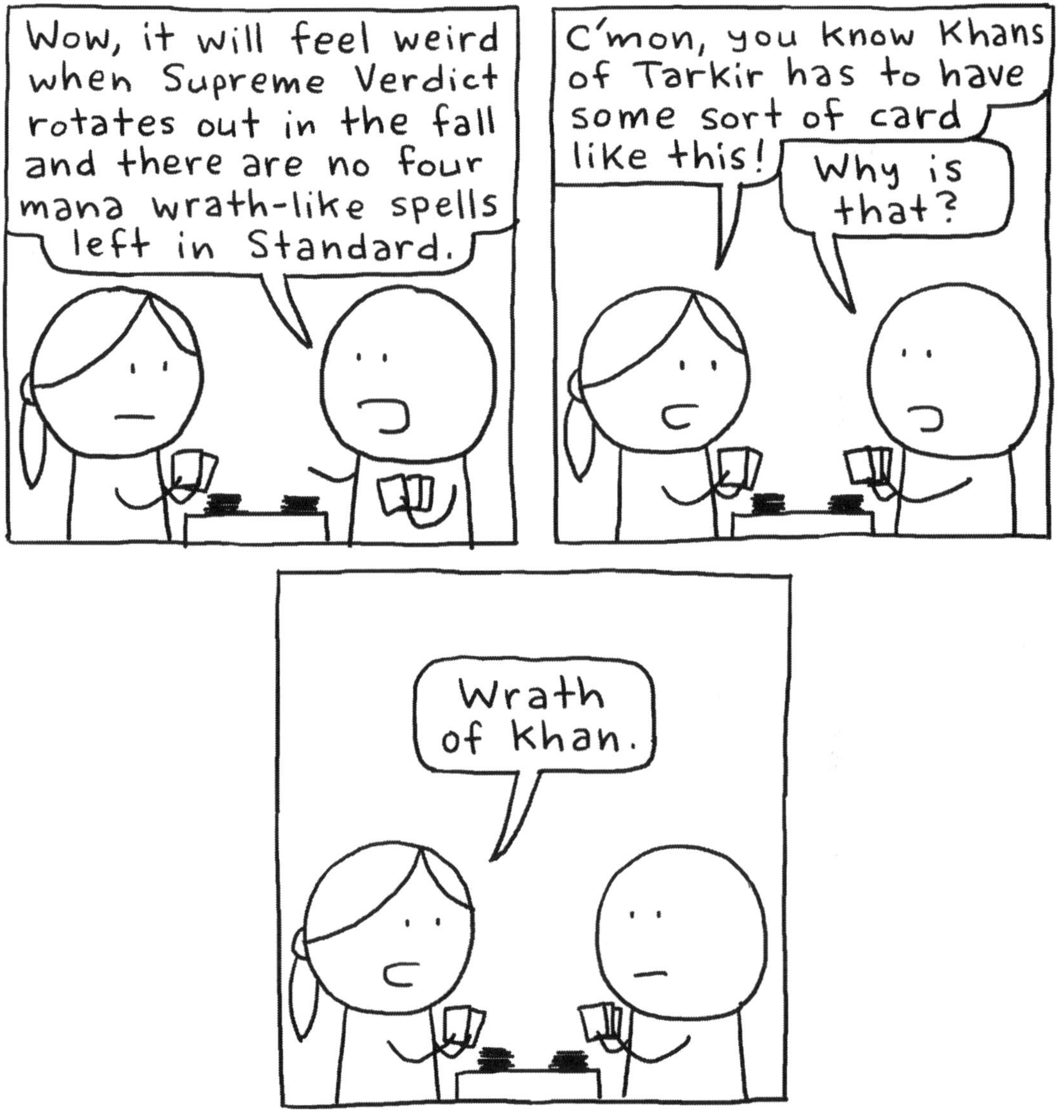
Wow, it will feel weird when Supreme Verdict rotates out in the fall and there are no four mana wrath-like spells left in Standard.
C'mon, you know Khans of Tarkir has to have some sort of card like this!
Why is that?
Wrath of khan.

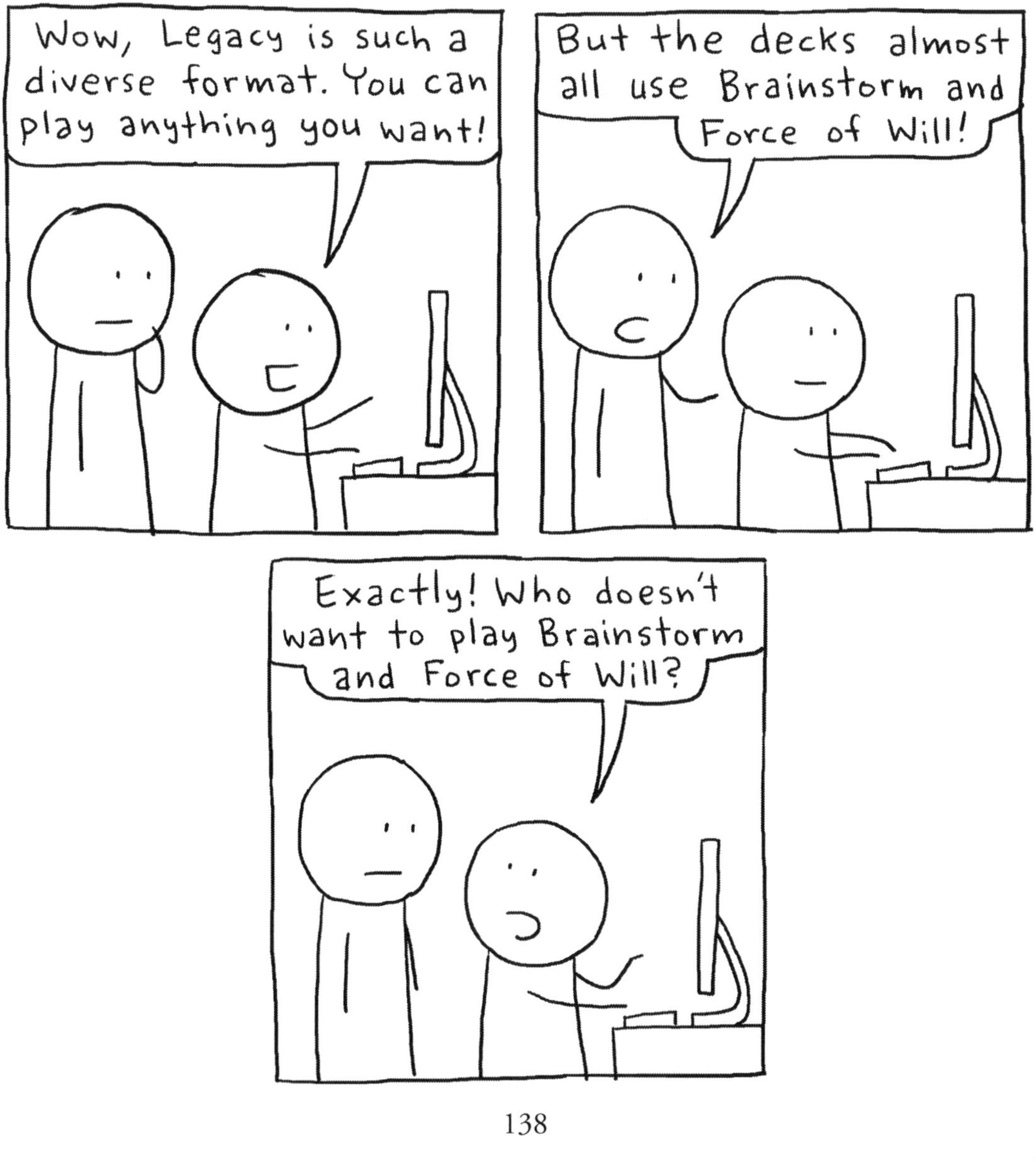
Wow, Legacy is such a diverse format. You can play anything you want!
But the decks almost all use Brainstorm and Force of Will!
Exactly! Who doesn't want to play Brainstorm and Force of Will?

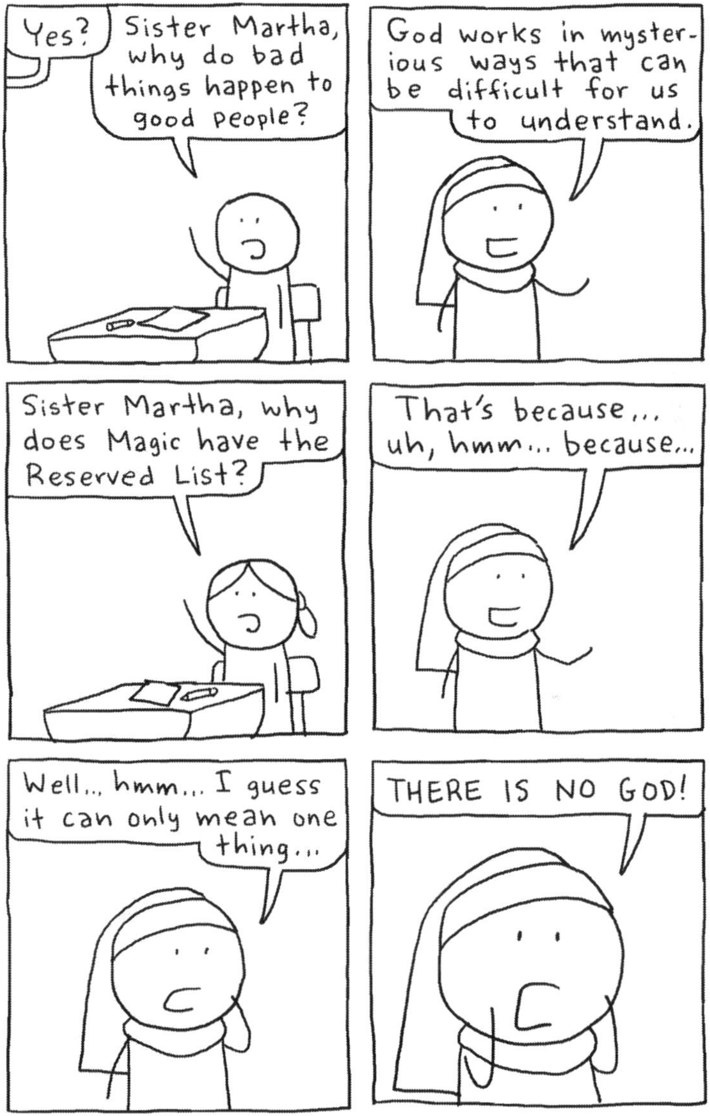
Yes?
Sister Martha, why do bad things happen to good people?
God works in mysterious ways that can be difficult for us to understand.
Sister Martha, why does Magic have the Reserved List?
That's because... uh, hmm... because...
Well... hmm... I guess it can only mean one thing...
THERE IS NO GOD!

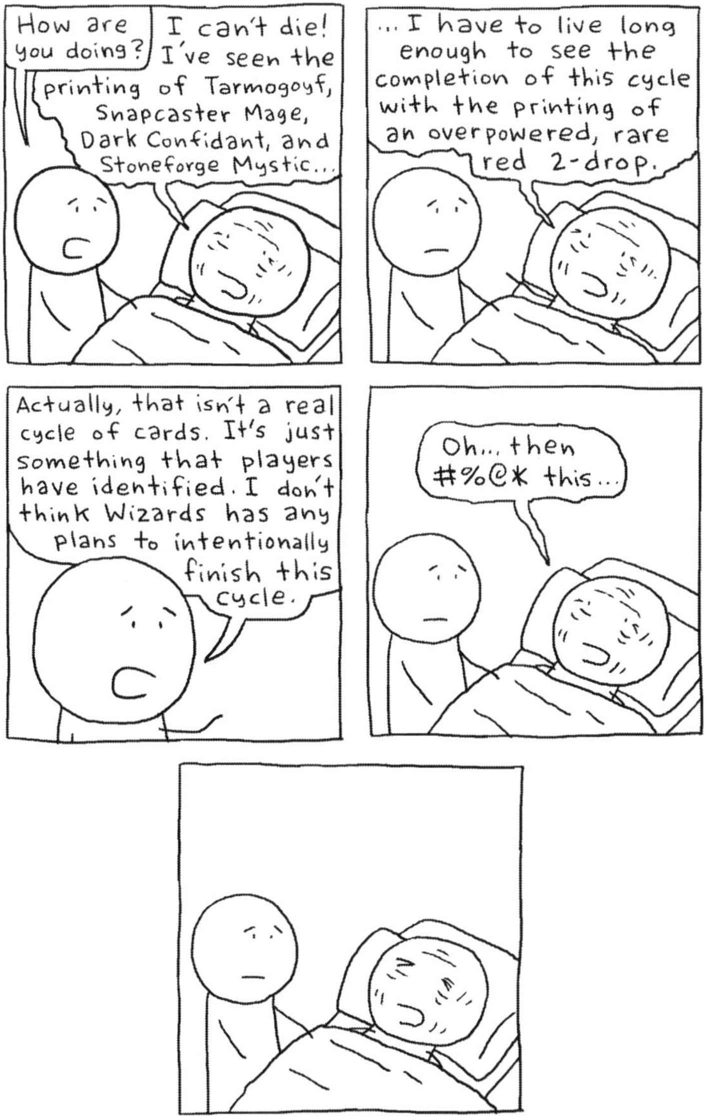
How are you doing?
I can't die! I've seen the printing of Tarmogoyf, Snapcaster Mage, Dark Confidant, and Stoneforge Mystic...
...I have to live long enough to see the completion of this cycle with the printing of an overpowered, rare red 2-drop.
Actually, that isn't a real cycle of cards. It's just something that players have identified. I don't think Wizards has any plans to intentionally finish this cycle.
Oh... then #%@* this...

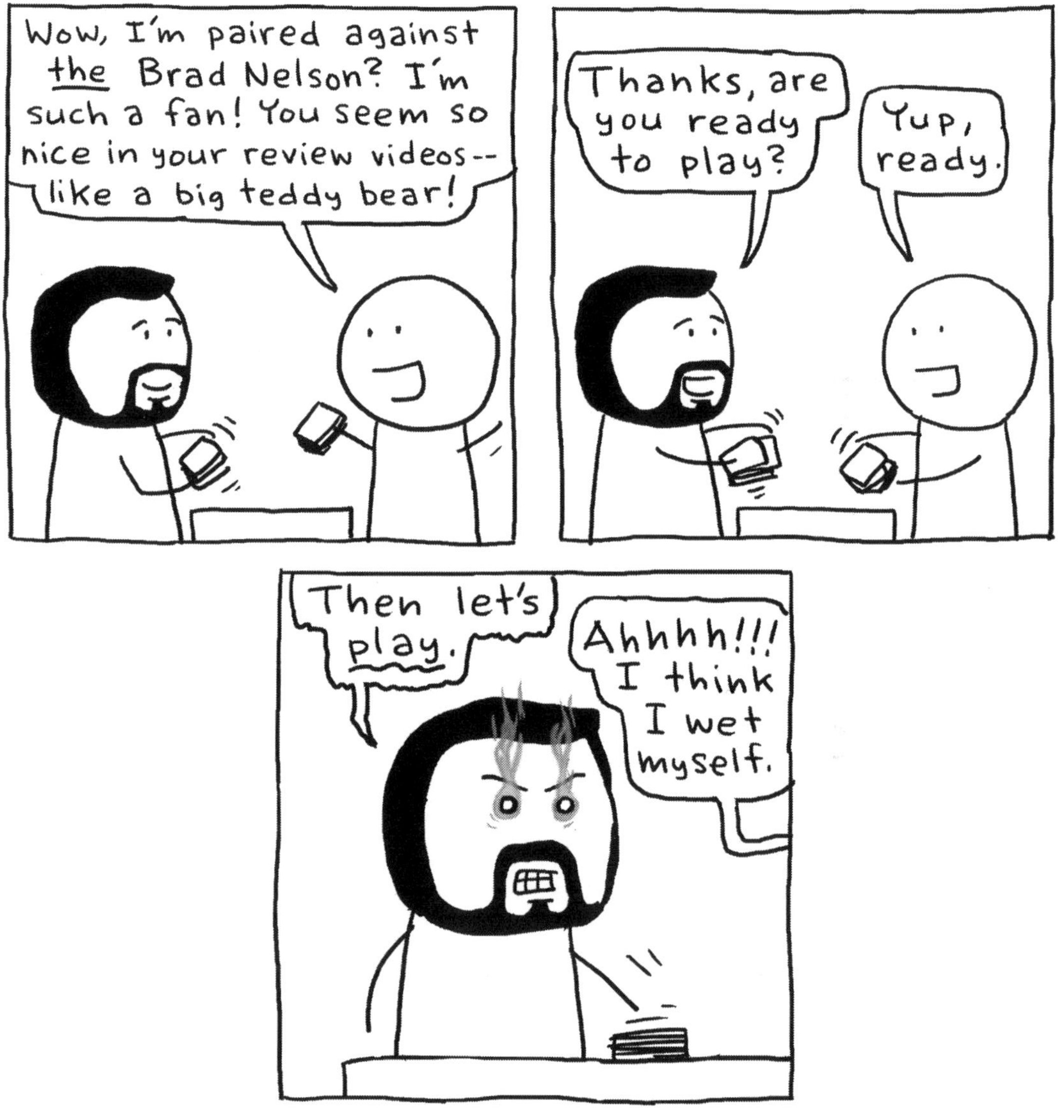
Wow, I'm paired against the Brad Nelson? I'm such a fan! You seem so nice in your review videos-- like a big teddy bear!
Thanks, are you ready to play?
Yup, ready.
Then let's play.
Ahhhh!!! I think I wet myself.

Cardboard Crack has been online since March 2013, exclusively featuring comics about the world's most addictive game, Magic: The Gathering. Since that time, the Cardboard Crack website has gained many thousands of followers and many millions of page views. It has received links from a wide variety of prominent personalities in the Magic community, from Aaron Forsythe (current director of Magic: The Gathering R&D) to Jon Finkel (widely regarded as one of the greatest Magic players of all-time). Cardboard Crack is also featured in the weekly newsletter of StarCityGames.com (the world's largest Magic store).

New comics can be found regularly at:
cardboard-crack.com
facebook.com/CardboardCrack

Check out these other Cardboard Crack books:
Cardboard Crack
I will never quit Cardboad Crack
Cardboard Crack anytime, anywhere

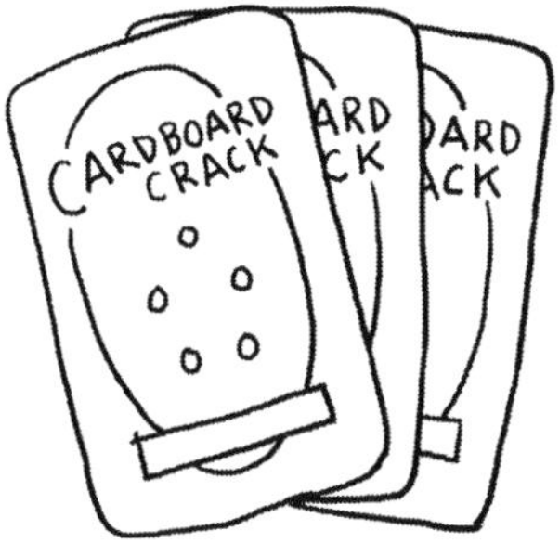
CARDBOARD CRACK
ARD CK
ARD CK

Made in the USA
Lexington, KY
28 November 2014